REEDS MARINA GUIDE 2012

The source directory for all sail & power boat owners

© Adlard Coles Nautical 2011

Adlard Coles Nautical,
36 Soho Square, London W1D 3QY
Tel: 0207 758 0200
Fax: 0207 758 0222/0333
e-mail: info@reedsalmanacs.co.uk
www.reedsalmanacs.co.uk

Cover photo: Port Pendennis
Tel: 01326 211211
www.portpendennis.com

Section 1

The Marinas and Services Section has been fully updated for the 2012 season. These useful pages provide chartlets and facility details for some 183 marinas around the shores of the UK and Ireland, including the Channel Islands, the perfect complement to any *Reeds Nautical Almanac*.

Section 2

The Marine Supplies & Services section lists more than 1000 services at coastal and other locations around the British Isles. It provides a quick and easy reference to manufacturers and retailers of equipment, services and supplies both nationally and locally together with emergency services.

Advertisement Sales

Enquiries about advertising space should be addressed to:

MS Publications, 2nd Floor Ewer House, 44-46 Crouch Street Colchester, Essex, CO3 3HH

Tel: +44(0)1206 506227
Fax: +44 (0)1206 500228

GW00702721

Section 1

Marinas and Services Section ....

Area Guide Chart 2

Area 1 - SW England
Area 1 Marina Chart 3
Falmouth Marina 5
Falmouth Visitors' Yacht H'n 7
Port Pendennis Marina 7
Mylor Yacht Harbour 9
Mayflower Marina 10
Q Anne's Battery 12
Sutton Harbour 12
Plymouth Yacht Haven 13
Darthaven Marina 14
Dart Marina 15
Noss Marina 15
Dartside Quay 16
Brixham Marina 16
Torquay Marina 16
Portland Marina 18
Weymouth Marina 18
Weymouth Harbour 18

Area 2 - Central S England
Ridge Wharf 23
Lake Yard Marina 23
Cobb's Quay Marina 24
Poole Quay Boat Haven 24
Port of Poole Marina 25
Parkstone Yacht Haven 25
Salterns Marina 25
Yarmouth Harbour/H Hayles ..25
Lymington Yacht Haven 27
Berthon Lymington Marina 27
Bucklers Hard 27
Cowes Yacht Haven 28
Shepards Wharf Marina 29
E Cowes Marina 29
Island Harbour Marina 30
Hythe Marina Village 30
Ocean Village Marina 30
Shamrock Quay.........................30
Kemps Quay 31
Saxon Wharf 31
Hamble Point Marina 32
Port Hamble Marina 33
Mercury Yacht Harbour 33
Universal Marina 33
Swanwick Marina 33
Ryde Leisure Harbour 34
Bembridge Marina 34
Haslar Marina 34
Gosport Marina 34
Endeavour Quay 35
Royal Clarence Marina 35
Port Solent Marina 36
Southsea Marina 36
Sparkes Marina 36
Northney Marina 37
Emsworth Yacht Harbour 37
Chichester Marina 38
Birdham Pool 38

Area 3 - SE England
Area 3 Marina Chart..................41
Littlehampton Marina 42
The Shipyard 42
Lady Bee Marina 42
Brighton Marina 43
Newhaven Marina 44
Sovereign Hbr Marina 44
Harbour of Rye 44
Dover Marina 45
Ramsgate Royal Hbr 45

Area 4 - E Engl
Area 4 Marina Ch
Gillingham Marina
Hoo Marina 49
Chatham Maritime Marina........49
Limehouse Basin 49
Gallions Point Marina 50
South Dock Marina 52
St Katharine Haven 52
Chelsea Harbour.......................53
Brentford Dock Marina 53
Penton Hook Marina 54
Windsor Marina 54
Bray Marina 54
Burnham Yacht Harbour 55
Essex Marina 55
Bridgemarsh Marina 55
Bradwell Marina 56
Heybridge Basin 56
Fambridge Yacht Haven 56
Blackwater Marina 58
Tollesbury Marina 58
Titchmarsh Marina 59
Walton Yacht Basin 59
Shotley Marina 60
Suffolk Yacht Harbour 60
Royal Harwich YC.....................61
Woolverstone Marina 61
Fox's Marina 62
Neptune Marina 62
Ipswich Haven Marina 63
Lowestoft Haven Marina 64
Hamilton Dock 64
Lowestoft CC 64
R Norfolk & Suffolk YC 64

Area 5 - NE England
Area 5 Marina Chart..................67
Wisbech Yacht Harbour 68
Boston Marina 68
Meridian Quay Marina 68
South Ferriby Marina 68
Hull Marina 69
Whitby Marina 70
Hartlepool Marina 70
Sunderland Marina 70
N Shields Royal Quays 70
St Peters Marina 71
R Northumberland Marina........71
Amble Marina 71

Area 6 - SE Scotland
Area 6 Marina Chart..................73
Port Edgar Marina 74
Arbroath Harbour 74

Area 7 - NE Scotland
Area 7 Marina Chart..................75
Peterhead Bay Marina 76
Banff Harbour Marina 77
Whitehills Marina 77
Nairn Marina 78
Lossiemouth Marina 78
Inverness Marina 78
Seaport Marina 78
Caley Marina 79
Wick Marina 79
Kirkwall/Stromness Marinas ..80

Area 8 - NW Scotland
Area 8 Marina Chart..................81
Oban Marina 82
Dunstaffnage Marina 82
Melfort Pier and Hbr.................82
Craobh Haven Marina 83
Ardfern Yacht Centre 83

Portavadie Marina ....
Tarbert Harbour 86
Holy Loch Marina 86
Rhu Marina 87
Sandpoint Marina 87
James Watt Dock Marina 87
Kip Marina 88
Largs Yacht Haven 88
Clyde Marina 89
Troon Yacht Haven 90
Maryport Marina 90

Area 10 - NW England
Area 10 Marina Chart 93
Whitehaven Marina 94
Glasson Dock 94
Peel Marina 95
Fleetwood Harbour Marina......95
Preston Marina 95
Liverpool Marina 96
Conwy Marina 97
Deganwy Marina 97
Holyhead Marina 97
Pwllheli Marina 98

Area 11 - South Wales
Area 11 Marina Chart 99
Aberystwyth Marina 100
Milford Marina 100
Neyland Yacht Haven 101
Swansea Marina 102
Penarth Marina 102
Cardiff Marina 103
Sharpness Marina 103
Bristol Marina 104
Portishead Quays Marina 104

Area 12 - S Ireland
Area 12 Marina Chart 105
Malahide Marina 107
Howth Marina 107
Dun Laoghaire Marina 108
Arklow Marina 108
Kilmore Quay 108
Waterford City Marina............109
Crosshaven BY Marina 109
Salve Marine 109
Royal Cork YC Marina 109
East Ferry Marina 110
Kinsale YC Marina 110
Castlepark Marina 110
Lawrence Cove Marina..........110
Cahersiveen Marina 111
Dingle Marina 111
Fenit Harbour..........................111
Kilrush Creek Marina 111

Area 13 - N Ireland
Area 13 Marina Chart 112
Galway City Marina 113
Coleraine Marina 113
Seatons Marina 113
Ballycastle Marina 113
Carrickfergus Marina 114
Bangor Marina.........................114
Carlingford Marina 115
Portaferry Marina 115
Phennick Cove, Ardglass 115

Area 14 - Channel Islands
Area 14 Marina Chart 116
Beaucette Marina 118
St Peter Port 119
St Peter Port Victoria Marina 120
St Helier Harbour....................120

Section 2

Marine Supplies and Services Section 123–160

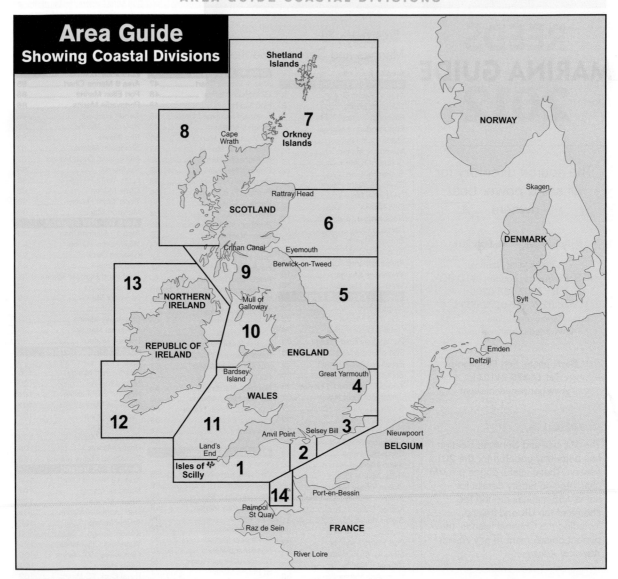

Area Guide
Showing Coastal Divisions

Shetland Islands
7
8
Cape Wrath
Orkney Islands
Rattray Head
SCOTLAND
6
Crinan Canal
Eyemouth
Berwick-on-Tweed
9
5
NORTHERN IRELAND
Mull of Galloway
10
REPUBLIC OF IRELAND
ENGLAND
Bardsey Island
Great Yarmouth
4
WALES
13
Anvil Point
Selsey Bill
3
12
11
Nieuwpoort
BELGIUM
Land's End
2
Isles of Scilly
1
14
Port-en-Bessin
Paimpol St Quay
Raz de Sein
FRANCE
River Loire
NORWAY
Skagen
DENMARK
Sylt
Emden
Delfzijl

Area 1 ......**South West England** ....Isles of Scilly to Anvil Point

Area 2 ......**Central Southern England** ....Anvil Point to Selsey Bill

Area 3 ......**South East England** ....Selsey Bill to North Foreland

Area 4 ......**East England** ....North Foreland to Great Yarmouth

Area 5 ......**North East England** ....Great Yarmouth to Berwick-upon-Tweed

Area 6 ......**South East Scotland**...Eyemouth to Rattray Head

Area 7 ......**North East Scotland** ....Rattray Head to Cape Wrath including Orkney & Shetland Is

Area 8 ......**North West Scotland** ....Cape Wrath to Crinan Canal

Area 9 ......**South West Scotland**...Crinan Canal to Mull of Galloway

Area 10 ....**North West England** ....Isle of Man & N Wales, Mull of Galloway to Bardsey Is

Area 11 ....**South Wales & Bristol Channel** ....Bardsey Island to Land's End

Area 12 ....**South Ireland** ....Malahide, clockwise to Liscannor Bay

Area 13 ....**North Ireland** ....Liscannor Bay, clockwise to Lambay Island

Area 14 ....**Channel Islands** ....Guernsey and Jersey

Key to Marina Plans symbols

Bottled gas		P	Parking
Chandler			Pub/Restaurant
Disabled facilities			Pump out
Electrical supply			Rigging service
Electrical repairs			Sail repairs
Engine repairs			Shipwright
First Aid			Shop/Supermarket
Fresh Water			Showers
Fuel - Diesel			Slipway
Fuel - Petrol		WC	Toilets
Hardstanding/boatyard			Telephone
Internet Café	@		Trolleys
Laundry facilities		V	Visitors berths
Lift-out facilities			Wi-Fi

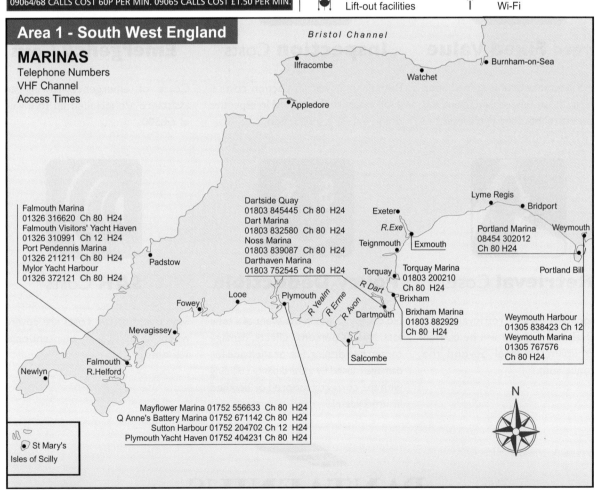

Area 1 - South West England

MARINAS
Telephone Numbers
VHF Channel
Access Times

Bristol Channel

Ilfracombe
Watchet
Burnham-on-Sea
Appledore

Falmouth Marina
01326 316620 Ch 80 H24
Falmouth Visitors' Yacht Haven
01326 310991 Ch 12 H24
Port Pendennis Marina
01326 211211 Ch 80 H24
Mylor Yacht Harbour
01326 372121 Ch 80 H24

Dartside Quay
01803 845445 Ch 80 H24
Dart Marina
01803 832580 Ch 80 H24
Noss Marina
01803 839087 Ch 80 H24
Darthaven Marina
01803 752545 Ch 80 H24

Exeter
R.Exe
Teignmouth
Exmouth

Lyme Regis
Bridport

Portland Marina
08454 302012
Ch 80 H24

Weymouth

Padstow

Torquay
R Dart
Torquay Marina
01803 200210
Ch 80 H24

Portland Bill

Looe
Fowey
Plymouth
R Yealm
R Erme
R Avon
Dartmouth

Brixham
Brixham Marina
01803 882929
Ch 80 H24

Weymouth Harbour
01305 838423 Ch 12
Weymouth Marina
01305 767576
Ch 80 H24

Mevagissey

Salcombe

Newlyn
Falmouth
R.Helford

N

Mayflower Marina 01752 556633 Ch 80 H24
Q Anne's Battery Marina 01752 671142 Ch 80 H24
Sutton Harbour 01752 204702 Ch 12 H24
Plymouth Yacht Haven 01752 404231 Ch 80 H24

St Mary's
Isles of Scilly

Pantaenius –
a strong **partner**

Agreed **Fixed Value**

A fixed insurance sum is agreed upon between the owner and Pantaenius, and this sum is reimbursed in the event of a total loss on the vessel.

Inspection Costs

Pantaenius covers inspection costs if your vessel runs aground irrespective of the excess contribution.

Emergency Costs

Costs of emergency towing and assistance are included up to a value of £4,500.

Retrieval Costs

Reasonable costs for retrieval, wreck removal, and disposal will be carried at an unlimited level beyond the insurance sum.

Policy Deductible

No excess applies in the event of a total loss, loss of personal effects, damage caused by lightning, fire or theft and for damage caused by a third party colliding with the correctly moored or berthed insured vessel.

SAR Costs

Search and rescue costs are covered when an EPIRB is unintentionally activated.

PANTAENIUS
Yacht Insurance

Germany · United Kingdom · Monaco · Denmark · Austria · Spain · Sweden · USA*

Marine Building · Victoria Wharf · Plymouth · Devon PL4 0RF · Phone +44-1752 22 36 56 · Fax +44-1752 22 36 37 · info@pantaenius.co.uk
Authorised and regulated by the Financial Services Authority

www.pantaenius.co.uk

2012/G1/e

FALMOUTH MARINA

Falmouth Marina
North Parade, Falmouth, Cornwall, TR11 2TD
Tel: 01326 316620 Fax: 01326 313939
Email: falmouth@premiermarinas.com
www.premiermarinas.com

VHF | Ch 80
ACCESS | H24

Falmouth Marina lies tucked away in sheltered waters at the southern end of the Fal Estuary. Welcoming to both visiting and residential yachts, its comprehensive facilities include a restaurant, convenience store and hairdresser, while just a 20-minute walk away is Falmouth's town centre where you will find no shortage of shops and eating places. Comprising more than 70 sq miles of navigable water, the Fal Estuary is an intriguing cruising area full of hidden creeks and inlets.

FACILITIES AT A GLANCE

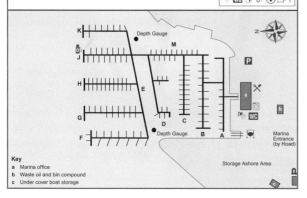

Key
a Marina office
b Waste oil and bin compound
c Under cover boat storage

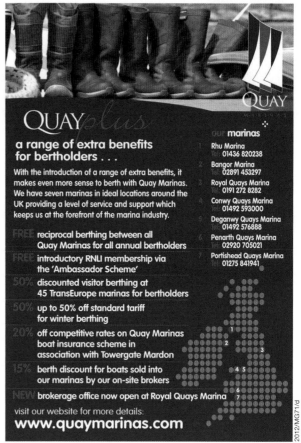

TYHA
Gold Anchor
Award Scheme
QUALITY ASSURED BERTHING

2012/MG25/d

WHAT IS THE GOLD ANCHOR AWARD SCHEME?

A voluntary assessment programme focused on customer service and providing Quality Assured Berthing for the visiting and resident boat owner.

The scheme is designed for the marina consumer by The Yacht Harbour Association incorporating the RYA berth holders charter. With 23 years experience of Gold Anchor standards, this is a point of reference for all boat owners to make an informed decision on where to berth. Ratings range from one to five gold anchors with the number of anchors indicating the facilities and services available to berth holders. Any award issued is a sure sign of a credible and quality marina.

Stage One
Marina Assessment
A comprehensive set of criteria that is checked and surveyed by an assessor.

Stage Two
Mystery Shop
A mystery shopper will visit the marina in the period between the application and the Gold Anchors being awarded. The results contribute to the final Gold Anchor rating.

Stage Three
Berth Holders Questionnaire
Berth holders are invited to complete an anonymous online questionnaire. With a minimum of 5% response, the results go directly to TYHA and contribute to the final Gold Anchor rating.

The Final Result
Concluding all three stages and compiling all scores the TYHA Gold Anchor panel consider all relevant information and an award is assigned according to the score achieved. The award is valid for three years during which the marina will undergo a further 2 mystery shops, the results of which will be used to recalculate the gold anchor rating.

Ratings are listed in this marina guide and at www.goldanchor.org

Chatham
MARINE

Every pair of our G2 deck shoes carries a unique 2 year guarantee.
Prices start from as little as £75.

To check your nearest stockist visit the Chatham Marine website
or call us on 0845 2700 217.

www.chatham-marine.co.uk

FALMOUTH VISITORS' YACHT HAVEN

Falmouth Visitors Yacht Haven
44 Arwenack Street
Tel: 01326 310991 Fax: 01326 211352
Email: admin@falmouthport.co.uk

VHF | Ch 12
ACCESS | H24

Run by Falmouth Harbour Commissioners (FHC), Falmouth Visitors' Yacht Haven has become increasingly popular since its opening in 1982, enjoying close proximity to the amenities and entertainments of Falmouth town centre. Sheltered by a breakwater, the Haven caters for 100 boats and offers petrol and diesel supplies as well as good shower and laundry facilities.

Falmouth Harbour is considered by some to be the cruising capital of Cornwall and its deep water combined with easily navigable entrance – even in the severest conditions – makes it a favoured destination for visiting yachtsmen.

FACILITIES AT A GLANCE

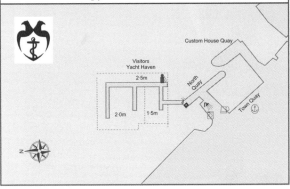

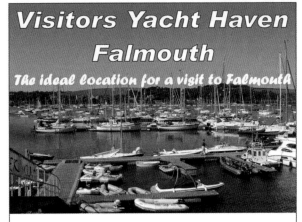
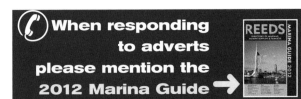

PORT PENDENNIS MARINA

Port Pendennis Marina
Challenger Quay, Falmouth, Cornwall, TR11 3YL
Tel: 01326 211211 Fax: 01326 311116
www.portpendennis.com

VHF | Ch 80
ACCESS | H24

Easily identified by the tower of the National Maritime Museum, Port Pendennis Marina is a convenient arrival or departure point for trans-Atlantic or Mediterranean voyages. Lying adjacent to the town centre, Port Pendennis is divided into an outer marina, with full tidal access, and inner marina, accessible three hours either side of HW. Among its impressive array of marine services is Pendennis Shipyard, one of Britain's most prestigious yacht builders, while other amenities on site include car hire, tennis courts and a yachtsman's lounge, from where you can send faxes or e-mails. Within walking distance of the marina are beautiful sandy beaches, an indoor swimming pool complex and castle.

FACILITIES AT A GLANCE

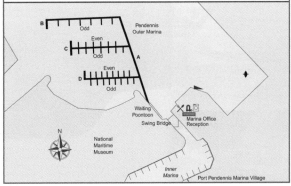

1

MYLOR YACHT HARBOUR

Mylor Yacht Harbour Marina
Mylor, Falmouth, Cornwall, TR11 5UF
Tel: 01326 372121 Fax: 01326 372120
Email: enquiries@mylor.com

VHF	Ch M, 80
ACCESS	H24

Situated on the western shore of Carrick Roads in the beautiful Fal Estuary, Mylor Yacht Harbour has been improved and expanded in recent years, now comprising two substantial breakwaters, three inner pontoons and approximately 250 moorings. With 24 hour access, good shelter and excellent facilities, it ranks among the most popular marinas on the SW Coast of England.

Formerly the Navy's smallest dockyard, established in 1805, Mylor is today a thriving yachting centre as well as home to the world's only remaining sailing oyster fishing fleet. With Falmouth just 10 mins away, local attractions include the Eden Project in St Austell and the National Maritime Museum in Falmouth.

FACILITIES AT A GLANCE

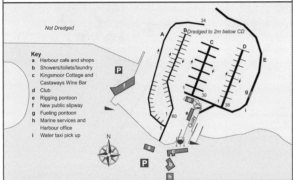

Key
a Harbour cafe and shops
b Showers/toilets/laundry
c Kingsmoor Cottage and
   Castaways Wine Bar
d Club
e Rigging pontoon
f New public slipway
g Fueling pontoon
h Marine services and
   Harbour office
i Water taxi pick up

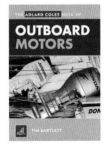
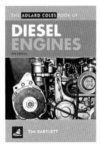

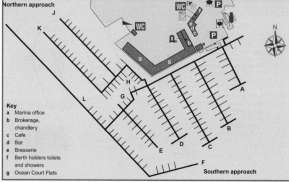

QUEEN ANNE'S BATTERY

Queen Anne's Battery
Plymouth, Devon, PL4 OLP
Tel: 01752 671142 Fax: 01752 266297
www.marinas.co.uk Email: qab@mdlmarinas.co.uk

VHF Ch 80
ACCESS H24

At the centre of Plymouth lies Queen Anne's Battery, comprising 280 resident berths as well as a visitor's basin with alongside pontoon berthing. Located just south of Sutton Harbour, all berths are well protected by a breakwater and double wavescreen.

As Plymouth Sound frequently provides the starting point for many prestigious international yacht races, the marina is often crowded with racers during the height of the season and its vibrant atmosphere can at times resemble a mini 'Cowes'.

FACILITIES AT A GLANCE

Key
a   Toilets and showers
b   Royal Western Yacht Club
c   Marina office and provisions shop
d   Bar/restaurant
e   Cafe

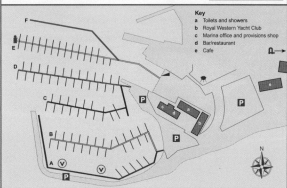

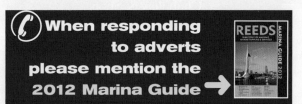
SUTTON HARBOUR

Sutton Harbour
The Jetty, Sutton Harbour, Plymouth, PL4 0DW
Tel: 01752 204702 Fax: 01752 204693
Email: marina@sutton-harbour.co.uk
www.sutton-harbour.co.uk

VHF Ch 12
ACCESS H24

Sutton Harbour Marina, located in the heart of Plymouth's historic Barbican area and a short stroll from the city centre, offers 5-star facilities in a sheltered location, surrounded by boutique waterfront bars and restaurants. Offering 490 pontoon berths with a minimum 3.5m depth, the harbour has 24-hr lock access on request with free flow approx 3hrs either side of high tide. The marina of choice for international yacht races such as The Transat and Fastnet. Visitors are invited to come and enjoy the unrivalled shelter, facilities, atmosphere and location that Sutton harbour offers.

FACILITIES AT A GLANCE

Key
a   Fish market
b   National Marine Aquarium
c   Customs House
d   The Cove
e   Marina office
f   Lock tower

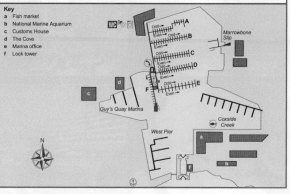

PLYMOUTH YACHT HAVEN

Plymouth Yacht Haven Ltd
Shaw Way, Mount Batten, Plymouth, PL9 9XH
Tel: 01752 404231 Fax: 01752 484177
www.yachthavens.com   Email: plymouth@yachthavens.com

VHF	Ch 80
ACCESS	H24

Situated at the mouth of the river Plym, Plymouth Yacht Haven offers good protection from the prevailing winds and is within close proximity of Plymouth Sound. This 450 berth marina can accommodate vessels up to 45m in length and 7m draught. Members of staff are on site 24/7 to welcome you as a visitor and to serve diesel. 2008 saw the opening of The Bridge Bar and Restaurant at the heart of the marina. Within easy access are coastal walks, a golf course, and health centre with heated swimming pool. The city of Plymouth and historic Barbican are a short water-taxi ride away.

With a 75ton travel hoist, undercover storage, and extensive range of marine services onsite, Plymouth Yacht Haven has the perfect yard for any maintenance required.

FACILITIES AT A GLANCE

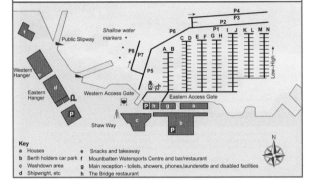

Key
a Houses
b Berth holders car park
c Washdown area
d Shipwright, etc
e Snacks and takeaway
f Mountbatten Watersports Centre and bar/restaurant
g Main reception - toilets, showers, phones,launderette and disabled facilities
h The Bridge restaurant

DARTHAVEN MARINA

Darthaven Marina
Brixham Road, Kingswear, Devon, TQ6 0SG
Tel: 01803 752242 Fax: 01803 752722
Email: darthaven@darthaven.co.uk
www.darthaven.co.uk

VHF	Ch 80
ACCESS	H24

Darthaven Marina is a family run business situated in the village of Kingswear on the east side of the River Dart. Within half a mile from Start Bay and the mouth of the river, it is the first marina you come to from seaward and is accessible at all states of the tide. Darthaven prides itself on being more than just a marina, offering a high standard of marine services with both electronic and engineering experts plus wood and GRP repairs on site. A shop, post office and five pubs are within a walking distance of the marina, while a frequent ferry service takes passengers across the river to Dartmouth.

FACILITIES AT A GLANCE

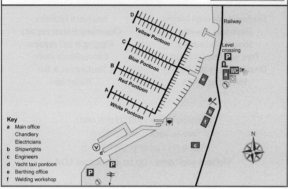

Key
a Main office
  Chandlery
  Electricians
b Shipwrights
c Engineers
d Yacht taxi pontoon
e Berthing office
f Welding workshop

Darthaven
The full-service marina in the Dart Harbour
Service provided where your boat is – or in our workshops at the marina and in Brixham

- Chandlery
- Engineering
- Electrical & electronics
- Shipwright & repairs
- Travel hoist (35 tonne)
- Fuel bug elimination
- Marine plumbing

VOLVO PENTA CENTRE · YANMAR · WESTERBEKE · DOOSAN · Raymarine · GARMIN · Webasto · B&G · PAGURO · WILLIAMS · SELVA Marine EUROPEAN POWER · express lube

Darthaven Marina, Brixham Road, Kingswear, Dartmouth, Devon TQ6 0SG
Main office 01803 752242   Engineering (24/7) 07973 280584   Chandlery 01803 752733
Berthing 01803 752545   Electrical & electronics (24/7) 07887 726093

British Marine

www.darthaven.co.uk

INVESTORS IN PEOPLE

2011/MG57/e

The Ship Inn
"The Village Inn"
Higher Street KINGSWEAR TQ6 0AG
Tel: 01803 752348

15th Century Inn with a superb local atmosphere.

CAMRA South Devon *Pub of the Year* 2006.
Good Beer Guide 2011.

Excellent local and national real ales, fine wines, traditional ciders and speciality whiskies and cognacs.

Eat in the Ship Restaurant or on the Terrace Deck with spectacular views of the River Dart and Dartmouth – the very best of local fish, shellfish, farm meats and poultry.

Booking essential

It's where the locals eat and meet

2012/MG106/e

Adlard Coles Nautical
THE BEST SAILING BOOKS

Course Book

'Masses of information'

Pass Your Day Skipper
4th edition
David Fairhall & Mike Peyton
978 1 4081 3113 8 **£12.99**

TO ORDER

Tel: **01256 302699**
email: **direct@macmillan.co.uk**
or **www.adlardcoles.com**

DART MARINA

Dart Marina
Sandquay Road, Dartmouth, Devon, TQ6 9PH
Tel: 01803 837161 Fax: 01803 835040
Email: yachtharbour@dartmarina.com
www.dartmarinayachtharbour.com

VHF | Ch 80
ACCESS | H24

Annual berth holders enjoy the finest marina location in the West Country, with the atmosphere and facilities of an exclusive club. The Yacht Harbour on the River Dart is a perfect retreat for simply relaxing and an ideal base for local boating and more ambitious cruising further afield. During the season there are a limited number of visitors' berths available and a waiting list for the 110 annual berths. The berths are accessible at any tide and are located in peaceful surroundings, just a short walk along the riverfront from Dartmouth's historic centre.

The showers and bathrooms are of high quality and some first class facilities are conveniently onsite - the Wildfire Bistro, Health Spa, River Restaurant and quayside dining.

FACILITIES AT A GLANCE

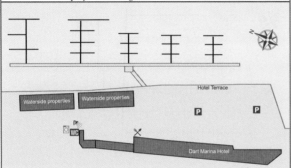

NOSS MARINA

Noss Marina
Bridge Road, Kingswear, Devon, TQ6 0EA
Tel: 01803 839087 Fax: 01803 835620
Email: info@nossmarina.co.uk
www.nossmarina.co.uk

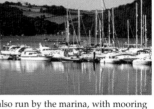

VHF | Ch 80
ACCESS | H24

Upstream of Dartmouth on the east shore of the River Dart is Noss Marina. Enjoying a peaceful rural setting, this marina is well suited to those who prefer a quieter atmosphere. Besides 180 fully serviced berths, 50 fore-and-aft moorings in the middle reaches of the river are also run by the marina, with mooring holders entitled to use all the facilities available to berth holders. During summer, a passenger ferry service runs regularly between Noss-on-Dart and Dartmouth, while a grocery service to your boat can be provided on request.

FACILITIES AT A GLANCE

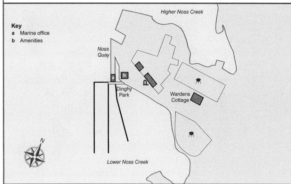

Key
a Marina office
b Amenities

DARTSIDE QUAY

Dartside Quay
Galmpton Creek, Brixham, Devon, TQ5 0EH
Tel: 01803 845445 Fax: 01803 843558
Email: dartsidequay@mdlmarinas.co.uk www.marinas.co.uk

VHF | Ch 80
ACCESS | H24

Located at the head of Galmpton Creek, Dartside Quay lies three miles up river from Dartmouth.

In a sheltered position and with beautiful views across to Dittisham, it offers extensive boatyard facilities. The 7-acre dry boat storage area has space for over 300 boats and is serviced by a 65-ton hoist operating from a purpose-built dock, a 16-ton trailer hoist and 13-ton crane.

There are also a number of summer mud moorings available and a well stocked chandlery, in fact if the item you want is not in stock we can order it in for you.

FACILITIES AT A GLANCE

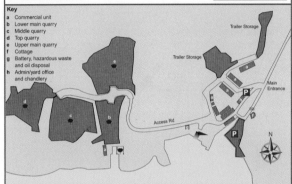

Key
a Commercial unit
b Lower main quarry
c Middle quarry
d Top quarry
e Upper main quarry
f Cottage
g Battery, hazardous waste and oil disposal
h Admin/yard office and chandlery

BRIXHAM MARINA

Brixham Marina
Berry Head Road, Brixham
Devon, TQ5 9BW
Tel: 01803 882929 Fax: 01803 882737
www.marinas.co.uk Email: brixham@mdlmarinas.co.uk

VHF | Ch 80
ACCESS | H24

Home to one of Britain's largest fishing fleets, Brixham Harbour is located on the southern shore of Tor Bay, which is well sheltered from westerly winds and where tidal streams are weak. Brixham Marina, housed in a separate basin to the work boats, provides easy access in all weather conditions and at all states of the tide. Established in 1989, it has become increasingly popular with locals and visitors alike, enjoying an idyllic setting right on the town's quayside.

Local attractions include a walk out to Berry Head Nature Reserve and a visit to the replica of Sir Francis Drake's ship, the *Golden Hind*.

FACILITIES AT A GLANCE

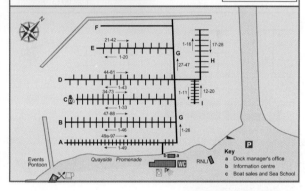

Key
a Dock manager's office
b Information centre
c Boat sales and Sea School

TORQUAY MARINA

Torquay Marina
Torquay, Devon, TQ2 5EQ
Tel: 01803 200210 Fax: 01803 200225
Email: torquaymarina@mdlmarinas.co.uk www.marinas.co.uk

VHF | Ch 80
ACCESS | H24

Tucked away in the north east corner of Tor Bay, Torquay Marina is well sheltered from the prevailing SW'ly winds, providing safe entry in all conditions and at any state of the tide. Located in the centre of Torquay, the marina enjoys easy access to the town's numerous shops, bars and restaurants.

Torquay is ideally situated for either exploring Tor Bay itself, with its many delightful anchorages, or else for heading further west to experience several other scenic harbours such as Dartmouth and Salcombe. It also provides a good starting point for crossing to Brittany, Normandy or the Channel Islands.

FACILITIES AT A GLANCE

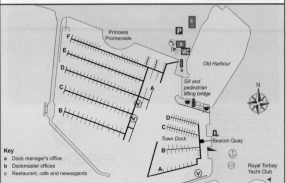

Key
a Dock manager's office
b Dockmaster offices
c Restaurant, cafe and newsagents

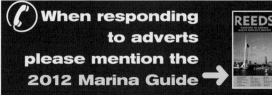

PORTLAND MARINA

Portland Marina
Osprey Quay, Portland, Dorset, DT5 1DX
Tel: 08454 302012 Fax: 08451 802012
www.deanreddyhoff.co.uk
Email: sales@portlandmarina.co.uk

VHF Ch 80
ACCESS H24

New for 2009, Portland Marina is an ideal location for both annual berthing and weekend stopovers. The marina offers first class facilities including washrooms, on-site bar and restaurant, lift out and storage up to 320T, dry stacking up to 10m, 24-hour manned security, fuel berth, sewage pump out, extensive car parking and a full range of marine services including a chandlery.

The marina is within walking distance of local pubs and restaurants on Portland with Weymouth's bustling town centre and mainline railway station just a short bus or ferry ride away.

FACILITIES AT A GLANCE

Key
a Admin Office, washrooms, showers and laundry
b Bar and Restaurant
c Business/retail units
d Refuse and recycling bins
e Commercial units
f Dry stack storage building
g Sunseeker

Berthing guide
From low at hammerheads
Odds outside
Evens inside

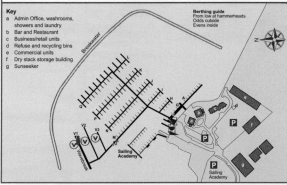

WEYMOUTH HARBOUR

Weymouth & Portland Borough Council
North Quay, Weymouth, Dorset, DT4 8TA
Tel: 01305 838423 Fax: 01305 767927
Email: berthingoffice@weymouth.gov.uk

VHF Ch 12
ACCESS H24

Weymouth Harbour which lies to the NE of Portland in the protected waters of Weymouth Bay, benefits from deep water at all states of the tide. Located in the heart of Weymouth old town, the Georgian harbour offers plenty of places to berth overnight, please make sure to

contact the berthing office on VHF Ch12 upon arrival. Vessels over 15m are advised to give prior notification of intended arrival. Pontoons on both quays benefit from free electricity and fresh water, as well as free showers and a coin-operated laundrette. Visiting yachtsmen are very welcome, both at the Royal Dorset Yacht Club and Weymouth Sailing Club, both situated directly on the quayside in the outer harbour.

FACILITIES AT A GLANCE

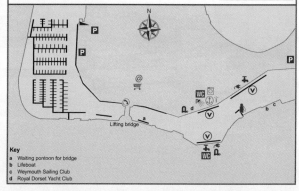

Key
a Waiting pontoon for bridge
b Lifeboat
c Weymouth Sailing Club
d Royal Dorset Yacht Club

WEYMOUTH MARINA

Weymouth Marina
70 Commercial Road, Dorset, DT4 8NA
Tel: 01305 767576 Fax: 01305 767575
www.weymouth-marina.co.uk
Email: sales@weymouth-marina.co.uk

VHF Ch 80
ACCESS H24

With more than 280 permanent and visitors' berths, Weymouth is a modern, purpose-built marina ideally situated for yachtsmen cruising between the West Country and the Solent. It is also conveniently placed for sailing to France or the Channel Islands.

Accessed via the town's historic lifting bridge, which opens every even hour 0800–2000 (plus 2100 Jun–Aug), the marina is dredged to 2.5m below chart datum. It provides easy access to the town centre, with its abundance of shops, pubs and restaurants, as well as to the traditional seafront where an impressive sandy beach is overlooked by an esplanade of hotels.

FACILITIES AT A GLANCE

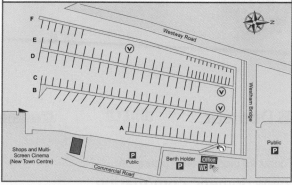

KINGFISHER MARINE

**CHANDLERS • MARINE ENGINEERS • RIGGERS
BOAT BUILDING & REPAIRS • BOAT LIFTING**

Visit our large quayside chandler's store where you'll find all the top brands in marine equipment and experienced marine engineers on hand to advise you.

Kingfisher Marine also offers full workshop facilities for all your servicing needs.

OPEN 7 DAYS A WEEK - ALL YEAR ROUND

10a Custom House Quay, Weymouth DT4 88G

www.kingfishermarine.co.uk

Telephone (01305) 766595

2012/MG103/e

ADLARD COLES NAUTICAL
WEATHER FORECASTS
BY FAX & TELEPHONE

Coastal/Inshore	2-day by Fax	5-day by Phone
South West	09065 222 348	09068 969 648
Mid Channel	09065 222 347	09068 969 647
Channel East	09065 222 346	09068 969 646
NE France	09065 501 611	09064 700 421
N France	09065 501 612	09064 700 422
N Brittany	09065 501 613	09064 700 423
Offshore	**2-5 day by Fax**	**2-5 day by Phone**
English Channel	09065 222 357	09068 969 657
Southern North Sea	09065 222 358	09068 969 658
Biscay	09065 222 360	09068 969 660

09064/68 CALLS COST 60P PER MIN. 09065 CALLS COST £1.50 PER MIN.

Key to Marina Plans symbols

Bottled gas		P	Parking
Chandler			Pub/Restaurant
Disabled facilities			Pump out
Electrical supply			Rigging service
Electrical repairs			Sail repairs
Engine repairs			Shipwright
First Aid			Shop/Supermarket
Fresh Water			Showers
Fuel - Diesel			Slipway
Fuel - Petrol		WC	Toilets
Hardstanding/boatyard			Telephone
Internet Café			Trolleys
Laundry facilities		V	Visitors berths
Lift-out facilities			Wi-Fi

Area 2 - Central Southern England

MARINAS
Telephone Numbers
VHF Channel
Access Times

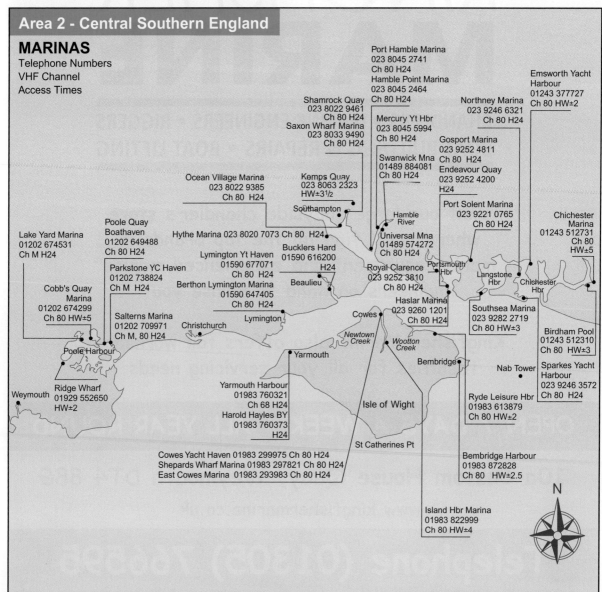

Port Hamble Marina 023 8045 2741 Ch 80 H24
Hamble Point Marina 023 8045 2464 Ch 80 H24
Shamrock Quay 023 8022 9461 Ch 80 H24
Saxon Wharf Marina 023 8033 9490 Ch 80 H24
Mercury Yt Hbr 023 8045 5994 Ch 80 H24
Swanwick Mna 01489 884081 Ch 80 H24
Northney Marina 023 9246 6321 Ch 80 H24
Emsworth Yacht Harbour 01243 377727 Ch 80 HW±2
Gosport Marina 023 9252 4811 Ch 80 H24
Endeavour Quay 023 9252 4200 H24
Ocean Village Marina 023 8022 9385 Ch 80 H24
Kemps Quay 023 8063 2323 HW±3½
Southampton
Hamble River
Port Solent Marina 023 9221 0765 Ch 80 H24
Chichester Marina 01243 512731 Ch 80 HW±5
Lake Yard Marina 01202 674531 Ch M H24
Poole Quay Boathaven 01202 649488 Ch 80 H24
Hythe Marina 023 8020 7073 Ch 80 H24
Bucklers Hard 01590 616200 H24
Universal Mna 01489 574272 Ch 80 H24
Portsmouth Hbr
Langstone Hbr
Chichester Hbr
Lymington Yt Haven 01590 677071 Ch 80 H24
Parkstone YC Haven 01202 738824 Ch M H24
Beaulieu
Royal Clarence 023 9252 3810 Ch 80 H24
Cobb's Quay Marina 01202 674299 Ch 80 HW±5
Berthon Lymington Marina 01590 647405 Ch 80 H24
Salterns Marina 01202 709971 Ch M, 80 H24
Lymington
Cowes
Haslar Marina 023 9260 1201 Ch 80 H24
Southsea Marina 023 9282 2719 Ch 80 HW±3
Christchurch
Newtown Creek
Wootton Creek
Birdham Pool 01243 512310 Ch 80 HW±3
Poole Harbour
Yarmouth
Bembridge
Nab Tower
Sparkes Yacht Harbour 023 9246 3572 Ch 80 H24
Weymouth
Ridge Wharf 01929 552650 HW±2
Yarmouth Harbour 01983 760321 Ch 68 H24
Harold Hayles BY 01983 760373 H24
Ryde Leisure Hbr 01983 613879 Ch 80 HW±2
Isle of Wight
St Catherines Pt
Cowes Yacht Haven 01983 299975 Ch 80 H24
Shepards Wharf Marina 01983 297821 Ch 80 H24
East Cowes Marina 01983 293983 Ch 80 H24
Bembridge Harbour 01983 872828 Ch 80 HW±2.5
Island Hbr Marina 01983 822999 Ch 80 HW±4
N

RELAX.

WITH 8 FIRST-CLASS MARINAS TO VISIT FINDING YOUR PERFECT HAVEN IS EASY.

EASTBOURNE	01323 470099
BRIGHTON	01273 819919
CHICHESTER	01243 512731
SOUTHSEA	023 9282 2719
PORT SOLENT	023 9221 0765
GOSPORT	023 9252 4811
SWANWICK	01489 884081
FALMOUTH	01326 316620

BUY 5 VISITOR NIGHTS AND STAY 7
SEE GREAT ESCAPES AT PREMIERMARINAS.COM

If you love boating, you'll love our first-class facilities and our passion for customer service. But we know that you look for value for money too. That's why we invite you to visit our website to find out more about our Great Escapes visitors offer. But if you are looking for a permanent berth you'll also be delighted by our berthing rates and our Premier Advantage Berth Holders' savings and benefits.

FUEL AT COST FREE STORAGE ASHORE **15% DISCOUNT ON BOATYARDS**
42 FREE VISITOR NIGHTS FLEXIBLE CONTRACTS 20% OFF MARINE INSURANCE

PREMIER MARINAS

2012/MG88/e

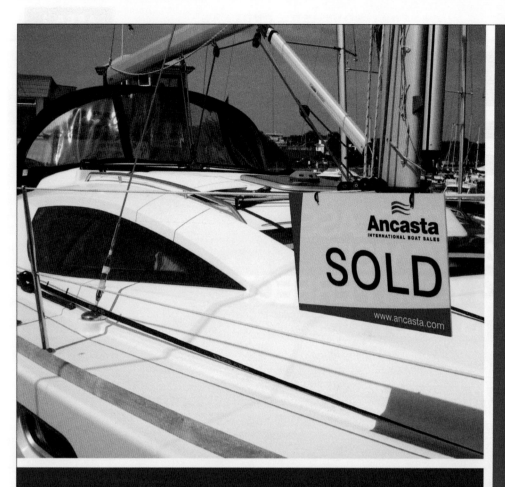

2

RIDGE WHARF YACHT CENTRE

Ridge Wharf Yacht Centre
Ridge, Wareham, Dorset, BH20 5BG
Tel: 01929 552650 Fax: 01929 554434
Email: office@ridgewharf.co.uk

VHF
ACCESS HW±2

On the south bank of the River Frome, which acts as the boundary to the North of the Isle of Purbeck, is Ridge Wharf Yacht Centre. Access for a 1.5m draught is between one and two hours either side of HW, with berths drying out to soft mud. The Yacht Centre cannot be contacted on VHF, so it is best to phone up ahead of time to inquire about berthing availability.

A trip upstream to the ancient market town of Wareham is well worth while, although owners of deep-draughted yachts may prefer to go by dinghy. Tucked between the Rivers Frome and Trent, it is packed full of cafés, restaurants and shops.

FACILITIES AT A GLANCE

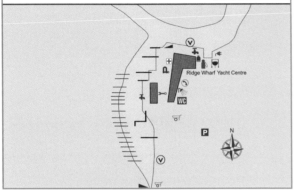

LAKE YARD MARINA

Lake Yard Marina
Lake Drive, Hamworthy, Poole, Dorset BH15 4DT
Tel: 01202 674531 Fax: 01202 677518
Email: office@lakeyard.com www.lakeyard.com

VHF Ch M
ACCESS H24

Lake Yard is situated towards the NW end of Poole Harbour, just beyond the SHM No 73. The entrance can be easily identified by 2FR (vert) and 2FG (vert) lights. Enjoying 24 hour access, the marina has no designated visitors' berths, but will accommodate visiting yachtsmen if resident berth holders are away. Its on site facilities include full maintenance and repair services as well as hard standing and a 50 ton boat hoist, although for the nearest fuel go to Corralls (Tel 01202 674551), opposite the Town Quay. Lake Yard's Waterfront Club, offering spectacular views across the harbour, opens seven days a week for lunchtime and evening meals.

FACILITIES AT A GLANCE

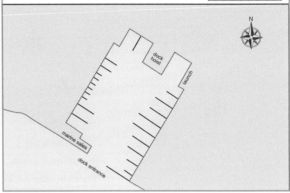

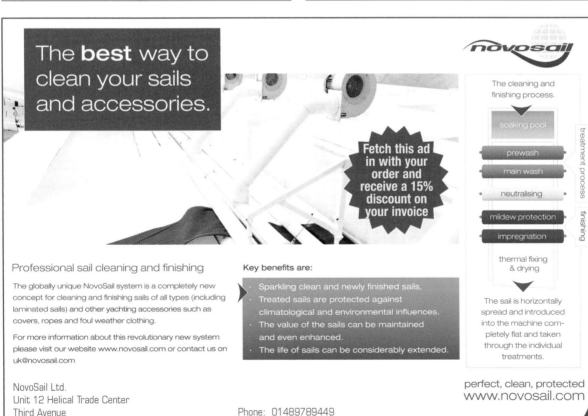

COBB'S QUAY MARINA

Cobb's Quay Marina
Hamworthy, Poole, Dorset, BH15 4EL
Tel: 01202 674299 Fax: 01202 665217
Email: cobbsquay@mdlmarinas.co.uk www.marinas.co.uk

VHF Ch 80
ACCESS HW±5

Lying on the west side of Holes Bay in Poole Harbour, Cobb's Quay is accessed via the lifting bridge at Poole Quay. With fully serviced pontoons for yachts up to 25m LOA, the marina can be entered five hours either side of high water and is normally able to accommodate visiting yachts. On site is the Boat House, which welcomes visitors to its bar and restaurant.

Cobb's Quay Marina also offers a convenient 240 berth Dry Stack system for motorboats up to 10 metres. Offering increased security and lower maintenance costs, the service includes unlimited launching on demand seven days a week. For location, Poole is one of the largest natural harbours in the world and is considered by many to be among the finest.

FACILITIES AT A GLANCE

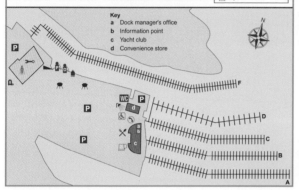

Key
a Dock manager's office
b Information point
c Yacht club
d Convenience store

POOLE QUAY BOAT HAVEN

c/o Poole Quay Boat Haven
Poole Town Quay, Poole, Dorset, BH15 1HJ
Tel: 01202 649488 Fax: 01202 785619
Email: info@poolequayboathaven.co.uk

VHF Ch 80
ACCESS H24

Once inside the Poole Harbour entrance small yachts heading for Poole Quay Boat Haven should use the Boat Channel running parallel south of the dredged Middle Ship Channel, which is primarily used by ferries sailing to and from the Hamworthy terminal. The marina can be accessed via the Little Channel and is easily identified by the large breakwater alongside the Quay. With deep water at all states of the tide the marina has berthing available for 125 yachts up to 35m, but due to its central location the marina can get busy so it is best to reserve a berth.

There is easy access to all of Poole Quay's facilities including restaurants, bars, Poole Pottery and the Waterfront Museum.

FACILITIES AT A GLANCE

2012/MG24/e

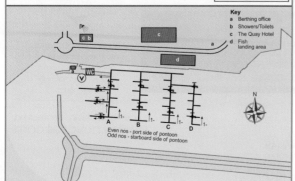

Key
a Berthing office
b Showers/Toilets
c The Quay Hotel
d Fish landing area

Even nos - port side of pontoon
Odd nos - starboard side of pontoon

2

PORT OF POOLE MARINA

c/o Poole Quay Boat Haven
Poole Town Quay, Poole, Dorset, BH15 1HJ
Tel: 01202 649488 Fax: 01202 785619
Email: info@poolequayboathaven.co.uk

VHF Ch 80
ACCESS H24

Beware of the chain ferry operating at the entrance to Poole harbour. Once inside small yachts heading for the marina should use the Boat Channel running parallel south of the Middle Ship Channel. The marina is to the east of the main ferry terminals and can be identified by a large floating breakwater at the entrance.

The marina has all tides deep water and berthing for 60 allocated permanent vessels with overflow from Town Quay berthing on the breakwater, wich is also suitable for super yachts.

A water taxi is available during daylight hours to access the quay for restaurants and shops, also accessible with a 10-15min walk round the quays.

FACILITIES AT A GLANCE

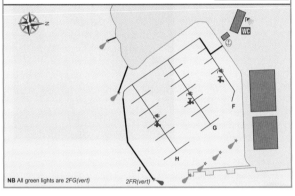

NB All green lights are 2FG(vert)   2FR(vert)

PARKSTONE YACHT HAVEN

Parkstone Yacht Club
Pearce Avenue, Parkstone, Poole, Dorset, BH14 8EH
Tel: 01202 738824 Fax: 01202 716394
Email: office@parkstoneyc.co.uk

VHF Ch M
ACCESS H24

Situated on the north side of Poole Harbour between Salterns Marina and Poole Quay Boat Haven, Parkstone Yacht Haven can be entered at all states of the tides. Its approach channel has been dredged to 2.0m and is clearly marked by buoys. Run by the Parkstone Yacht Club, the Haven provides 200 deep water berths for members and visitors' berths. Other services include a new office facility with laundry and WCs, bar, restaurant, shower/changing rooms and wi-fi. With a busy sailing programme for over 2,500 members, the Yacht Club plays host to a variety of events including Poole Week, which is held towards the end of August. Please phone for availability.

FACILITIES AT A GLANCE

Western Point

Parkstone Yacht Club

1.5m
2.0m
2.0m

Elm Park

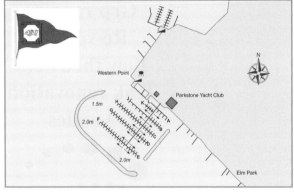

SALTERNS MARINA

Salterns Marina
40 Salterns Way, Lilliput, Poole
Dorset, BH14 8JR
Tel: 01202 709971 Fax: 01202 700398
Email: marina@salterns.co.uk www.salterns.co.uk

VHF Ch M, 80
ACCESS H24

Holding both the Blue Flag and Five Gold Anchor awards, Salterns Marina provides a service which is second to none. Located off the North Channel, it is approached from the No 31 SHM and benefits from deep water at all states of the tide. Facilities include 220 alongside pontoon berths as well as 75 swinging moorings with a free launch service. However, with very few designated visitors' berths, it is best to contact the marina ahead of time for availability. Fuel, diesel and gas can all be obtained 24 hours a day and the well-stocked chandlery, incorporating a coffee shop, stays open seven days a week.

FACILITIES AT A GLANCE

Key
a Marina office
    Reception
    Chandlery
    Salterns Brokerage
    Coffee shop
    Toilets/Showers
    Marine Sales
    Laundry
Sales Offices:
    Princess
    Golden Arrow Electronics
    Nordic Marine
    Wessex Marine
    Poole Aquatic Ltd
    North Haven
    Crest Marine

b Fuel pumps
    Yacht hoist
c Crest Marine
d Dinghy racks
e Toilets & showers
f Salterns Hotel
g Boatyard workshop
h 45 tonne travel hoist
i Boatyard office
    Engine & boat sales

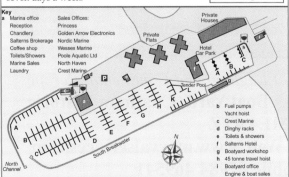

YARMOUTH HBR/HAROLD HAYLES BY

Yarmouth Harbour
Yarmouth, Isle of Wight, PO41 0NT
Tel: 01983 760321 Fax: 01983 761192
info@yarmouth-harbour.co.uk
www.yarmouth-harbour.co.uk

VHF Ch 68
ACCESS H24

Harold Hayles Ltd
The Quay, Yarmouth, Isle of Wight, PO41 0RS
Tel: 01983 760373 Fax: 01983 760666
Email: info@spurscutters.co.uk
www.spurscutters.co.uk

VHF
ACCESS H24

The most western harbour on the Isle of Wight, Yarmouth is not only a convenient passage stopover but has become a very desirable destination in its own right, with virtually all weather and tidal access, although strong N to NE'ly winds can produce a considerable swell. The HM launch patrols the harbour entrance and will direct visiting yachtsmen to a pontoon berth or pile. The pretty harbour and town offer plenty of fine restaurants and amenities.

Walkashore pontoon moorings are available from the local boatyard, Harold Hayles Ltd, in the SW corner of the harbour. Pre-booking is preferred for both individuals or rallies.

FACILITIES AT A GLANCE

Car Ferry Terminal

Town Quay

South Quay

Key
a Royal Solent Yacht Club
b Harbour office
c Yarmouth Sailing Club
d Harold Hayles Boatyard

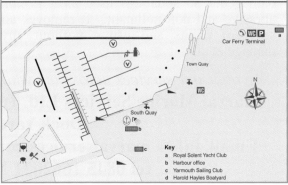

2

LYMINGTON YACHT HAVEN

Lymington Yacht Haven
King's Saltern Road, Lymington, S041 3QD
Tel: 01590 677071 Fax: 01590 678186
Email: lymington@yachthavens.com www.yachthavens.com

⚓⚓⚓⚓

VHF | Ch 80
ACCESS | H24

The attractive old market town of Lymington lies at the western end of the Solent, just three miles from the Needles Channel. Despite the numerous ferries plying to and from the Isle of Wight, the river is well sheltered and navigable at all states of the tide, proving a popular destination with visiting yachtsmen. LPG is available.

Lymington Yacht Haven is the first of the two marinas from seaward, situated on the port hand side. Offering easy access to the Solent, it is a 10-minute walk to the town centre and supermarkets.

FACILITIES AT A GLANCE

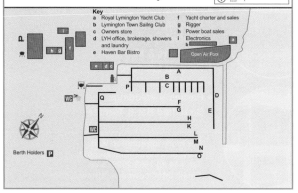

Key
a Royal Lymington Yacht Club
b Lymington Town Sailng Club
c Owners store
d LYH office, brokerage, showers and laundry
e Haven Bar Bistro
f Yacht charter and sales
g Rigger
h Power boat sales
i Electronics

BERTHON LYMINGTON MARINA

Berthon Lymington Marina Ltd
The Shipyard, Lymington, Hampshire, SO41 3YL
Tel: 01590 647405 Fax: 01590 676353
www.berthon.co.uk Email: marina@berthon.co.uk

VHF | Ch 80
ACCESS | H24

Situated approximately half a mile up river of Lymington Yacht Haven, on the port hand side, is Lymington Marina. Easily accessible at all states of the tide, it offers between 60 to 70 visitors' berths, with probably the best

washrooms in the Solent. Its close proximity to the town centre and first rate services mean that booking is essential on busy weekends. Lymington Marina's parent, Berthon Boat Co, has state of the art facilities and a highly skilled work force of 100+ to deal with any repair, maintenance or refit.

Lymington benefits from having the New Forest on its doorstep and the Solent Way footpath provides an invigorating walk to and from Hurst Castle.

FACILITIES AT A GLANCE

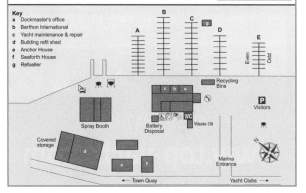

Key
a Dockmaster's office
b Berthon International
c Yacht maintenance & repair
d Building refit shed
e Anchor House
f Seaforth House
g Refueller

BUCKLERS HARD MARINA

Bucklers Hard
Beaulieu, Brockenhurst, Hampshire, SO42 7XB
Tel: 01590 616200 Fax: 01590 616211
www.bucklershard.co.uk Email: river@beaulieu.co.uk

VHF
ACCESS | H24

Meandering through the New Forest, the Beaulieu River is considered by many to be one of the most attractive harbours on the mainland side of the Solent. Two miles upstream from the mouth of the river lies Bucklers Hard, an historic

18th century village where shipwrights skilfully constructed warships for Nelson's fleet. The Maritime Museum, showing the history of boat-building in the village, is open throughout the year.

The marina is manned 24/7 and offers deep water to visitors at all states of the tide, although the bar at the river's entrance should be avoided two hours either side of LW.

FACILITIES AT A GLANCE

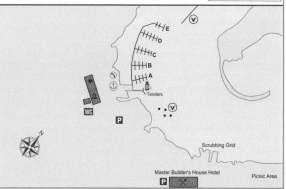

COWES YACHT HAVEN

Cowes Yacht Haven
Vectis Yard, Cowes, Isle of Wight, PO31 7BD
Tel: 01983 299975 Fax: 01983 200332
www.cowesyachthaven.com
Email: berthing@cowesyachthaven.com

VHF	Ch 80
ACCESS	H24

Situated virtually at the centre of the Solent, Cowes is best known as Britain's premier yachting centre and offers all types of facilities to yachtsmen. Cowes Yacht Haven, operating 24 hours a day, has very few permanent moorings and is dedicated to catering for visitors and events. At peak times it can become very crowded and for occasions such as Skandia Cowes Week you need to book up in advance.

FACILITIES AT A GLANCE

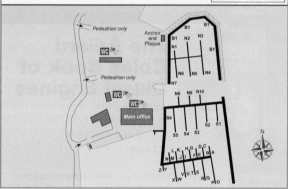

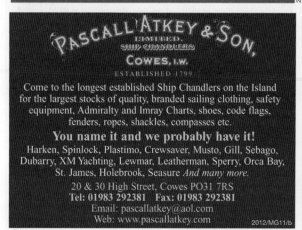

2

SHEPARDS WHARF MARINA

Shepards Wharf Boatyard
Medina Road, Cowes, Isle of Wight, PO31 7HT
Tel: 01983 297821 Fax: 01983 294814
www.shephards.co.uk

VHF	Ch 80
ACCESS	H24

A cable upstream of Cowes Yacht Haven, still on the starboard side, is Shepards Wharf. Incorporating several visitor pontoon berths, its facilities include water as well as full boatyard services ranging from a chandler and sailmaker to a 20-ton boat hoist. Fuel can be obtained from Lallows Boatyard (Tel 01983 292111) or Cowes Yacht Haven. For berthing availability, visiting yachtsmen should contact Cowes Harbour Control on VHF Ch 69 or Tel 01983 293952.

Shepards Wharf is within easy walking distance of Cowes town centre, where among the restaurants to be highly recommended are the Red Duster and Murrays Seafoods on the High Street and Tonino's on Shooters Hill. Also worth visiting are the Maritime Museum, exhibiting the Uffa Fox boats *Avenger* and *Coweslip*, and the Sir Max Aitken Museum. Sir Max contributed enormously to ocean yacht racing and the museum is dedicated to his collection of nautical instruments, paintings and maritime artefacts.

FACILITIES AT A GLANCE

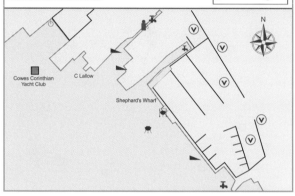

EAST COWES MARINA

East Cowes Marina
Britannia Way, East Cowes, Isle of Wight, PO32 6UB
Tel: 01983 293983 Fax: 01983 299276
www.eastcowesmarina.co.uk
Email: sales@eastcowesmarina.co.uk

VHF	Ch 80
ACCESS	H24

Accommodating around 235 residential yachts and 150 visiting boats at all states of the tide, East Cowes Marina is situated on the quiet and protected east bank of the Medina River, about a quarter mile above the chain ferry. The on-site chandlery stocks essential marine equipment and a small convenience store is just five minutes walk away. The new centrally heated shower and toilet facilities ensure the visitor a warm welcome at any time of the year, as does the on-site pub and restaurant.

Several water taxis provide a return service to Cowes, ensuring a quick and easy way of getting to the town centre.

FACILITIES AT A GLANCE

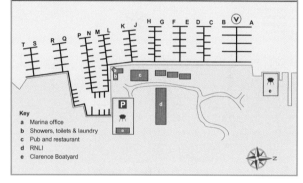

Key
a Marina office
b Showers, toilets & laundry
c Pub and restaurant
d RNLI
e Clarence Boatyard

ISLAND HARBOUR MARINA

Island Harbour Marina
Mill Lane, Binfield, Newport, Isle of Wight, PO30 2LA
Tel: 01983 822999 Fax: 01983 526020
Email: info@island-harbour.co.uk

VHF | Ch 80
ACCESS | HW±4

Situated in beautiful rolling farmland about half a mile south of Folly Inn, Island Harbour Marina provides around 200 visitors' berths. Protected by a lock that is operated daily from 0700 – 2100 during the summer and from 0800 – 1730 during the winter, the marina is accessible for about four hours either side of HW for draughts of 1.5m.

Due to its remote setting, the marina's on site restaurant also sells essential provisions and newspapers. A half hour walk along the river brings you to Newport, the capital and county town of the Isle of Wight.

FACILITIES AT A GLANCE

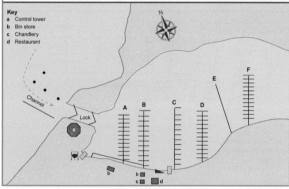

Key
a Control tower
b Bin store
c Chandlery
d Restaurant

HYTHE MARINA VILLAGE

Hythe Marina Village
Shamrock Way, Hythe, Southampton, SO45 6DY
Tel: 023 8020 7073 Fax: 023 8084 2424
Email: hythe@mdlmarinas.co.uk www.marinas.co.uk

VHF | Ch 80
ACCESS | H24

Situated on the western shores of Southampton Water, Hythe Marina Village is approached by a dredged channel leading to a lock basin. The lock gates are controlled 24 hours a day throughout the year, with a waiting pontoon to the south of the approach basin.

Hythe Marina Village incorporates full marine services as well as on site restaurants and shops. Forming an integral part of the New Forest Waterside, Hythe is the perfect base from which to explore Hampshire's pretty inland villages and towns, or alternatively you can catch the ferry to Southampton's Town Quay.

FACILITIES AT A GLANCE

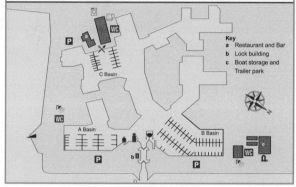

Key
a Restaurant and Bar
b Lock building
c Boat storage and Trailer park

OCEAN VILLAGE MARINA

Ocean Village Marina
2 Channel Way, Southampton, SO14 3TG
Tel: 023 8022 9385 Fax: 023 8023 3515
Email: oceanvillage@mdlmarinas.co.uk www.marinas.co.uk

VHF | Ch 80
ACCESS | H24

The entrance to Ocean Village Marina lies on the port side of the River Itchen, just before the Itchen Bridge. With the capacity to accommodate large yachts and tall ships, the marina, accessible 24 hours a day, is a renowned home for international yacht races.

Situated at the heart of a waterside development incorporating shops, cinemas, restaurants and housing as well as The Royal Southampton Yacht Club, Ocean Village offers a vibrant atmosphere along with high quality service.

FACILITIES AT A GLANCE

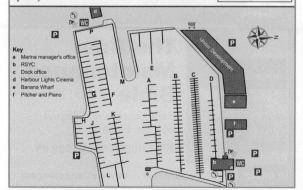

Key
a Marina manager's office
b RSYC
c Dock office
d Harbour Lights Cinema
e Banana Wharf
f Pitcher and Piano

SHAMROCK QUAY

Shamrock Quay
William Street, Northam, Southampton, Hants, SO14 5QL
Tel: 023 8022 9461 Fax: 023 8021 3808
Email: shamrockquay@mdlmarinas.co.uk www.marinas.co.uk

VHF | Ch 80
ACCESS | H24

Shamrock Quay, lying upstream of the Itchen Bridge on the port hand side, offers excellent facilities to yachtsmen. It also benefits from being accessible and manned 24 hours a day. On-site there is a 75-ton travel hoist and a 47-ton boat mover, and for dining out there is a choice of restaurants and bars.

The city centre is about two miles away, where among the numerous attractions are the Maritime Museum at Town Quay, the Medieval Merchant's House in French Street and the Southampton City Art Gallery in the Civic Centre.

FACILITIES AT A GLANCE

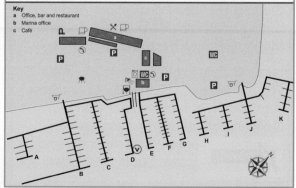

Key
a Office, bar and restaurant
b Marina office
c Café

KEMPS QUAY

Kemp's Shipyard Ltd
Quayside Road, Southampton, SO18 1BZ
Tel: 023 8063 2323 Fax: 023 8022 6002
Email: enquiries@kempsquay.com

VHF
ACCESS HW±3.5

At the head of the River Itchen on the starboard side is Kemps Quay, a family-run marina with a friendly, old-fashioned feel. Accessible only 3½ hrs either side of HW, it has a limited number of deep water berths, the rest being half tide, drying out to soft mud. Its restricted access is, however, reflected in the lower prices.

Although situated on the outskirts of Southampton, a short bus or taxi ride will soon get you to the city centre. Besides a nearby BP Garage selling bread and milk, the closest supermarkets can be found in Bitterne Shopping Centre, which is five minutes away by bus.

FACILITIES AT A GLANCE

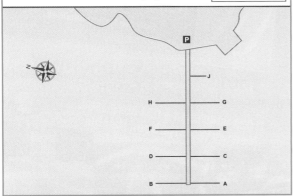

SAXON WHARF

Saxon Wharf
Lower York Street, Northam
Southampton, SO14 5QF
Tel: 023 8033 9490 Fax: 023 8033 5215
Email: saxonwharf@mdlmarinas.co.uk www.marinas.co.uk

VHF Ch 80
ACCESS H24

Saxon Wharf is situated towards the top of the River Itchen at the head of Southampton Water and boasts the largest Dry Stack facility in Europe, which offers secure dry berthing and on-demand launching and lifting for boats up to 13m. Equipped with 50m marina berths and heavy duty pontoons, it is intended to accommodate superyachts and larger vessels. Boasting a 200-ton boat hoist and several marine specialists, including Southampton Yacht Services, it is the ideal place for the refit and restoration of big boats, whether it be a quick liftout or a large scale project. Located close to Southampton city centre and airport, Saxon Wharf is easily accessible by road, rail or air.

FACILITIES AT A GLANCE

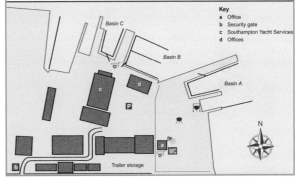

Key
a   Office
b   Security gate
c   Southampton Yacht Services
d   Offices

Basin C

Basin B

Basin A

Trailer storage

HAMBLE POINT MARINA

Hamble Point Marina
School Lane, Hamble, Southampton, SO31 4NB
Tel: 023 8045 2464 Fax: 023 8045 6440
Email: hamblepoint@mdlmarinas.co.uk www.marinas.co.uk

VHF | Ch 80
ACCESS | H24

Situated virtually opposite Warsash, this is the first marina you will come to on the western bank of the Hamble. Accommodating yachts and power boats up to 30m in length, it offers easy access to the Solent.

Boasting extensive facilities including 116 Dry Stack berths for motorboats up to 10 metres, the marina is within a 20-minute walk of Hamble Village, where services include a plethora of pubs and restaurants as well as a bank and a convenience store.

FACILITIES AT A GLANCE

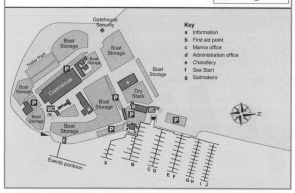

Key
a Information
b First aid point
c Marina office
d Administration office
e Chandlery
f Sea Start
g Sailmakers

2

PORT HAMBLE MARINA

Port Hamble Marina
Satchell Lane, Hamble, Southampton, SO31 4QD
Tel: 023 8045 2741 Fax: 023 8045 5206
Email: porthamble@mdlmarinas.co.uk www.marinas.co.uk

⚓⚓⚓⚓⚓
VHF | Ch 80
ACCESS | H24

On the west bank of the River Hamble, Port Hamble is the closest marina to the picturesque Hamble Village, therefore proving extremely popular with visiting yachtsmen. As this marina is extremely popular with visitors, especially in the summer months, it is best to contact the marina ahead of time.

Besides exploring the River Hamble, renowned for its maritime history which began as far back as the ninth century when King Alfred's men sank some 20 Viking long ships at Bursledon, other nearby places of interest include the 13th century Netley Abbey, allegedly haunted by Blind Peter the monk, and the Royal Victoria Country Park.

FACILITIES AT A GLANCE

Key
a Dock manager's office
b Boat sales
c Royal Air Force YC
d Bar/restaurant

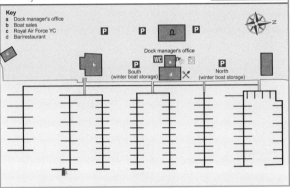

MERCURY YACHT HARBOUR

Mercury Yacht Harbour
Satchell Lane, Hamble, Southampton, SO31 4HQ
Tel: 023 8045 5994 Fax: 023 8045 7369
Email: mercury@mdlmarinas.co.uk www.marinas.co.uk

⚓⚓⚓⚓⚓
VHF | Ch 80
ACCESS | H24

Mercury Yacht Harbour is the third marina from seaward on the western bank of the River Hamble, tucked away in a picturesque, wooded site adjacent to Badnam Creek. Enjoying deep water at all states of the tide, it accommodates yachts up to 24m LOA and boasts an extensive array of facilities.

Hamble Village is a 20-minute walk away, although the on-site chandlery does stock a small amount of essential items, and for a good meal look no further than The Waters Edge Bar and Restaurant whose balcony offers striking views over the water.

FACILITIES AT A GLANCE

Key
a Toilets and showers
b Launderette
c Chandlery
d Restaurant and bar
e Marine surveyor
f Dockmaster,
   marina manager's office
g Waste disposal
h Recycling area

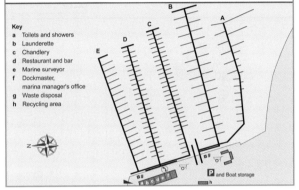

UNIVERSAL MARINA

Universal Marina
Crableck Lane, Sarisbury Green, Southampton, SO31 7ZN
Tel: 01489 574272 Fax: 01489 574273
Email: info@universalmarina.co.uk

VHF | Ch 80
ACCESS | H24

Universal Marina is one of the few remaining independent marinas offering south coast moorings. Universal Marina's unique location is unbeatable, tucked in between the oak trees on the East Bank of the Hamble where 68 acres of natural wildlife and marshlands surrounds the busy and friendly marina. Positioned only minutes off the M27, it is one of the most accessible marinas on the south coast. The 250 berth complex, features all the latest facilities required by the modern day boat owner, recently upgraded pontoons, power, water and wifi available to each berth. Visitors are welcome & although there are no dedicated visitor berths these are available by prior arrangement.

FACILITIES AT A GLANCE

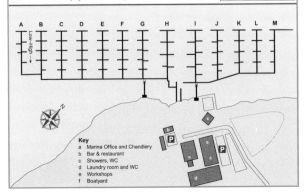

Key
a Marina Office and Chandlery
b Bar & restaurant
c Showers, WC
d Laundry room and WC
e Workshops
f Boatyard

SWANWICK MARINA

Swanwick Marina
Swanwick, Southampton, Hampshire, SO31 1ZL
Tel: 01489 884081 Fax: 01489 579073
Email: swanwick@premiermarinas.com
www.premiermarinas.com

VHF | Ch 80
ACCESS | H24

Situated on the east bank of the River Hamble next to Bursledon Bridge, Swanwick Marina is accessible at all states of the tide and can accommodate yachts up to 20m LOA.

The marina's fully-licensed bar and bistro, Velshedas, over-looking the river, is open for breakfast, lunch and dinner during the summer. Alternatively, just a short row or walk away is the celebrated Jolly Sailor pub in Bursledon on the west bank, made famous for being the local watering hole in the British television series *Howard's Way*.

FACILITIES AT A GLANCE

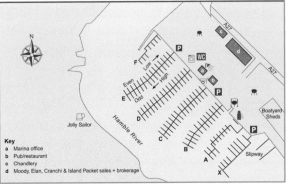

Key
a Marina office
b Pub/restaurant
c Chandlery
d Moody, Elan, Cranchi & Island Packet sales + brokerage

RYDE LEISURE HARBOUR

Ryde Harbour
The Esplanade, Ryde, Isle of Wight, PO33 1JA
Tel: 01983 613879 Fax: 01983 613903
www.rydeharbour.com Email: ryde.harbour@iow.gov.uk

VHF	Ch 80
ACCESS	HW±2

Known as the 'gateway to the Island', Ryde, with its elegant houses and abundant shops, is among the Isle of Wight's most popular resorts. Its well-protected harbour is conveniently close to the exceptional beaches as well as to the town's restaurants and amusements.

Drying to 2.5m and therefore only accessible to yachts that can take the ground, the harbour accommodates 90 resident boats as well as up to 75 visiting yachts. Fin keel yachts may dry out on the harbour wall.

Ideal for family cruising, Ryde offers a wealth of activities, ranging from ten pin bowling and ice skating to crazy golf and tennis.

FACILITIES AT A GLANCE

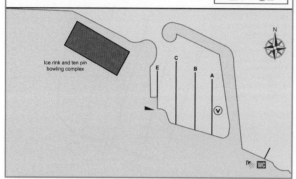

Ice rink and ten pin bowling complex

BEMBRIDGE HARBOUR

Bembridge Harbour
Harbour Office, The Duver, St Helens, Ryde
Isle of Wight, PO33 1YB
Tel: 01983 872828 Fax: 01983 872922
Email: chris@bembridgeharbour.co.uk
www.bembridgeharbour.co.uk

VHF	Ch 80
ACCESS	HW±2.5

Bembridge is a compact, pretty harbour whose entrance, although restricted by the tides (recommended entry for a 1.5m draught is 2½hrs before HW), is well sheltered in all but north north easterly gales. Offering excellent sailing clubs, beautiful beaches and fine restaurants, this Isle of Wight port is a first class haven with plenty of charm. With approximately 100 new visitors' berths on the Duver Marina pontoons, the marina at St Helen's Quay, at the western end of the harbour, is now allocated to annual berth holders only.

FACILITIES AT A GLANCE

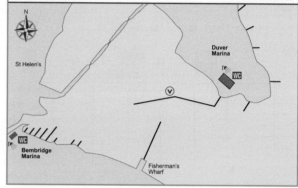

St Helen's

Duver Marina

WC

Bembridge Marina

Fisherman's Wharf

HASLAR MARINA

Haslar Marina
Haslar Road, Gosport, Hampshire, PO12 1NU
Tel: 023 9260 1201 Fax: 023 9260 2201
www.haslarmarina.co.uk Email: sales@haslarmarina.co.uk

VHF	Ch 80
ACCESS	H24

This modern, purpose-built marina lies to port on the western side of Portsmouth Harbour entrance and is easily recognised by its prominent lightship incorporating a bar and restaurant. Accessible at all states of the tide, Haslar's extensive facilities do not however include fuel, the nearest being at the Gosport Marina only a few cables north.

Within close proximity is the Royal Navy Submarine Museum and the Museum of Naval Firepower 'Explosion' both worth a visit.

FACILITIES AT A GLANCE
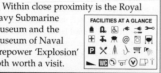

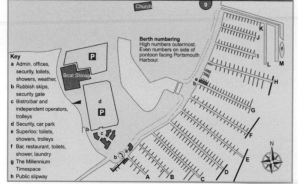

Church

Berth numbering
High numbers outermost.
Even numbers on side of pontoon facing Portsmouth Harbour.

Boat Storage

Key
a Admin. offices, security, toilets, showers, weather,
b Rubbish skips, security gate
c Bistro/bar and independent operators, trolleys
d Security, car park
e Superloo: toilets, showers, trolleys
f Bar, restaurant, toilets, shower, laundry
g The Millennium Timespace
h Public slipway

GOSPORT MARINA

Premier Gosport Marina
Mumby Road, Gosport, Hampshire, PO12 1AH
Tel: 023 9252 4811 Fax: 023 9258 9541
Email: gosport@premiermarinas.com
www.premiermarinas.com

VHF	Ch 80
ACCESS	H24

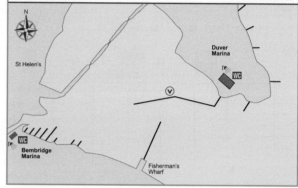

A few cables north of Haslar Marina, again on the port hand side, lies Gosport Marina. Boasting 519 fully-serviced visitors' berths, its extensive range of facilities incorporates a fuel barge on its southern breakwater as well as shower and laundry amenities. Numerous boatyard and engineering specialists are also located in and around the premises.

Within easy reach of the marina is Gosport town centre, offering a cosmopolitan selection of restaurants along with several supermarkets and shops.

FACILITIES AT A GLANCE

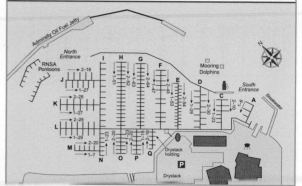

Admiralty Oil Fuel Jetty

North Entrance

RNSA Pontoons

Mooring Dolphins

South Entrance

Breakwater

Drystack holding

Drystack

ROYAL CLARENCE MARINA

Royal Clarence Marina, Royal Clarence Yard
Weevil Lane, Gosport, Hampshire PO12 1AX
Tel: 02392 523523 Fax: 02392 523523
Email: berthing@royalclarencemarina.org
www.royalclarencemarina.org

| VHF | Ch 80 |
| ACCESS | H24 |

Royal Clarence Marina
benefits from a unique setting
within a deep-water basin in
front of the Royal Navy's
former victualling yard. Only
10 minutes from the entrance
to Portsmouth Harbour, it
forms part of a £100 million
redevelopment scheme which
will incorporate residential homes, waterfront bars and restaurants as
well as shopping outlets. Among its facilities are
fully serviced finger pontoon berths up to 18m in
length, while over 150m of alongside berthing will
accommodate Yacht Club rallies and other maritime
events.

FACILITIES AT A GLANCE

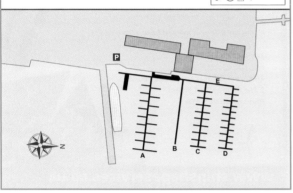

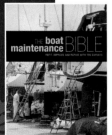
ENDEAVOUR QUAY

Endeavour Quay
Mumby Road, Gosport, Hampshire, PO12 1AH
Tel: 023 9258 4200 Email: enquiries@endeavourquay.co.uk
www.endeavourquay.co.uk

| VHF | |
| ACCESS | H24 |

Endeavour Quay commands a prime
location in Portsmouth Harbour on the
Gosport waterfront with unrestricted access
to its modern facilities by deep water. It is
also a site of significant yacht building
heritage being the birthplace of the famous
yacht builders Camper & Nicholsons.

Now modernised, the marina provides a
wide range of professional services from
boat lifting (180 tons max) craneage, deep
water berthing and outside/undercover
storage. The open yard policy and the wide range
of onsite marine related businesses makes
Endeavour Quay an ideal location for emergency
repairs to complex refit and specialist work for all
types of vessels.

FACILITIES AT A GLANCE

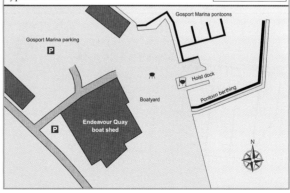

Gosport Marina pontoons

Gosport Marina parking

Hoist dock

Boatyard

Pontoon berthing

Endeavour Quay
boat shed

PORT SOLENT MARINA

Port Solent Marina
South Lockside, Portsmouth, PO6 4TJ
Tel: 023 9221 0765 Fax: 023 9232 4241
www.premiermarinas.com
Email: portsolent@premiermarinas.com

VHF Ch 80
ACCESS H24

Port Solent Marina is located to the north east of Portsmouth Harbour, not far from the historic Portchester Castle. Accessible via a 24-hour lock, this purpose built marina offers a full range of facilities. The Boardwalk comprises an array of shops and restaurants, while close by is a David Lloyd Health Centre and a large Odeon cinema.

No visit to Portsmouth Harbour is complete without a trip to the Historic Dockyard, home to Henry VIII's *Mary Rose*, Nelson's HMS *Victory* and the first iron battleship, HMS *Warrior*, built in 1860.

FACILITIES AT A GLANCE

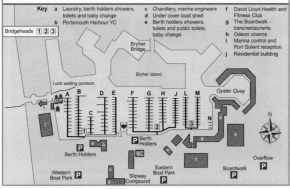

Key
a Laundry, berth holders showers, toilets and baby change
b Portsmouth Harbour YC
c Chandlery, marine engineers
d Under cover boat shed
e Berth holders showers, toilets and public toilets, baby change
f David Lloyd Health and Fitness Club
g The Boardwalk - bars/restaurants
h Odeon cinema
i Marina control and Port Solent reception
j Residential building

Bridgeheads 1 2 3

SOUTHSEA MARINA

Southsea Marina
Fort Cumberland Road, PO4 9RJ
Tel: 02392 822719 Fax: 02392 822220
Email: southsea@premiermarinas.com
www.premiermarinas.com

VHF Ch 80
ACCESS HW±3

Southsea Marina is a small and friendly marina located on the western shore of Langstone Harbour, an expansive tidal bay situated between Hayling Island and Portsmouth. The channel is clearly marked by seven starboard and nine port hand markers. A tidal gate allows unrestricted movement in and out of the marina up to 3 hours either side of HW operates the entrance. The minimum depth in the marina entrance during this period is 1.6m and a waiting pontoon is available. There are excellent on site facilities including a bar, restaurant and chandlery.

FACILITIES AT A GLANCE

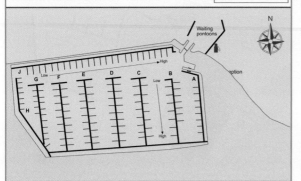

SPARKES MARINA

Sparkes Marina
38 Wittering Road, Hayling Island, Hampshire, PO11 9SR
Tel: 023 9246 3572 Fax: 023 9246 5741
Email: sparkes@mdlmarinas.co.uk www.marinas.co.uk

VHF Ch 80
ACCESS H24

Just inside the entrance to Chichester Harbour, on the eastern shores of Hayling Island, lies Sparkes Marina. One of two marinas in Chichester to have full tidal access, its facilities include a wide range of marine services. Also on-site is Marina Jaks, a first class restaurant that has been recommended by the Which Good Food Guide 2007 and 2008. Within fairly close proximity are a convenience store and various takeaway restaurants.

FACILITIES AT A GLANCE

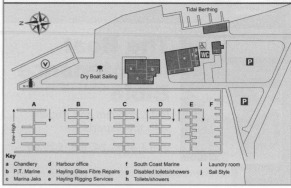

Key
a Chandlery
b P.T. Marine
c Marina Jaks
d Harbour office
e Hayling Glass Fibre Repairs
f Hayling Rigging Services
g South Coast Marine
h Disabled toilets/showers
i Laundry room
j Sail Style
k Toilets/showers

NORTHNEY MARINA

Northney Marina
Northney Road, Hayling Island, Hampshire, PO11 0NH
Tel: 023 9246 6321 Fax: 023 9246 1467
Email: northney@mdlmarinas.co.uk
www.northneymarina.co.uk

| VHF | Ch 80 |
| ACCESS | H24 |

One of two marinas in Chichester Harbour to be accessible at all states of the tide, Northney Marina is on the northern shore of Hayling Island in the well marked Sweare Deep Channel, which branches off to port almost at the end of the Emsworth Channel.

With an excellent facilities block, the marina incorporates a provisions store and laundry area as well as fantastic ablution facilities. There is also an events area for rallies.

FACILITIES AT A GLANCE

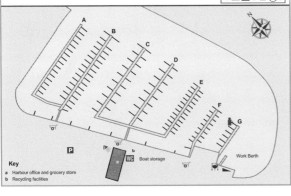

Key
a Harbour office and grocery store
b Recycling facilities

EMSWORTH YACHT HARBOUR

Emsworth Yacht Harbour Ltd
Thorney Road, Emsworth, Hants, PO10 8BP
Tel: 01243 377727 Fax: 01243 373432
Email: info@emsworth-marina.co.uk
www.emsworth-marina.co.uk

| VHF | |
| ACCESS | HW±2 |

Accessible about one and a half to two hours either side of high water, Emsworth Yacht Harbour is a sheltered site, offering good facilities to yachtsmen.

Created in 1964 from a log pond, the marina is within easy walking distance of the pretty little town of Emsworth, which boasts at least 10 pubs, several high quality restaurants and two well-stocked convenience stores.

FACILITIES AT A GLANCE

Key
a Ground floor - toilets and showers
   1st floor - harbour office
b Home Marine -
   outboard engine repairs

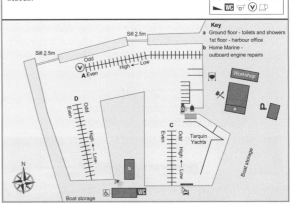

CHICHESTER MARINA

Chichester Marina
Birdham, Chichester, West Sussex, PO20 7EJ
Tel: 01243 512731 Fax: 01243 513472
Email: chichester@premiermarinas.com
www.premiermarinas.com

⚓⚓⚓⚓

VHF	Ch 80
ACCESS	HW±5

Chichester Marina, nestling in an enormous natural harbour, has more than 1,000 berths, making it one of the largest in the UK. Its approach channel can be easily identified by the CM SHM pile. The channel was dredged to 0.5m below CD in 2004, giving access of around five hours either side of HW at springs. Besides the wide ranging marine facilities, there are also a restaurant and small convenience store on site. Chichester, which is only about a five minute bus or taxi ride away, has several places of interest, the most notable being the cathedral.

FACILITIES AT A GLANCE

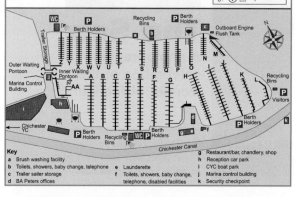

Key
a Brush washing facility
b Toilets, showers, baby change, telephone
c Trailer sailer storage
d BA Peters offices
e Launderette
f Toilets, showers, baby change, telephone, disabled facilities
g Restaurant/bar, chandlery, shop
h Reception car park
i CYC boat park
j Marina control building
k Security checkpoint

BIRDHAM POOL MARINA

Birdham Pool Marina
Birdham Pool, Chichester, Sussex
Tel: 01243 512310 Fax: 01243 513163
Email: info@birdhampool.co.uk

VHF	Ch 80
ACCESS	HW±3

Birdham Pool must be among Britain's most charming and rustic marinas. Its recently dredged channel allows access for up to four hours either side of HW via a lock. Any visiting yachtsman will not be disappointed by its unique and picturesque setting. The marina boasts a boatyard with skilled craftsmen offering a wide range of services as well as fuel. The channel is marked by green piles that should be left no more than 3m to starboard.

FACILITIES AT A GLANCE

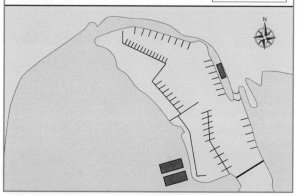

Key to Marina Plans symbols

Bottled gas		P	Parking
Chandler		Pub/Restaurant	
Disabled facilities		Pump out	
Electrical supply		Rigging service	
Electrical repairs		Sail repairs	
Engine repairs		Shipwright	
First Aid		Shop/Supermarket	
Fresh Water		Showers	
Fuel - Diesel		Slipway	
Fuel - Petrol		WC Toilets	
Hardstanding/boatyard		Telephone	
Internet Café		Trolleys	
Laundry facilities		Visitors berths	
Lift-out facilities		Wi-Fi	

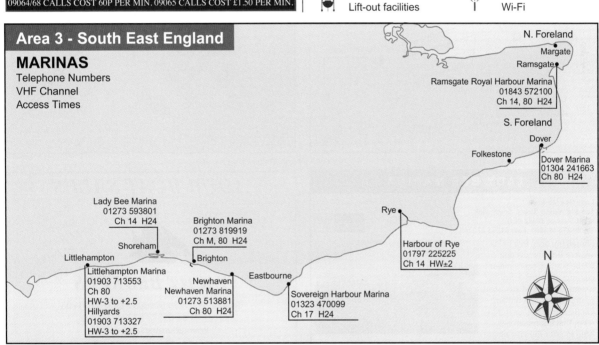

Area 3 - South East England

MARINAS
Telephone Numbers
VHF Channel
Access Times

N. Foreland
Margate
Ramsgate
Ramsgate Royal Harbour Marina
01843 572100
Ch 14, 80 H24

S. Foreland
Dover
Folkestone
Dover Marina
01304 241663
Ch 80 H24

Lady Bee Marina
01273 593801
Ch 14 H24

Brighton Marina
01273 819919
Ch M, 80 H24

Rye

Harbour of Rye
01797 225225
Ch 14 HW±2

Shoreham
Brighton

Littlehampton
Littlehampton Marina
01903 713553
Ch 80
HW-3 to +2.5
Hillyards
01903 713327
HW-3 to +2.5

Newhaven
Newhaven Marina
01273 513881
Ch 80 H24

Eastbourne

Sovereign Harbour Marina
01323 470099
Ch 17 H24

N

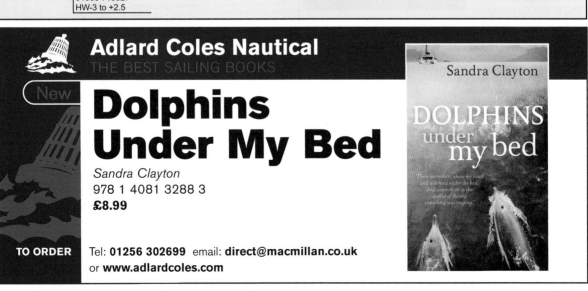

LITTLEHAMPTON MARINA

Littlehampton Marina
Ferry Road, Littlehampton, W Sussex
Tel: 01903 713553 Fax: 01903 732264
Email: sales@littlehamptonmarina.co.uk

VHF	Ch 80
ACCESS	HW-3 to +2.5

A typical English seaside town with funfair, promenade and fine sandy beaches, Littlehampton lies roughly midway between Brighton and Chichester at the mouth of the River Arun. It affords a convenient stopover for yachts either east or west bound, providing you have the right tidal conditions to cross the entrance bar with its charted depth of 0.7m. The marina lies about three cables above Town Quay and Fisherman's Quay, both of which are on the starboard side of the River Arun, and is accessed via a retractable footbridge that opens on request to the HM (note that you should contact him by 1630 the day before you require entry).

FACILITIES AT A GLANCE

Key
a Marina offices
b Cafe

THE SHIPYARD

The Shipyard
Rope Walk, Littlehampton, West Sussex, BN17 5DG
Tel: 01903 713327
Email: info@littlehamptonshipyard.co.uk

VHF	
ACCESS	HW-3 to +2.5

Formerly Hillyards, The Shipyard is a full service boatyard with moorings and storage for up to 50 boats. Based on the south coast within easy reach of London and the main yachting centres of the UK and Europe, The Shipyard provides a comprehensive range of marine services.

The buildings of the boatyard are on the River Arun, a short distance from the English Channel. They provide the ideal conditions to accommodate and service craft up to 36m in length and with a maximum draft 3.5m. There is also craning services for craft up to 40 tons and the facilities to slip vessels up to 27m. In addition there are secure facilities to accommodate vessels up to 54m in dry dock.

FACILITIES AT A GLANCE

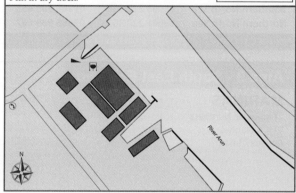

LADY BEE MARINA

Lady Bee Marina
138-140 Albion Street, Southwick
West Sussex, BN42 4EG
Tel: 01273 593801 Fax: 01273 870349

VHF	Ch 14
ACCESS	H24

Shoreham, only five miles west of Brighton, is one of the South Coast's major commercial ports handling, among other products, steel, grain, tarmac and timber. On first impressions it may seem that Shoreham has little to offer the visiting yachtsman, but once through the lock and into the eastern arm of the River Adur, the quiet Lady Bee Marina, with its Spanish waterside restaurant, can make this harbour an interesting alternative to the lively atmosphere of Brighton Marina. Run by the Harbour Office, the marina meets all the usual requirements, although fuel is available in cans from Southwick garage or from Corral's diesel pump situated in the western arm.

FACILITIES AT A GLANCE

Key
a Sussex Yacht Club
b Riverside Boatyard

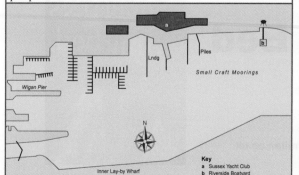

BRIGHTON MARINA

Brighton Marina
West Jetty, Brighton, East Sussex, BN2 5UP
Tel: 01273 819919 Fax: 01273 675082
Email: brighton@premiermarinas.com
www.premiermarinas.com

⚓⚓⚓⚓⚓

VHF	Ch M, 80
ACCESS	H24

Brighton Marina is the largest marina in the country and with its extensive range of shops, restaurants and facilities, is a popular and convenient stop-over for east and west-going passagemakers. Note, however, that it is not advisable to attempt entry in strong S to SE winds.

Only half a mile from the marina is the historic city of Brighton itself, renowned for being a cultural centre with a cosmopolitan atmosphere. Among its numerous attractions are the exotic Royal Pavilion, built for King George IV in the 1800s, and the Lanes, with its multitude of antiques shops.

FACILITIES AT A GLANCE

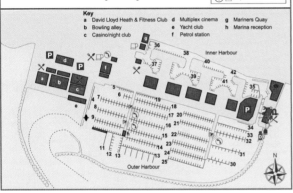

Key
a David Lloyd Heath & Fitness Club
b Bowling alley
c Casino/night club
d Multiplex cinema
e Yacht club
f Petrol station
g Mariners Quay
h Marina reception

NEWHAVEN MARINA

Newhaven Marina
The Yacht Harbour, Fort Road, Newhaven
East Sussex, BN9 9BY
Tel: 01273 513881 Fax: 01273 510493
Email: john.stirling@seacontainers.com

| VHF | Ch 80 |
| ACCESS | H24 |

Some seven miles from Brighton, Newhaven lies at the mouth of the River Ouse. With its large fishing fleet and regular ferry services to Dieppe, the harbour has over the years become progressively commercial, therefore care is needed to keep clear of large vessels under manoeuvre. The marina lies approximately quarter of a mile from the harbour entrance on the west bank and was recently dredged to allow full tidal access except on LWS.

FACILITIES AT A GLANCE

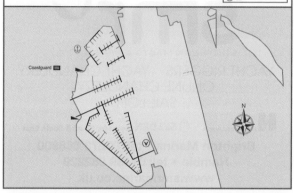

Coastguard

SOVEREIGN HARBOUR MARINA

Sovereign Harbour Marina
Pacific Drive, Eastbourne, East Sussex, BN23 5BJ
Tel: 01323 470099 Fax: 01323 470077
Email: sovereignharbour@premiermarinas.com
www.premiermarinas.com

| VHF | Ch 17 |
| ACCESS | H24 |

Opened in 1993 and taken over by Premier Marinas in 2007, Sovereign Harbour is situated to the eastern end of Eastbourne and is accessible at all states of the tide and weather except for in strong NE to SE'ly winds. Entered via a lock at all times of the day or night, the Five Gold Anchor Award marina is part of one of the largest waterfront complexes in the UK, enjoying close proximity to shops, restaurants and a multiplex cinema. A short bus or taxi ride takes you to Eastbourne, where you will find shops and eating places to suit all tastes and budgets.

FACILITIES AT A GLANCE

Key
a   The Waterfront, shops, restaurants, pubs and offices
b   Harbour office - weather information and visitor's information
c   Cinema
d   Retail park - supermarket and post office
e   Restaurant
f   Toilets, showers, launderette and disabled facilities
g   24 hr fuel pontoon (diesel, petrol and holding tank pump out)
h   Recycling centre
i   Boatyard, boatpark, marine engineers, riggers and electricians
NB Berth numbering runs from low outer to high inner

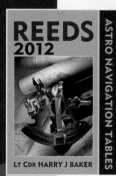

HARBOUR OF RYE

Harbour of Rye
New Lydd Road, Camber, E Sussex, TN31 7QS
Tel: 01797 225225 Fax: 01797 227429
Email: rye.harbour@environment-agency.gov.uk
www.environment-agency.gov.uk/harbourofrye

| VHF | Ch 14 |
| ACCESS | HW±2 |

The Strand Quay moorings are located in the centre of the historic town of Rye with all of its amenities a short walk away. The town caters for a wide variety of interests with the nearby Rye Harbour Nature Reserve, a museum, numerous antique shops and plentiful pubs, bars and restaurants. Vessels, up to a length of 15 metres, wishing to berth in the soft mud in or near the town of Rye should time their arrival at the entrance for not later than one hour after high water. Larger vessels should make prior arrangements with the Harbour Master. Fresh water, electricity, shower and toilet facilities are available.

FACILITIES AT A GLANCE

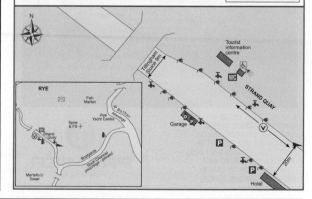

DOVER MARINA

Dover Harbour Board
Harbour House, Dover, Kent, CT17 9TF
Tel: 01304 241663 Fax: 01304 242549
Email: marina@doverport.co.uk

VHF Ch 80
ACCESS H24

Nestling under the famous White Cliffs, Dover sits between South Foreland to the NE and Folkestone to the SW. Boasting a maritime history stretching back as far as the Bronze Age, Dover is today one of Britain's busiest commercial ports, with a continuous stream of ferries and cruise liners plying to and from their European destinations. However, over the past years the harbour has made itself more attractive to the cruising yachtsman, with the marina, set well away from the busy ferry terminal, offering three sheltered berthing options in the Tidal Harbour, Granville Dock and Wellington Dock.

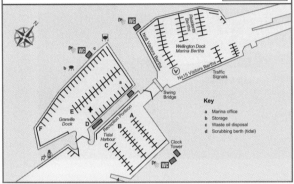

ROYAL HARBOUR MARINA

Royal Harbour Marina, Ramsgate
Harbour Office, Military Road, Ramsgate, Kent, CT11 9LQ
Tel: 01843 572105 Fax: 01843 590941
Email: portoframsgate@thanet.gov.uk
www.portoframsgate.co.uk

VHF Ch 14, 80
ACCESS H24

Steeped in maritime history, Ramsgate was awarded 'Royal' status in 1821 by George IV in recognition of the warm welcome he received when sailing from Ramsgate to Hanover with the Royal Squadron. Offering good shelter and modern facilities, the Royal Harbour comprises an inner marina, entered approximately HW±2. Permission to enter or leave the Royal Harbour must be obtained from Port Control on channel 14 and berthing instructions can be obtained from the Dockmaster on channel 80.

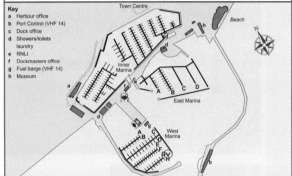

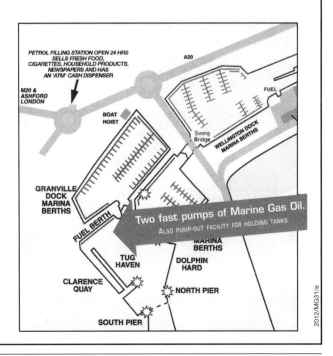

EAST ENGLAND - North Foreland to Great Yarmouth

Key to Marina Plans symbols

Bottled gas		Parking	
Chandler		Pub/Restaurant	
Disabled facilities		Pump out	
Electrical supply		Rigging service	
Electrical repairs		Sail repairs	
Engine repairs		Shipwright	
First Aid		Shop/Supermarket	
Fresh Water		Showers	
Fuel - Diesel		Slipway	
Fuel - Petrol		Toilets	
Hardstanding/boatyard		Telephone	
Internet Café		Trolleys	
Laundry facilities		Visitors berths	
Lift-out facilities		Wi-Fi	

4

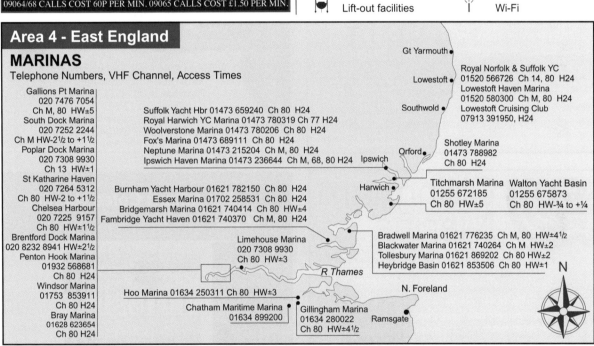

Area 4 - East England

MARINAS
Telephone Numbers, VHF Channel, Access Times

Gallions Pt Marina
020 7476 7054
Ch M, 80 HW±5
South Dock Marina
020 7252 2244
Ch M HW-2½ to +1½
Poplar Dock Marina
020 7308 9930
Ch 13 HW±1
St Katharine Haven
020 7264 5312
Ch 80 HW-2 to +1½
Chelsea Harbour
020 7225 9157
Ch 80 HW±1½
Brentford Dock Marina
020 8232 8941 HW±2½
Penton Hook Marina
01932 568681
Ch 80 H24
Windsor Marina
01753 853911
Ch 80 H24
Bray Marina
01628 623654
Ch 80 H24

Suffolk Yacht Hbr 01473 659240 Ch 80 H24
Royal Harwich YC Marina 01473 780319 Ch 77 H24
Woolverstone Marina 01473 780206 Ch 80 H24
Fox's Marina 01473 689111 Ch 80 H24
Neptune Marina 01473 215204 Ch M, 80 H24
Ipswich Haven Marina 01473 236644 Ch M, 68, 80 H24

Burnham Yacht Harbour 01621 782150 Ch 80 H24
Essex Marina 01702 258531 Ch 80 H24
Bridgemarsh Marina 01621 740414 Ch 80 HW±4
Fambridge Yacht Haven 01621 740370   Ch M, 80 H24

Limehouse Marina
020 7308 9930
Ch 80 HW±3

Hoo Marina 01634 250311 Ch 80 HW±3

Chatham Maritime Marina
01634 899200

Gillingham Marina
01634 280022
Ch 80 HW±4½

Gt Yarmouth
Lowestoft
Southwold

Royal Norfolk & Suffolk YC
01520 566726 Ch 14, 80 H24
Lowestoft Haven Marina
01520 580300 Ch M, 80 H24
Lowestoft Cruising Club
07913 391950, H24

Shotley Marina
01473 788982
Ch 80 H24

Orford
Ipswich
Harwich

Titchmarsh Marina   Walton Yacht Basin
01255 672185   01255 675873
Ch 80 HW±5   Ch 80 HW-¾ to +¼

Bradwell Marina 01621 776235 Ch M, 80 HW±4½
Blackwater Marina 01621 740264 Ch M HW±2
Tollesbury Marina 01621 869202 Ch 80 HW±2
Heybridge Basin 01621 853506 Ch 80 HW±1

R Thames

N. Foreland

Ramsgate

N

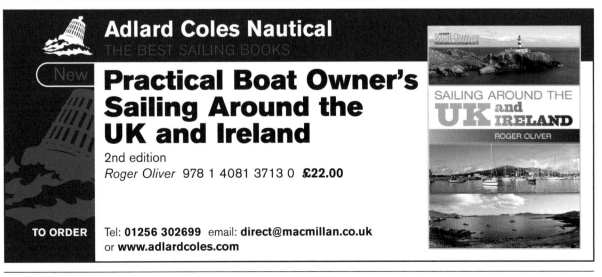

GILLINGHAM MARINA

Gillingham Marina
173 Pier Road, Gillingham, Kent, ME7 1UB
Tel: 01634 280022 Fax: 01634 280164
Email: berthing@gillingham-marina.co.uk
www.gillingham-marina.co.uk

⚓ ⚓ ⚓ ⚓ ⚓

VHF	Ch 80
ACCESS	HW±4.5

Gillingham Marina comprises a locked basin, accessible four and a half hours either side of high water, and a tidal basin upstream which can be entered approximately two hours either side of high water. Deep water moorings in the river cater for yachts arriving at other times.

Visiting yachts are usually accommodated in the locked basin, although it is best to contact the marina ahead of time. Lying on the south bank of the River Medway, the marina is approximately eight miles from Sheerness, at the mouth of the river, and five miles downstream of Rochester Bridge. Facilities include a well-stocked chandlery, brokerage and an extensive workshop.

FACILITIES AT A GLANCE

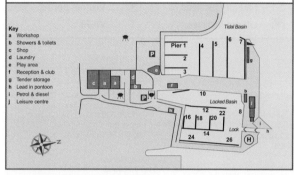

Key
a Workshop
b Showers & toilets
c Shop
d Laundry
e Play area
f Reception & club
g Tender storage
h Lead in pontoon
i Petrol & diesel
j Leisure centre

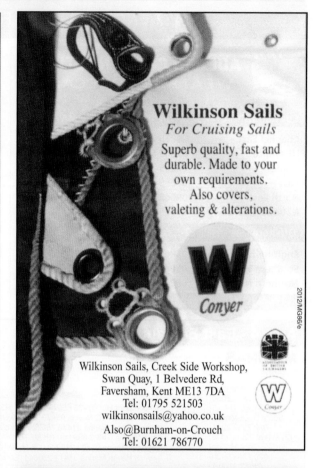

HOO MARINA

Hoo Marina
Vicarage Lane, Hoo, Rochester, Kent, ME3 9LE
Tel: 01634 250311 Fax: 01634 251761
Email: jcmarine@btconnect.com

VHF Ch 80
ACCESS HW±3

Hoo is a small village on the Isle of Grain, situated on a drying creek on the north bank of the River Medway approximately eight miles inland from Sheerness. Its marina was the first to be constructed on the East Coast and comprises finger berths supplied by all the usual services. It can be approached either straight across the mudflats near HW or, for a 1.5m draught, three hours either side of HW via a creek known locally as Orinoco. The entrance to this creek, which is marked by posts that must be left to port, is located a mile NW of Hoo Ness.

Grocery stores can be found either in the adjacent chalet park or else in Hoo Village, while the Hoo Ness Yacht Club welcomes visitors to its bar and restaurant. There are also frequent bus services to the nearby town of Rochester.

FACILITIES AT A GLANCE

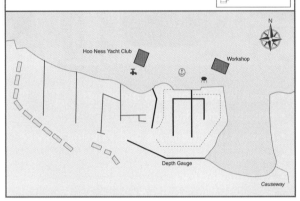

CHATHAM MARITIME MARINA

Chatham Maritime Marina, The Lock Building,
Leviathan Way, Chatham Maritime, Chatham, Medway, ME4 4LP
Tel: 01634 899200 Fax: 01634 899201
Email: chatham@mdlmarinas.co.uk www.marinas.co.uk

VHF Ch 80
ACCESS H24

Chatham Maritime Marina is situated on the banks of the River Medway in Kent, providing an ideal location from which to explore the surrounding area. There are plenty of secluded anchorages in the lower reaches of the Medway Estuary, while the river is navigable for some 13 miles from its mouth at Sheerness right up to Rochester, and even beyond for those yachts drawing less than 2m. Only 45 minutes from London by road, the marina is part of a multi-million pound leisure and retail development, currently accommodating 300 yachts.

FACILITIES AT A GLANCE

4

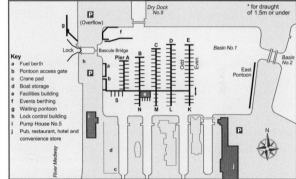

Key
a Fuel berth
b Pontoon access gate
c Crane pad
d Boat storage
e Facilities building
f Events berthing
g Waiting pontoon
h Lock control building
i Pump House No.5
j Pub, restaurant, hotel and convenience store

LIMEHOUSE MARINA

Limehouse Marina
46 Goodhart Place, London, E14 8EG
Tel: 020 7308 9930 Fax: 020 7363 0428
www.bwml.co.uk

VHF Ch 80
ACCESS HW±3

Limehouse Marina, situated where the canal system meets the Thames, is now considered the 'Jewel in the Crown' of the British inland waterways network. With complete access to 2,000 miles of inland waterway systems and with access to the Thames at most stages of the tide except around low water, the marina provides a superb location for river, canal and sea-going pleasure craft alike. Boasting a wide range of facilities and up to 90 berths, Limehouse Marina is housed in the old Regent's Canal Dock.

FACILITIES AT A GLANCE

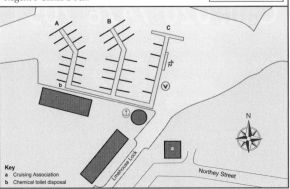

Key
a Cruising Association
b Chemical toilet disposal

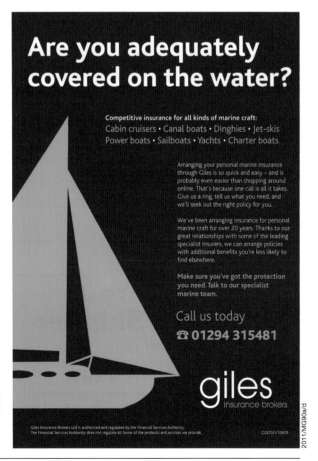

GALLIONS POINT MARINA

Gallions Point Marina, Gate 14, Royal Albert Basin
Woolwich Manor Way, North Woolwich
London, E16 2QY. Tel: 020 7476 7054 Fax: 020 7474 7056
Email: info@gallionspointmarina.co.uk
www.gallionspointmarina.co.uk

VHF	Ch M, 80
ACCESS	HW±5

Gallions Point Marina lies about 500 metres downstream of the Woolwich Ferry on the north side of Gallions Reach. Accessed via a lock at the entrance to the Royal Albert Basin, the marina offers deep water pontoon berths as well as hard standing. Future plans to improve facilities include the development of a bar/restaurant, a chandlery and an RYA tuition school.

FACILITIES AT A GLANCE

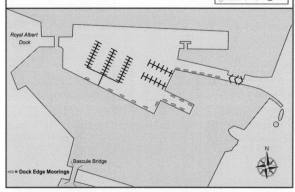

Royal Albert Dock

Bascule Bridge

= Dock Edge Moorings

N

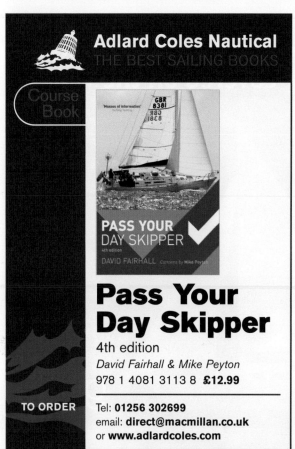

SOUTH DOCK MARINA

South Dock Marina
Rope Street, Off Plough Way
London, SE16 7SZ
Tel: 020 7252 2244 Fax: 020 7237 3806
Email: christopher.magro@southwark.gov.uk

VHF	Ch M
ACCESS	HW-2.5 to +1.5

South Dock Marina is housed in part of the old Surrey Dock complex on the south bank of the River Thames. Its locked entrance is immediately downstream of Greenland Pier, just a few miles down river of Tower Bridge. For yachts with a 2m draught, the lock can be entered HW-2½ to HW+1½ London Bridge, although if you arrive early there is a holding pontoon on the pier. The marina can be easily identified by the conspicuous arched rooftops of Baltic Quay, a luxury waterside apartment block. Once inside this secure, 200-berth marina, you can take full advantage of all its facilities as well as enjoy a range of restaurants and bars close by or visit historic maritime Greenwich.

FACILITIES AT A GLANCE

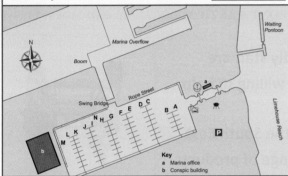

Key
a Marina office
b Conspic building

ST KATHARINE HAVEN

St Katharine's Marina Ltd
50 St Katharine's Way, London, E1W 1LA
Tel: 020 7264 5312 Fax: 020 7702 2252
Email: haven.reception@skdocks.co.uk
www.skdocks.co.uk

VHF	Ch 80
ACCESS	HW -2 to +1.5

St Katharine Docks has played a significant role in worldwide trade and commerce for over 1,000 years. Formerly a working dock, today it is an attractive waterside development housing a mixture of shops, restaurants, luxury flats and offices as well as a state-of-the-art marina. St Katharine Haven is ideally situated for exploring central London and taking full advantage of the West End's theatres and cinemas. Within easy walking distance are Tower Bridge, the Tower of London and the historic warship HMS *Belfast*. No stay at the docks is complete without a visit to the famous Dickens Inn, an impressive three storey timber building incorporating a pizza bar and stylish restaurant.

FACILITIES AT A GLANCE

Key
a Ivory House
b Dickens Inn
c Haven office
d Tower Hotel

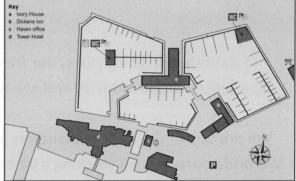

4

CHELSEA HARBOUR MARINA

Chelsea Harbour Marina
Estate Managements Office
C2-3 The Chambers, London, SW10 0XF
Tel: 07770 542783 Fax: 020 7352 7868
Email: harboumaster@chelsea-harbour.co.uk

VHF
ACCESS HW±1.5

Chelsea Harbour is widely thought of as one of London's most significant maritime sites. It is located in the heart of SW London, therefore enjoying easy access to the amenities of Chelsea and the West End. On site is the Chelsea Harbour Design Centre, where 80 showrooms exhibit the best in British and International interior design, offering superb waterside views along with excellent cuisine in the Wyndham Grand.

The harbour lies approximately 48 miles up river from Sea Reach No 1 buoy in the Thames Estuary and is accessed via the Thames Flood Barrier in Woolwich Reach. With its basin gate operating one and a half hours either side of HW (+ 20 minutes at London Bridge), the marina welcomes visiting yachtsmen.

FACILITIES AT A GLANCE

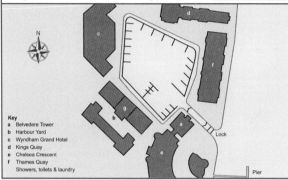

Key
a Belvedere Tower
b Harbour Yard
c Wyndham Grand Hotel
d Kings Quay
e Chelsea Crescent
f Thames Quay
   Showers, toilets & laundry

Lock

Pier

Sailing Information

Location and Access:
From the sea, Chelsea Harbour is 48 nautical miles upriver from Sea Reach No: 1 Buoy in the Thames Estuary. For vessels entering or leaving the Thames, the recommended overnight mooring, if required, is at Queenbough at the river entrance to the River Medway. Vessels bound for Chelsea Harbour will pass through the Thames Floor Barrier located in Woolwich Reach. Traffic is controlled by London VTS (VHF Ch 14), and vessels equipped with VHF are required to call up Barrier Control on passing Margaret Ness when proceeding upstream, or on passing Blackwall Point when heading downstream. There is a speed limit of 8 knots on the tideway above Wandsworth Bridge.

Visitors:
Visitor yachtsmen from home and abroad are most welcome to Chelsea Harbour Marina, and are able to make prior arrangements by telephoning the Harbour Master's office on +44 (0) 7770 542783

Basin Gate Operation:
Approximately 1? hours either side of high water +20 minutes at London Bridge. With spring tide it may be necessary to close the outer gates around high water to control marina level.

Marina Lock Dimensions (Maximum for Craft):
Beam 5.5m (18')
Draught 2.5m (8')

Recommended Charts and Publications:
Admiralty: 1183, 2151 2484, 3319
Imray: C1, C2.

Cruising Opportunities:
Chelsea Harbour is ideally located for day, weekend or longer trips either upstream to Kew, Richmond, Hampton Court, or downstream to Rochester.

2012/MG3/e

BRENTFORD DOCK MARINA

Brentford Dock Marina
2 Justine Close, Brentford, Middlesex, TW8 8QE
Tel: 020 8232 8941 Fax: 020 8560 5486 Mob: 07920 143 987
E-mail: brentforddockmarina@gmail.com

VHF
ACCESS HW±2.5

Brentford Dock Marina is situated on the River Thames at the junction with the Grand Union Canal. Its hydraulic lock is accessible for up to two and a half hours either side of high water, although boats over 9.5m LOA enter on high water by prior arrangement. There is a Spar grocery store on site. The main attractions within the area are the Royal Botanic Gardens at Kew and the Kew Bridge Steam Museum at Brentford.

FACILITIES AT A GLANCE

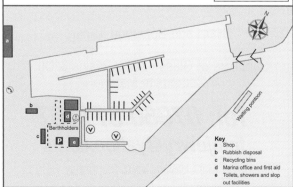

Waiting pontoon

Key
a Shop
b Rubbish disposal
c Recycling bins
d Marina office and first aid
e Toilets, showers and slop
   out facilities

Berthholders

PENTON HOOK MARINA

Penton Hook Marina
Staines Road, Chertsey, Surrey, KT16 8PY
Tel: 01932 568681 Fax: 01932 567423
Email: pentonhook@mdlmarinas.co.uk
www.marinas.co.uk

VHF Ch 80
ACCESS H24

Penton Hook Marina is situated on what is considered to be one of the most attractive reaches of the River Thames, close to Chertsey and about a mile downstream of Runnymede. Providing unrestricted access to the River Thames through a deep water channel below Penton Hook Lock, the marina can accommodate ocean-going craft of up to 21m LOA and is ideally placed for a visit to Thorpe Park, reputedly one of Europe's most popular family leisure attractions.

FACILITIES AT A GLANCE

Key
a Information point
b Dock manager's office
c Yacht club
d Repairs and under cover storage

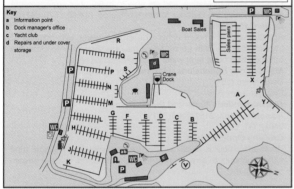

WINDSOR MARINA

Windsor Marina
Maidenhead Road, Windsor
Berkshire, SL4 5TZ
Tel: 01753 853911
Email: windsor@mdlmarinas.co.uk www.marinas.co.uk

VHF Ch 80
ACCESS H24

Situated on the outskirts of Windsor town on the south bank of the River Thames, Windsor Marina enjoys a peaceful garden setting. On site are the Windsor Yacht Club as well as boat lifting and repair facilities, a chandlery and brokerage.

A trip to the town of Windsor, comprising beautiful Georgian and Victorian buildings, would not be complete without a visit to Windsor Castle. With its construction inaugurated over 900 years ago by William the Conqueror, it is the oldest inhabited castle in the world and accommodates a priceless art and furniture collection.

FACILITIES AT A GLANCE

Key
a Boat sales & engineers
b Recycling bins
c Dock office
d Trimmers
e Yacht club

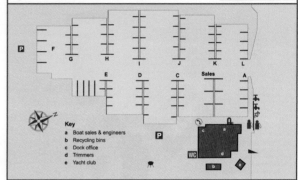

BRAY MARINA

Bray Marina
Monkey Island Lane, Bray
Berkshire, SL6 2EB
Tel: 01628 623654 Fax: 01628 773485
Email: bray@mdlmarinas.co.uk www.marinas.co.uk

VHF
ACCESS H24

Bray Marina is situated in a country park setting among shady trees, providing berth holders with a delightfully tranquil mooring. From the marina there is direct access to the Thames and there are extensive well-maintained facilities available for all boat owners. Also on site is the highly acclaimed Riverside Brasserie. Twice winner of the AA rosette award for culinary excellence and short-listed for the Tatler best country restaurant, the Brasserie is especially popular with Club Outlook members who enjoy a 15% discount. The 400-berth marina boasts an active club, which holds social functions as well as boat training lessons and handling competitions, a chandlery and engineering services.

FACILITIES AT A GLANCE

Key
a Boat storage
b Boat sales office
c Marina office, small chandlery, toilets, showers, repairs and engineering
d Battery, hazardous waste, oil and fuel disposal

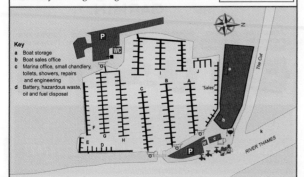

4

BURNHAM YACHT HARBOUR MARINA

Burnham Yacht Harbour Marina Ltd
Burnham-on-Crouch, Essex, CM0 8BL
Tel: 01621 782150 Fax: 01621 785848
Email: admin@burnhamyachtharbour.co.uk

VHF Ch 80
ACCESS H24

Boasting four major yacht clubs, each with comprehensive racing programmes, Burnham-on-Crouch has come to be regarded by some as 'the Cowes of the East Coast'. At the western end of the town lies Burnham Yacht Harbour, dredged 2.2m below datum. Offering a variety of on site facilities, its entrance can be easily identified by a yellow pillar buoy with an 'X' topmark.

The historic town, with its 'weatherboard' and early brick buildings, elegant quayside and scenic riverside walks, exudes plenty of charm. Among its attractions are a sports centre, a railway museum and a two-screen cinema.

FACILITIES AT A GLANCE

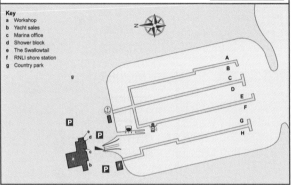

Key
a Workshop
b Yacht sales
c Marina office
d Shower block
e The Swallowtail
f RNLI shore station
g Country park

Burnham Yacht Harbour Marina Ltd
The finest marina in Essex on the delightful River Crouch offering all services

- Access at all states of the tide
- On site Chandlery, Brokerage, Restaurant/Bar
- 100 ton slipway, 35 ton Travelhoist
- Experienced engineers, shipwrights, riggers and outfitters
- Free wireless internet connectivity
- 10 minutes walk from the picturesque town and all its amenities

Harbourmaster:
**01621 786832
VHF Channel 80**

Tel: 01621 782150 • Fax: 01621 785848
Email: admin@burnhamyachtharbour.co.uk
www.burnhamyachtharbour.co.uk

ESSEX MARINA

Essex Marina
Wallasea Island, Essex, SS4 2HF
Tel: 01702 258531 Fax: 01702 258227
Email: info@essexmarina.co.uk
www.essexmarina.co.uk

VHF Ch 80
ACCESS H24

Surrounded by beautiful countryside in an area of Special Scientific Interest, Essex Marina is situated in Wallasea Bay, about half a mile up river of Burnham on Crouch. Boasting 500 deep water berths, including 50 swinging moorings, the marina can be accessed at all states of the tide. On site are a 70 ton boat hoist, a chandlery and brokerage service as well as the Essex Marina Yacht Club.

Buses run frequently to Southend-on-Sea, just seven miles away, while a ferry service takes passengers across the river on weekends to Burnham, where you will find numerous shops and restaurants. Benefiting from its close proximity to London (just under an hour's drive away) and Rochford Airport (approximately four miles away), the marina provides a suitable location for crew changeovers.

FACILITIES AT A GLANCE

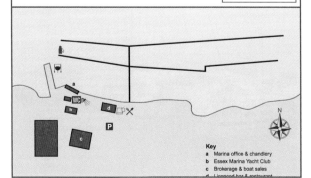

Key
a Marina office & chandlery
b Essex Marina Yacht Club
c Brokerage & boat sales
d Licensed bar & restaurant

BRIDGEMARSH MARINA

Bridgemarsh Marine
Fairholme, Bridge Marsh Lane, Althorne, Essex
Tel: 01621 740414 Mobile: 07968 696815 Fax: 01621 742216

VHF Ch 80
ACCESS HW±4

On the north side of Bridgemarsh Island, just beyond Essex Marina on the River Crouch, lies Althorne Creek. Here Bridgemarsh Marine accommodates over 100 boats berthed alongside pontoons supplied with water and electricity. A red beacon marks the entrance to the creek, with red can buoys identifying the approach channel into the marina. Accessible four hours either side of high water, the marina has an on site yard with two docks, a slipway and crane. The village of Althorne is just a short walk away, from where there are direct train services (taking approximately one hour) to London.

FACILITIES AT A GLANCE

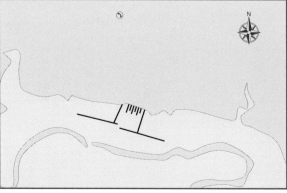

HEYBRIDGE BASIN

Heybridge Basin
Lock Hill, Heybridge Basin, Maldon, Essex, CM9 4RY
Tel: 01621 853506
Email: martin.maudsley@waterways.org.uk
www.essexwaterways.com

VHF	Ch 80
ACCESS	HW±1

Towards the head of the River Blackwater, not far from Maldon, lies Heybridge Basin. Situated at the lower end of the 14–mile long Chelmer and Blackwater Navigation Canal, it can be reached via a lock about one hour

either side of HW for a yacht drawing around 2m. If you arrive too early, there is good holding ground in the river just outside the lock. Incorporating as many as 200 berths, the basin has a range of facilities, including shower and laundry amenities. It is strongly recommendedthat you book 24 hours in advance for summer weekends.

FACILITIES AT A GLANCE

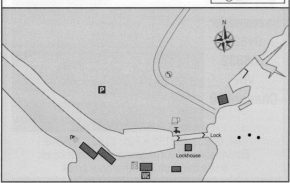

BRADWELL MARINA

Bradwell Marina, Port Flair Ltd, Waterside
Bradwell-on-Sea, Essex, CM0 7RB
Tel: 01621 776235 Fax: 01621 776393
Email: info@bradwellmarina.com
www.bradwellmarina.com

VHF	Ch M, 80
ACCESS	HW±4.5

Opened in 1984, Bradwell is a privately-owned marina situated in the mouth of the River Blackwater, serving as a convenient base from which to explore the Essex coastline or as a departure point for cruising further afield to Holland and Belgium. The yacht basin can be accessed four and a half hours either side of HW and offers plenty of protection from all wind directions. With a total of 300 fully serviced berths, generous space has been allocated for manoeuvring between pontoons. Overlooking the marina is Bradwell Club House, incorporating a bar, restaurant, launderette and ablution facilities.

FACILITIES AT A GLANCE

Key
a   Clubhouse
b   Tower office

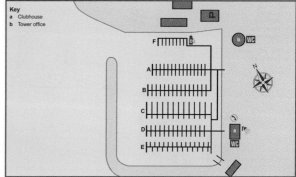

FAMBRIDGE YACHT HAVEN

Fambridge Yacht Haven
Church Road, North Fambridge, Essex, CM3 6LR
Tel: 01621 740370 Fax: 01621 742359
Email: danyal@fambridgeyachthaven.com

VHF	Ch M, 80
ACCESS	H24

Just under a mile upstream of North Fambridge, Stow Creek branches off to the north of the River Crouch. The creek, marked with occasional starboard hand buoys and leading lights, leads to the entrance to Fambridge Yacht Haven, which enjoys an unspoilt, tranquil setting between saltings and farmland. Home to West Wick Yacht Club, the marina has 220 berths and can accommodate vessels up to 17m LOA.

The nearby village of North Fambridge features the Ferryboat Inn, a favourite haunt with the boating fraternity. Only six miles down river lies Burnham-on-Crouch, while the Essex and Kent coasts are within easy sailing distance.

FACILITIES AT A GLANCE

Key
a   Marina reception
b   Waste
c   West Wick YC
d   Boat Shed Essex
e   Marina maintenance,
     workshop & stores
f   Under cover storage

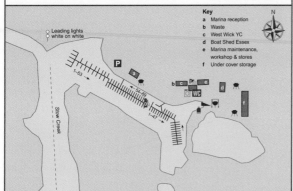

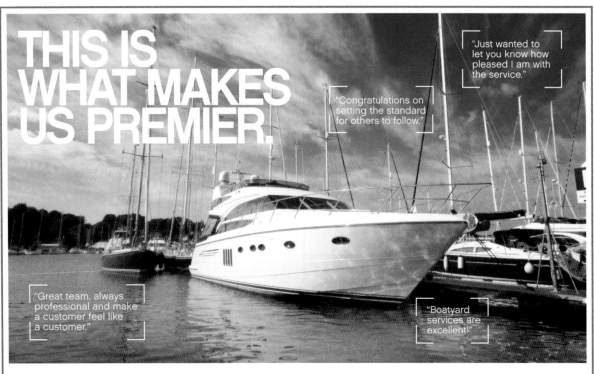

BLACKWATER MARINA

Blackwater Marina
Marine Parade, Maylandsea, Essex
Tel: 01621 740264 Tel: 01621 742122
Email: info@blackwater-marina.co.uk

VHF | Ch M
ACCESS | HW±2

Blackwater Marina is a place where families in day boats mix with Smack owners and yacht crews; here seals, avocets and porpoises roam beneath the big, sheltering East Coast skies and here the area's rich heritage of working Thames Barges and Smacks remains part of daily life today. But it isn't just classic sailing boats that thrive on the Blackwater. An eclectic mix of motor cruisers, open boats and modern yachts enjoy the advantages of a marina sheltered by its natural habitat, where the absence of harbour walls allows uninterrupted views of some of Britain's rarest wildlife and where the 21st century shoreside facilities are looked after by experienced professionals, who are often found sailing on their days off.

FACILITIES AT A GLANCE

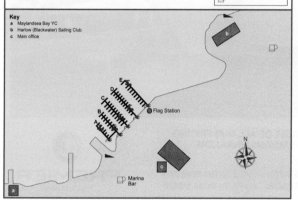

Key
a Maylandsea Bay YC
b Harlow (Blackwater) Sailing Club
c Main office

Flag Station

Marina Bar

TOLLESBURY MARINA

Tollesbury Marina
The Yacht Harbour, Tollesbury, Essex, CM9 8SE
Tel: 01621 869202 Fax: 01621 868494
email: marina@woodrolfe.com www.woodrolfe.com

VHF | Ch M, 80
ACCESS | HW±2

Tollesbury Marina lies at the mouth of the River Blackwater in the heart of the Essex countryside. Within easy access from London and the Home Counties, it has been designed as a leisure centre for the whole family, with on-site activities comprising tennis courts and a covered heated swimming pool as well as a convivial bar and restaurant. Accommodating over 240 boats, the marina can be accessed two hours either side of HW and is ideally situated for those wishing to explore the River Crouch to the south and the Rivers Colne, Orwell and Deben to the north.

FACILITIES AT A GLANCE

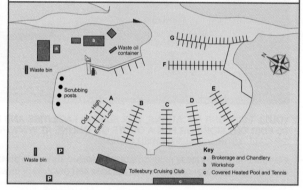

Waste oil container

Waste bin

Scrubbing posts

Odd → high
Even → Low

Waste bin

Tollesbury Cruising Club

Key
a Brokerage and Chandlery
b Workshop
c Covered Heated Pool and Tennis

TITCHMARSH MARINA

Titchmarsh Marina Ltd
Coles Lane, Walton on the Naze, Essex, CO14 8SL
Tel: 01255 672185 Fax: 01255 851901
Email: info@titchmarshmarina.co.uk
www.titchmarshmarina.co.uk

| VHF | Ch 80 |
| ACCESS | HW±5 |

Titchmarsh Marina sits on the south side of The Twizzle in the heart of the Walton Backwaters. As the area is designated as a 'wetland of international importance', the marina has been designed and developed to function as a natural harbour. The 420 berths are well sheltered by the high-grassed clay banks, offering good protection in all conditions. Access to Titchmarsh is over a sill, which has a depth of about 1m at LWS, but once inside the basin, the depth increases to around 2m. Among the excellent facilities on site are the well stocked Marinestore Chandlery and Harbour Lights Restaurant & Bar serving carvery meals daily.

FACILITIES AT A GLANCE

Key
a Harbour master, chandlery (+ cycle hire) marine engineers, marine electronics
b Hardstanding
c Harbour Lights - restaurant and bar

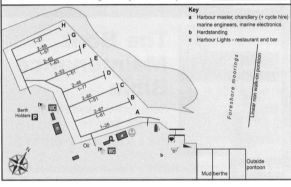

WALTON YACHT BASIN

Walton and Frinton Yacht Trust
Mill Lane, Walton on the Naze, CO14 8PF
Managed by Bedwell & Co Tel: 01255 675873
Fax: 01255 677405 After hours Tel: 01255 672655

| VHF | |
| ACCESS | HW-0.75,HW+0.25 |

Walton Yacht Basin lies at the head of Walton Creek, an area made famous in Arthur Ransome's *Swallows & Amazons* and *Secret Waters*. The creek can only be navigated two hours either side of HW, although yachts heading for the Yacht Basin should arrive on a rising tide as the entrance gate is kept shut once the tide turns in order to retain the water inside. Before entering the gate, moor up against the Club Quay to enquire about berthing availability.

A short walk away is the popular seaside town of Walton, full of shops, pubs and restaurants. Its focal point is the pier which, overlooking superb sandy beaches, offers various attractions including a ten-pin bowling alley. Slightly further out of town, the Naze affords pleasant coastal walks with striking panoramic views.

FACILITIES AT A GLANCE

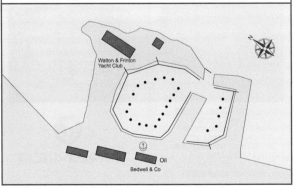

SHOTLEY MARINA

Shotley Marina Ltd
Shotley Gate, Ipswich,Suffolk, IP9 1QJ
Tel: 01473 788982 Fax: 01473 788868
Email: sales@shotleymarina.co.uk
www.shotleymarina.co.uk www.eastcoastmarinas.co.uk

VHF	Ch 80
ACCESS	H24

Based in the well protected Harwich Harbour where the River Stour joins the River Orwell, Shotley Marina is only eight miles from the county town of Ipswich. Entered via a lock at all states of the tide, its first class facilities include extensive boat repair and maintenance services as well as a well-stocked chandlery and on site bar and restaurant. The marina is strategically placed for sailing up the Stour to Manningtree, up the Orwell to Pin Mill or exploring the Rivers Deben, Crouch and Blackwater as well as the Walton Backwaters.

FACILITIES AT A GLANCE

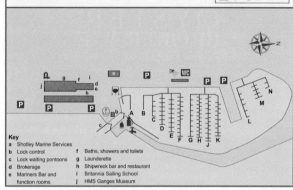

Key
a Shotley Marine Services
b Lock control
c Lock waiting pontoons
d Brokerage
e Mariners Bar and function rooms
f Baths, showers and toilets
g Launderette
h Shipwreck bar and restaurant
i Britannia Sailing School
j HMS Ganges Museum

SUFFOLK YACHT HARBOUR

Suffolk Yacht Harbour Ltd
Levington, Ipswich, Suffolk, IP10 0LN
Tel: 01473 659240 Fax: 01473 659632
Email: enquiries@syharbour.co.uk
www.syharbour.co.uk

VHF	Ch 80
ACCESS	H24

A friendly, independently-run marina on the East Coast of England, Suffolk Yacht Harbour enjoys a beautiful rural setting on the River Orwell, yet is within easy access of Ipswich, Woodbridge and Felixstowe. With approximately 500 berths, the marina offers extensive facilities while the Haven Ports Yacht Club provides a bar and restaurant.

FACILITIES AT A GLANCE

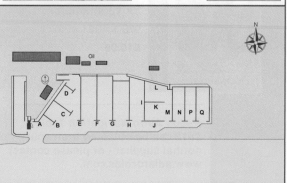

ROYAL HARWICH YACHT CLUB MARINA

Royal Harwich Yacht Club Marina
Marina Road, Woolverstone, Suffolk, IP9 1BA
Tel: 01473 780319 Fax: 01473 780919
www.rhyc.demon.co.uk
Email: secretary@rhyc.demon.co.uk

| VHF | Ch 77 |
| ACCESS | H24 |

This 54 berth marina is ideally situated at a mid point on the Orwell between Levington and Ipswich. The facility is owned and run by the Royal Harwich Yacht Club and enjoys a full catering and bar service in the Clubhouse. The marina benefits from full tidal access, and can accommodate yachts up to 14.5m on the hammerhead. Within the immediate surrounds, there are boat repair services, and a well stocked chandlery. The marina is situated a mile's walk from the world famous Pin Mill and is a favoured destination with visitors from Holland, Belgium and Germany. The marina welcomes racing yachts and cruisers, and is able to accommodate multiple bookings.

FACILITIES AT A GLANCE

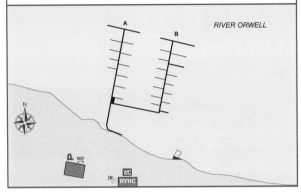

RIVER ORWELL

WOOLVERSTONE MARINA

Woolverstone Marina
Woolverstone, Ipswich, Suffolk, IP9 1AS
Tel: 01473 780206 Fax: 01473 780273
Email: woolverstone@mdlmarinas.co.uk www.marinas.co.uk

| VHF | Ch 80 |
| ACCESS | H24 |

Set in 22 acres of parkland, within close proximity to the Royal Harwich Yacht Club, Woolverstone Marina boasts 235 pontoon berths as well as 110 swinging moorings, all of which are served by a water taxi. Besides boat repair services, an on-site chandlery and excellent ablution facilities, the marina also incorporates a yacht brokerage and the Buttermans bar and restaurant, which overlooks the river and serves fine food prepared with fresh local produce.

Woolverstone's location on the scenic R. Orwell makes it ideally placed for exploring the various cruising grounds along the East Coast, including the adjacent R. Stour, the Colne and Blackwater estuaries to the south and the R. Deben to the north.

FACILITIES AT A GLANCE

Key
a   Marina office, toilets, showers, launderette and boat sales
b   Buttermans Bar Restaurant
c   Royal Harwich Yacht Club

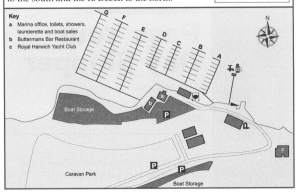

FOX'S MARINA

Fox's Marina & Boatyard
The Strand, Ipswich, Suffolk, IP2 8SA
Tel: 01473 689111 Fax: 01473 601737
Email: foxs@foxsmarina.com www.foxsmarina.com

VHF	Ch 80
ACCESS	H24

Located on the picturesque River Orwell, Fox's provides good shelter in all conditions and access at all states of tide. 100 pontoon berths and ashore storage for 200 vessels. A 70 tonne hoist provides the ability to handle boats up to 80ft in length.

The on-site chandlery is the largest on the east coast with a prominent position overlooking the marina. Fox's offer a full range of in-house boatyard services and with 10,000 sq ft of heated workshop space are specialists in repairs and refits of sailing yachts and motor boats. Other service on hand include experienced riggers and electronics engineers as well as marine engineers, and custom fabrication of stainless steel.

There are regular bus services to Ipswich, which is only about one to two miles away.

FACILITIES AT A GLANCE

Key
a Chandlery
b Harbourmaster office
c Yacht Club

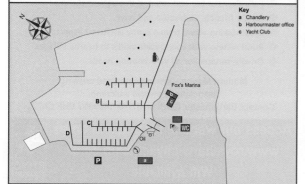

NEPTUNE MARINA

Neptune Marina Ltd
Neptune Quay, Ipswich, IP4 1AX
Tel: 01473 215204 Fax: 01473 215206
Email: enquiries@neptune-marina.com

VHF	Ch M, 80
ACCESS	H±2.5

The Wet Dock at Ipswich, which was opened in 1850, became the largest in Europe and was in use right up until the 1930s. Now the dock incorporates Neptune Marina, situated at Neptune Quay on the Historic Waterfront, and ever increasing shoreside developments. This 26-acre dock is accessible through a 24-hr lock gate, with a waiting pontoon outside. The town centre is a 10 minute walk away, while Cardinal Park, a relatively new complex housing an 11-screen cinema and several eating places, is nearby. There are also a number of other excellent restaurants along the quayside and adjacent to the Marina. The Neptune Marina building occupies an imposing position in the NE corner of the dock with quality coffee shop and associated retail units.

FACILITIES AT A GLANCE

Key
a Old Custom House
b Conference centre
c Floating French restaurant
d Bistro
e Bellway apartments
f Neptune Marina office & facilities
g Marina storage yard

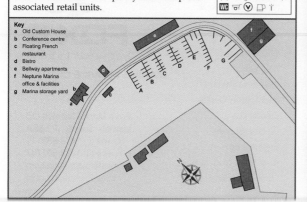

IPSWICH HAVEN MARINA

Ipswich Haven Marina
Associated British Ports
New Cut East, Ipswich, Suffolk, IP3 0EA
Tel: 01473 236644 Fax: 01473 236645
Email: ipswichhaven@abports.co.uk

⚓⚓⚓⚓

VHF	Ch M, 68 & 80
ACCESS	H24

Lying at the heart of Ipswich, the Haven Marina enjoys close proximity to all the bustling shopping centres, restaurants, cinemas and museums that this County Town of Suffolk has to offer. The main railway station is only a 10-minute walk away, where there are regular connections to London, Cambridge and Norwich, all taking just over an hour to get to.

Within easy reach of Holland, Belgium and Germany, East Anglia is proving an increasingly popular cruising ground. The River Orwell, displaying breathtaking scenery, was voted one of the most beautiful rivers in Britain by the RYA.

FACILITIES AT A GLANCE

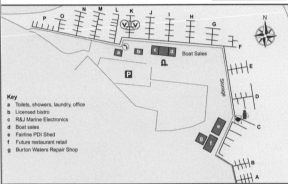

Key
a Toilets, showers, laundry, office
b Licensed bistro
c R&J Marine Electronics
d Boat sales
e Fairline PDI Shed
f Future restaurant retail
g Burton Waters Repair Shop

HAMILTON DOCK

Hamilton Dock, c/o Lowestoft Haven Marina
School Road, Lowestoft, Suffolk, NR33 9NB
Tel: 01502 580300 Fax: 01502 581851
Email: lowestofhaven@abports.co.uk

VHF	Ch M, 80
ACCESS	H24

Lowestoft Haven Marina's Hamilton Dock is based in an old fish dock in the outer harbour and offers easy access to the open sea making it an ideal overnight location, whilst its in town position means all the facilities of the town centre are at your doorstep.

The marina's 47 berths can accommodate vessels from 10 - 28m and is especially geared up for club bookings. It offers a full range of modern facilities and is complimented by the main marina at School Road for boatyard facilities.

FACILITIES AT A GLANCE

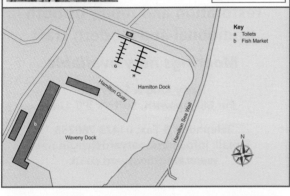

Key
a   Toilets
b   Fish Market

LOWESTOFT HAVEN MARINA

Lowestoft Haven Marina
School Road, Lowestoft, Suffolk, NR33 9NB
Tel: 01502 580300 Fax: 01502 581851
Email: lowestofhaven@abports.co.uk

VHF	Ch M, 80
ACCESS	H24

Lowestoft Haven Marina is based on Lake Lothing with easy access to both the open sea and the Norfolk Broads. The town centres of both Lowestoft and Oulton Broad are within a short distance of the marina. The marina's 140 berths can accommodate vessels from 7-20m. Offering a full range of modern facilities the marina welcomes all visitors.

FACILITIES AT A GLANCE

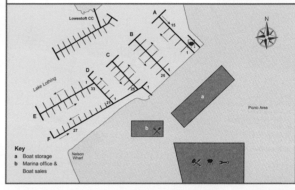

Key
a   Boat storage
b   Marina office & Boat sales

ROYAL NORFOLK & SUFFOLK YACHT CLUB

Royal Norfolk and Suffolk Yacht Club
Royal Plain, Lowestoft, Suffolk, NR33 0AQ
Tel: 01502 566726 Fax: 01502 517981
Email: marinaoffice@rnsyc.org.uk

VHF	Ch 14, 80
ACCESS	H24

With its entrance at the inner end of the South Pier, opposite the Trawl Basin on the north bank, the Royal Norfolk and Suffolk Yacht Club marina occupies a sheltered position in Lowestoft Harbour. Lowestoft has always been an appealing destination to yachtsmen due to the fact that it can be accessed at any state of the tide, 24 hours a day. Note, however, that conditions just outside the entrance can get pretty lively when the wind is against tide. The clubhouse is enclosed in an impressive Grade 2 listed building overlooking the marina and its facilities include a bar and restaurant as well as a formal dining room with a full à la carte menu.

FACILITIES AT A GLANCE

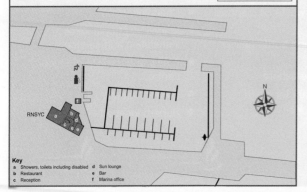

RNSYC

Key
a   Showers, toilets including disabled
b   Restaurant
c   Reception
d   Sun lounge
e   Bar
f   Marina office

LOWESTOFT CRUISING CLUB

Lowestoft Cruising Club
Off Harbour Road, Oulton Broad, Lowestoft, Suffolk, NR32 3LY
Tel: 07913 391950
www.lowestoftcruisingclub.co.uk

VHF	
ACCESS	H24

Lowestoft Cruising Club welcomes visitors and can offer a friendly atmosphere, some of the finest moorings and at very competitive rates. Whatever the weather, these moorings provide a calm, safe haven for visiting yachts and with the Mutford lock only 250 metres away, easy access onto the Norfolk and Suffolk Broads. Facilities include electricity and water, plus excellent showers, toilets and secure car parking. These moorings are the nearest ones to the railway stations (to Norwich and Ipswich), bus routes, shops, banks, pubs and restaurants in Oulton Broad.

FACILITIES AT A GLANCE

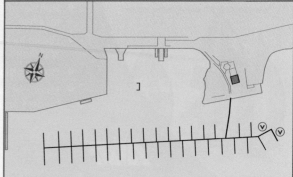

People who *love and understand* boats...

// Boatbuilding and Design

// Refit and Restoration

// Repair and Maintenance

// Spar Making and Rigging

// Marine Electronics Supply and Install

// Marine Engineering

// New Electrical Installations and Re-design

// Engine Rebuild and Repair

// Osmosis Treatment and Re-spray

// Teak Deck Repair and Renovation

// Delivery and Collection

// Pre-purchase Inspection and Survey

4

// Well stocked chandlery

// Diesel available direct to boat

// Lift out and launch facilities

// Boat and Trailer Park

// Storage ashore for 60 boats

// Welcoming and friendly service

To contact us with an enquiry call 01502 724721 or 07867 556640, email info@harbourmarine.co.uk
HMS Ltd, Blackshore, Southwold Harbour, Suffolk, IP18 6TA.

2012/MG139/vv

QUAY*plus*

a range of extra benefits for bertholders . . .

With the introduction of a range of extra benefits, it makes even more sense to berth with Quay Marinas. We have seven marinas in ideal locations around the UK providing a level of service and support which keeps us at the forefront of the marina industry.

FREE reciprocal berthing between all Quay Marinas for all annual bertholders

FREE introductory RNLI membership via the 'Ambassador Scheme'

50% discounted visitor berthing at 45 TransEurope marinas for bertholders

50% up to 50% off standard tariff for winter berthing

20% off competitive rates on Quay Marinas boat insurance scheme in association with Towergate Mardon

15% berth discount for boats sold into our marinas by our on-site brokers

NEW brokerage office now open at Royal Quays Marina

visit our website for more details:

www.quaymarinas.com

our marinas

1 Rhu Marina
Tel: 01436 820238

2 Bangor Marina
Tel: 02891 453297

3 Royal Quays Marina
Tel: 0191 272 8282

4 Conwy Quays Marina
Tel: 01492 593000

5 Deganwy Quays Marina
Tel: 01492 576888

6 Penarth Quays Marina
Tel: 02920 705021

7 Portishead Quays Marina
Tel: 01275 841941

2012/MG136/r

NORTH EAST ENGLAND - Great Yarmouth to Berwick-upon-Tweed

Key to Marina Plans symbols

Bottled gas		P	Parking
Chandler			Pub/Restaurant
Disabled facilities			Pump out
Electrical supply			Rigging service
Electrical repairs			Sail repairs
Engine repairs			Shipwright
First Aid			Shop/Supermarket
Fresh Water			Showers
Fuel - Diesel			Slipway
Fuel - Petrol		WC	Toilets
Hardstanding/boatyard			Telephone
Internet Café			Trolleys
Laundry facilities		V	Visitors berths
Lift-out facilities			Wi-Fi

5

Area 5 - North East England

MARINAS
Telephone Numbers
VHF Channel
Access Times

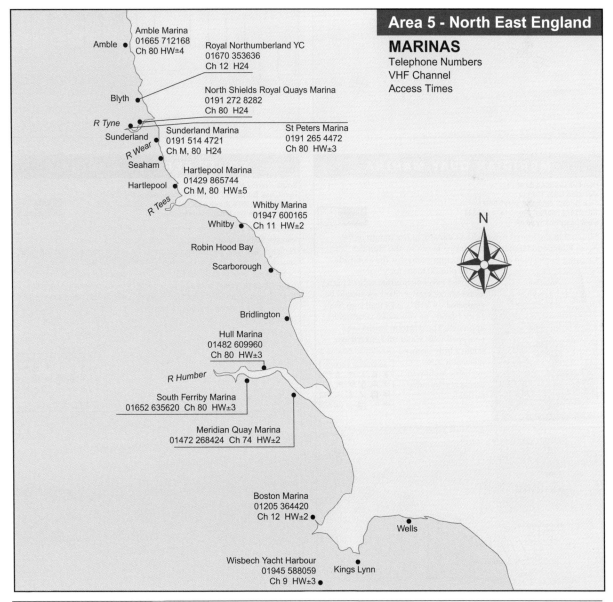

Amble
Amble Marina
01665 712168
Ch 80 HW±4

Royal Northumberland YC
01670 353636
Ch 12 H24

Blyth

North Shields Royal Quays Marina
0191 272 8282
Ch 80 H24

R Tyne

Sunderland Marina
0191 514 4721
Ch M, 80 H24

St Peters Marina
0191 265 4472
Ch 80 HW±3

Sunderland

R Wear

Seaham

Hartlepool

Hartlepool Marina
01429 865744
Ch M, 80 HW±5

R Tees

Whitby Marina
01947 600165
Ch 11 HW±2

Whitby

Robin Hood Bay

Scarborough

N

Bridlington

Hull Marina
01482 609960
Ch 80 HW±3

R Humber

South Ferriby Marina
01652 635620 Ch 80 HW±3

Meridian Quay Marina
01472 268424 Ch 74 HW±2

Boston Marina
01205 364420
Ch 12 HW±2

Wells

Wisbech Yacht Harbour
01945 588059
Ch 9 HW±3

Kings Lynn

WISBECH YACHT HARBOUR

Wisbech Yacht Harbour
Harbour Master, Harbour Office, Dock Cottage
Wisbech, Cambridgeshire PE13 3JJ
Tel: 01945 588059 Fax: 01945 580589
Email: cdorrington@fenland.gov.uk www.fenland.gov.uk

VHF	Ch 9
ACCESS	HW±3

Regarded as the capital of the
English Fens, Wisbech is situated
about 25 miles north east of
Peterborough and is a market
town of considerable character
and historical significance. Rows
of elegant houses line the banks
of the River Nene, with the North
and South Brink still deemed two
of the finest Georgian streets in England.

Wisbech Yacht Harbour, linking Cambridgeshire with the sea,
is proving increasingly popular as a haven for small
craft, despite the busy commercial shipping. In
recent years the facilities have been developed and
improved upon and the HM is always on hand to
help with passage planning both up or downstream.

FACILITIES AT A GLANCE

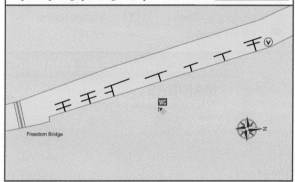

Freedom Bridge

BOSTON MARINA

Boston Marina
5/7 Witham Bank East, Boston, Lincs, PE21 9JU
Tel: 01205 364420 Fax: 01205 364420
www.bostonmarina.net Email: bostonmarina@5witham.fsnet

VHF	Ch 12
ACCESS	H±2

Boston Marina, located near
Boston Grand Sluice in
Lincolnshire, is an ideal
location for both seagoing
vessels and for river boats
wanting to explore the heart
of the Fens. The on site
facilities include a fully-
stocked chandlery and
brokerage service, while
nearby is the well-established and recently refurbished Witham bar and
restaurant.

The old maritime port of Boston has numerous
modern-day and historical attractions, one of the
most notable being St Botolph's Church, better
known as the 'Boston Stump'.

FACILITIES AT A GLANCE

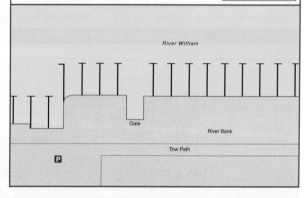

River Witham

Gate

River Bank

Tow Path

MERIDIAN QUAY MARINA

Humber Cruising Assn
Meridian Quay Marina
Fish Docks, Grimsby, DN31 3SD
Tel: 01472 268424 Fax: 01472 269832
www.hcagrimsby.co.uk

VHF	Ch 74
ACCESS	HW±2

Situated in the locked fish dock of Grimsby, at the mouth of the
River Humber, Meridian Quay Marina is run by the Humber
Cruising Association and comprises approximately 200 alongside

berths plus 30 more for visitors.
Accessed two hours either side of high
water via lock gates, the lock should be
contacted on VHF Ch 74 (call sign 'Fish
Dock Island') as you make your final
approach. The pontoon berths are
equipped with water and electricity,
while a fully licensed clubhouse boasts a
television. Also
available are internet
access and laundry
facilities.

FACILITIES AT A GLANCE

No1
Fish Dock

North Quay

Key
a Office
b Clubhouse/bar

No3
Fish Dock

**Meridian Quay
Marina**

West Quay

East Quay

South Quay

No2 Fish
Dock

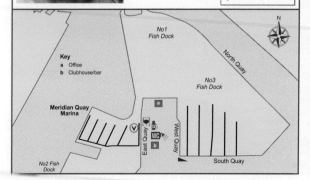

SOUTH FERRIBY MARINA

South Ferriby Marina
Red Lane, Barton on Humber, Lincolnshire, DN18 6JH
Tel: 01652 635620 (Lock 635219) Mobile: 07828 312071
Email: patrick@humbermarina.com

VHF	Ch 74
ACCESS	HW±3

South Ferriby Marina is run by Teresa and Patrick Ferguson, an
established company since 1967 and today offers a comprehensive
range of services, including heated workshops, cranage, boat storage,
morrings boat sales and chandlery.

Situated at Barton upon Humber, the marina lies on the south
bank of the River Humber at the southern crossing of the Humber
Bridge, approximately eight miles south west of Kingston upon Hull.
Good public transport links to nearby towns and villages include
train services to Cleethorpes and Grimsby, and bus connections to
Scunthorpe and Hull.

FACILITIES AT A GLANCE

Lock

Moorings

Conveyor

Key
a Chandlery
b Shipwrights workshop

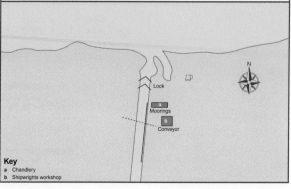

HULL MARINA

Hull Marina
W 13, Kingston Street, Hull, HU1 2DQ
Tel: 01482 609960 Fax: 01482 224148
www.bwml.co.uk
Email: hull.marina@bwml.co.uk

| VHF | Ch 80 |
| ACCESS | HW±3 |

Situated on the River Humber, Hull Marina is literally a stone's throw from the bustling city centre with its array of arts and entertainments. Besides the numerous historic bars and cafés surrounding the marina itself, there are plenty of traditional taverns to be sampled in the Old Town, while also found here is the Street Life Museum, vividly depicting the history of the city.

Yachtsmen enter the marina via a tidal lock, operating HW±3, and should try to give 15 minutes' notice of arrival via VHF Ch 80. Hull is perfectly positioned for exploring the Trent, Ouse and the Yorkshire coast as well as across the North Sea to Holland or Belgium.

FACILITIES AT A GLANCE

Key
a   Reception
b   Boatshed
c   Kildale Marine
d   Lock control &
     lock keeper's cottage

WHITBY MARINA

Whitby Marina
Whitby Harbour Office, Endeavour Wharf
Whitby, North Yorkshire YO21 1DN
Harbour Office: 01947 602354 Marina: 01947 600165
Email: port.services@scarborough.gov.uk

VHF	Ch 11
ACCESS	HW±2

The only natural harbour between the Tees and the Humber, Whitby lies some 20 miles north of Scarborough on the River Esk. The historic town is said to date back as far as the Roman times, although it is better known for its abbey, which was founded over 1,300 years ago by King Oswy of Northumberland. Another place of interest is the Captain Cook Memorial Museum, a tribute to Whitby's greatest seaman.

A swing bridge divides the harbour into upper and lower sections, with the marina being in the Upper Harbour. The bridge opens on request (VHF Ch 11) each half hour for two hours either side of high water.

FACILITIES AT A GLANCE

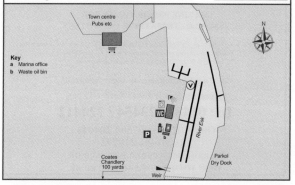

Key
a   Marina office
b   Waste oil bin

HARTLEPOOL MARINA

Hartlepool Marina
Lock Office, Slake Terrace, Hartlepool, TS24 0UR
Tel: 01429 865744
Email: enquiries@hartlepool-marina.com

VHF	Ch M, 80
ACCESS	HW±5

Hartlepool Marina is a major boating facility on the North East coast with over 500 fully serviced berths surrounded by a cosmopolitan mix of bars restaurants and hotels. The Historic Quay is nearby with the 17th Century warship, Trincomelee. A tourist town with shopping centre is an easy walk away. Beautiful crusing water north and south access channel dredged to chart datum.

The marina can be accessed five hours either side of high water via a lock: note that yachtsmen wishing to enter should contact the marina on VHF Ch 80 about 15 minutes before arrival.

FACILITIES AT A GLANCE

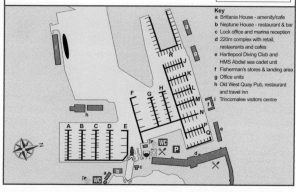

Key
a   Brittania House - amenity/cafe
b   Neptune House - restaurant & bar
c   Lock office and marina reception
d   220m complex with retail,
    restaurants and cafes
e   Hartlepool Diving Club and
    HMS Abdiel sea cadet unit
f   Fisherman's stores & landing area
g   Office units
h   Old West Quay Pub, restaurant
    and travel inn
i   Trincomalee visitors centre

SUNDERLAND MARINA

The Marine Activities Centre
Sunderland Marina, Sunderland, SR6 0PW
Tel: 0191 514 4721 Fax: 0191 514 1847
Email: mervyn.templeton@marineactivitiescentre.co.uk

VHF	Ch M, 80
ACCESS	H24

Sunderland Marina sits on the north bank of the River Wear and is easily accessible through the outer breakwater at all states of the tide. Among the extensive range of facilities on site are a newsagent, café, hairdresser and top quality Italian restaurant. Other pubs, restaurants, hotels and cafés are located nearby on the waterfront. Both the Wear Boating Association and the Sunderland Yacht Club are also located in the vicinity and welcome yachtsmen to their respective bars and lounges.

FACILITIES AT A GLANCE

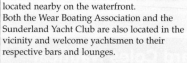

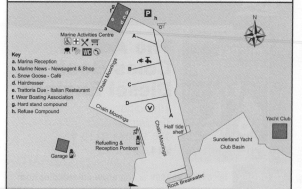

Key
a. Marina Reception
b. Marine News - Newsagent & Shop
c. Snow Goose - Café
d. Hairdresser
e. Trattoria Due - Italian Restaurant
f. Wear Boating Association
g. Hard stand compound
h. Refuse Compound

NORTH SHIELDS ROYAL QUAYS MARINA

North Shields Royal Quays Marina
Coble Dene Road, North Shields, NE29 6DU
Tel: 0191 272 8282 Fax: 0191 272 8288
www.quaymarinas.com
Email: royalquaysmarina@quaymarinas.com

VHF	Ch 80
ACCESS	H24

North Shields Royal Quays Marina enjoys close proximity to the entrance to the River Tyne, allowing easy access to and from the open sea as well as being ideally placed for cruising further up the Tyne. Just over an hour's motoring upstream brings you to the heart of the city of Newcastle, where you can tie up on a security controlled visitors' pontoon right outside the Pitcher and Piano Bar.

With a reputation for a high standard of service, the marina accommodates 300 pontoon berths, all of which are fully serviced. It is accessed via double sector lock gates which operate at all states of the tide and 24 hours a day.

FACILITIES AT A GLANCE

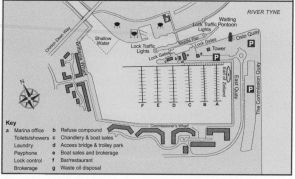

Key
a   Marina office   b   Refuse compound
    Toilets/showers   c   Chandlery & boat sales
    Laundry   d   Access bridge & trolley park
    Payphone   e   Boat sales and brokerage
    Lock control   f   Bar/restaurant
    Brokerage   g   Waste oil disposal

ST PETERS MARINA

**St Peters Marina, St Peters Basin
Newcastle upon Tyne, NE6 1HX
Tel: 0191 2654472 Fax: 0191 2762618
Email: info@stpetersmarina.co.uk
www.stpetersmarina.co.uk**

VHF | Ch 80
ACCESS | HW±3

Nestling on the north bank of the River Tyne, some eight miles upstream of the river entrance, St Peters Marina is a fully serviced, 150-berth marina with the capacity to accommodate large vessels of up to 37m LOA. Situated on site is the Bascule Bar and Bistro, while a few minutes away is the centre of Newcastle. This city, along with its surrounding area, offers an array of interesting sites, among which are Hadrian's Wall, the award winning Gateshead Millennium Bridge and the Baltic Art Centre.

FACILITIES AT A GLANCE

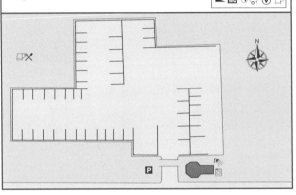

ROYAL NORTHUMBERLAND YACHT CLUB

**Royal Northumberland Yacht Club
South Harbour, Blyth, Northumberland, NE24 3PB
Tel: 01670 353636**

VHF | Ch 12
ACCESS | H24

The Royal Northumberland Yacht Club is based at Blyth, a well-sheltered port that is accessible at all states of the tide and in all weathers except for when there is a combination of low water and strong south-easterly winds. The yacht club is a private club with some 75 pontoon berths and a further 20 fore and aft moorings.

Visitors usually berth on the north side of the most northerly pontoon and are welcome to use the clubship, HY *Tyne* – a wooden lightship built in 1880 which incorporates a bar, showers and toilet facilities. The club also controls its own boatyard, providing under cover and outside storage space plus a 20 ton boat hoist.

FACILITIES AT A GLANCE

5

AMBLE MARINA

**Amble Marina Ltd
Amble, Northumberland, NE65 0YP
Tel: 01665 712168 Fax:01665 713363
Email: marina@amble.co.uk   www.amble.co.uk**

VHF | Ch 80
ACCESS | HW±4

Amble Marina is a small family run business offering peace, security and a countryside setting at the heart of the small town of Amble. It is located on the banks of the beautiful River Coquet and at the start of the Northumberland coast's area of outstanding natural beauty. Amble Marina has 250 fully serviced berths for residential and visiting yachts. Cafes, bars, restaurants and shops are all within a short walk.

From your berth watch the sun rise at the entrance to the harbour and set behind Warkworth Castle or walk on wide empty beaches. There is so much to do or if you prefer simply enjoy the peace, tranquillity and friendliness at Amble Marina.

FACILITIES AT A GLANCE

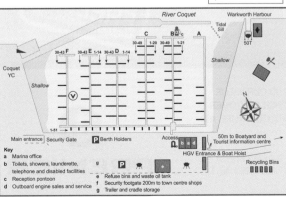

Key
a   Marina office
b   Toilets, showers, launderette, telephone and disabled facilities
c   Reception pontoon
d   Outboard engine sales and service
e   Refuse bins and waste oil tank
f   Security footgate 200m to town centre shops
g   Trailer and cradle storage

2012/MG22/e

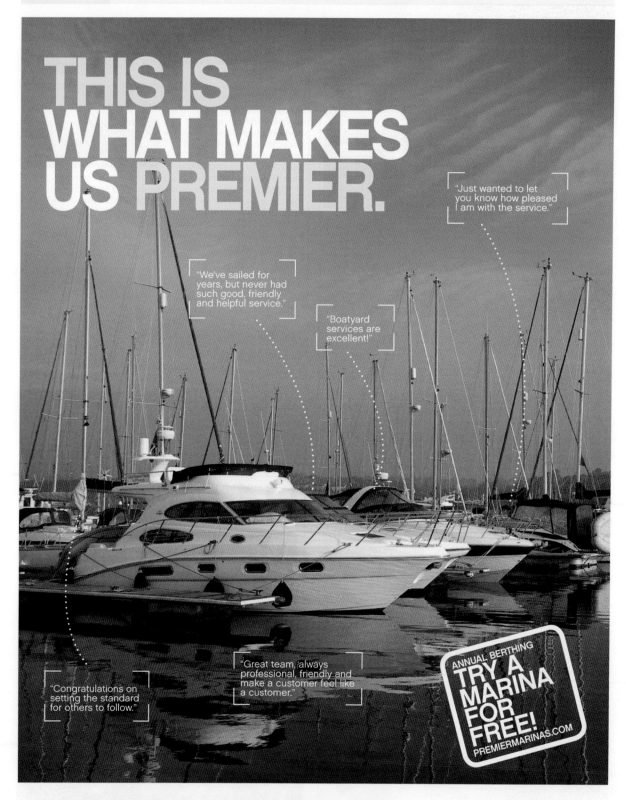

THIS IS WHAT MAKES US PREMIER.

"Just wanted to let you know how pleased I am with the service."

"We've sailed for years, but never had such good, friendly and helpful service."

"Boatyard services are excellent!"

"Great team, always professional, friendly and make a customer feel like a customer."

"Congratulations on setting the standard for others to follow."

ANNUAL BERTHING
TRY A MARINA FOR FREE!
PREMIERMARINAS.COM

YOU'LL LOVE OUR FIRST-CLASS MARINAS, OUR SUPERB FACILITIES AND OUR VALUE FOR MONEY PRICING, BUT BEST OF ALL, YOU'LL LOVE OUR PASSION FOR CUSTOMER SERVICE. FOR A 12-MONTH BERTHING QUOTE OR A 'FREE TRIAL NIGHT' GO ONLINE AT PREMIERMARINAS.COM OR CALL YOUR LOCAL PREMIER MARINA

EASTBOURNE **01323 470099** BRIGHTON **01273 819919** CHICHESTER **01243 512731**
SOUTHSEA **023 9282 2719** PORT SOLENT **023 9221 0765** GOSPORT **023 9252 4811**
SWANWICK **01489 884081** FALMOUTH **01326 316620**

PREMIER
MARINAS

2012/MG148/k

SOUTH EAST SCOTLAND - Eyemouth to Rattray Head

Key to Marina Plans symbols

	Bottled gas	P	Parking
	Chandler		Pub/Restaurant
	Disabled facilities		Pump out
	Electrical supply		Rigging service
	Electrical repairs		Sail repairs
	Engine repairs		Shipwright
	First Aid		Shop/Supermarket
	Fresh Water		Showers
	Fuel - Diesel		Slipway
	Fuel - Petrol	WC	Toilets
	Hardstanding/boatyard		Telephone
@	Internet Café		Trolleys
	Laundry facilities	V	Visitors berths
	Lift-out facilities		Wi-Fi

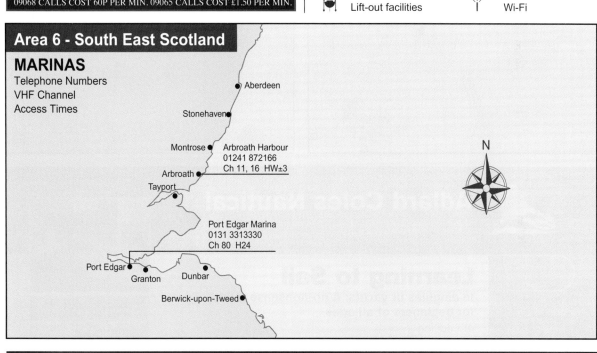

Area 6 - South East Scotland

MARINAS
Telephone Numbers
VHF Channel
Access Times

Aberdeen

Stonehaven

Montrose ● Arbroath Harbour
01241 872166
Ch 11, 16 HW±3
Arbroath ●
Tayport

Port Edgar Marina
0131 3313330
Ch 80 H24

Port Edgar ●
Granton ● Dunbar
Berwick-upon-Tweed ●

N

6

PORT EDGAR MARINA

Port Edgar Marina
Shore Road, South Queensferry
West Lothian, EH3 9SX
Tel: 0131 331 3330 Fax: 0131 331 4878
Email: admin.pe@edinburghleisure.co.uk

VHF | Ch 80
ACCESS | H24

Port Edgar is a large watersports centre and marina found on the south bank of the sheltered Firth of Forth. Situated in the village of South Queensferry, just west of the Forth Road Bridge, it is managed by Edinburgh Leisure on behalf of the City of Edinburgh Council and is reached via a deep water channel just west of the suspension bridge.

The nearby village offers a sufficient range of shops and restaurants, while Port Edgar is only a 20-minute walk from Dalmeny Station from where trains run regularly to Edinburgh.

FACILITIES AT A GLANCE

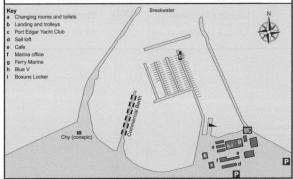

Key
a Changing rooms and toilets
b Landing and trolleys
c Port Edgar Yacht Club
d Sail loft
e Cafe
f Marina office
g Ferry Marine
h Blue V
i Bosuns Locker

ARBROATH HARBOUR

Arbroath Harbour
Harbour Office, Arbroath, DD11 1PD
Tel: 01241 872166 Fax: 01241 878472
Email: harbourmaster@angus.gov.uk

VHF | Ch 11, 16
ACCESS | HW±3

Arbroath harbour has 59 floating pontoon berths with security entrance which are serviced with electricity and fresh water to accommodate all types of leisure craft. Half height dock gates with walkway are located between the inner and outer harbours, which open and close at half tide, maintaining a minimum of 2.5m of water in the inner harbour.

The town of Arbroath offers a variety of social and sporting amenities to visiting crews and a number of quality pubs, restaurants, the famous twelfth century Abbey and Signal Tower Museum are located close to the harbour. Railway and bus stations are only 1km from the harbour with direct north and south connections.

FACILITIES AT A GLANCE

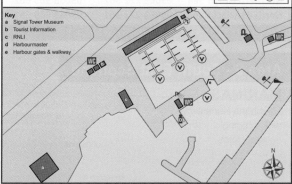

Key
a Signal Tower Museum
b Tourist Information
c RNLI
d Harbourmaster
e Harbour gates & walkway

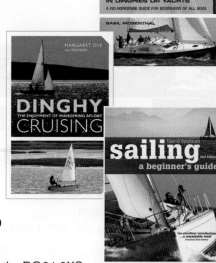

NORTH EAST SCOTLAND - Peterhead to Cape Wrath & Orkney & Shetland Is

ADLARD COLES NAUTICAL
WEATHER FORECASTS
BY FAX & TELEPHONE

Coastal/Inshore	2-day by Fax	5-day by Phone
North East	09065 222 343	09068 969 643
Scotland East	09065 222 342	09068 969 642
Scotland North	09065 222 341	09068 969 641
Minch	09065 222 354	09068 969 654
National (3-5 day)	09065 222 340	09068 969 640
Offshore	2-5 day by Fax	2-5 day by Phone
Southern North Sea	09065 222 358	09068 969 658
Northern North Sea	09065 222 362	09068 969 662
North West Scotland	09065 222 361	09068 969 661
Irish Sea	09065 222 359	09068 969 659

09068 CALLS COST 60P PER MIN. 09065 CALLS COST £1.50 PER MIN.

Key to Marina Plans symbols

Bottled gas		P	Parking
Chandler			Pub/Restaurant
Disabled facilities			Pump out
Electrical supply			Rigging service
Electrical repairs			Sail repairs
Engine repairs			Shipwright
First Aid			Shop/Supermarket
Fresh Water			Showers
Fuel - Diesel			Slipway
Fuel - Petrol		WC	Toilets
Hardstanding/boatyard			Telephone
@ Internet Café			Trolleys
Laundry facilities		V	Visitors berths
Lift-out facilities			Wi-Fi

Area 7 - North East Scotland

MARINAS
Telephone Numbers
VHF Channel
Access Times

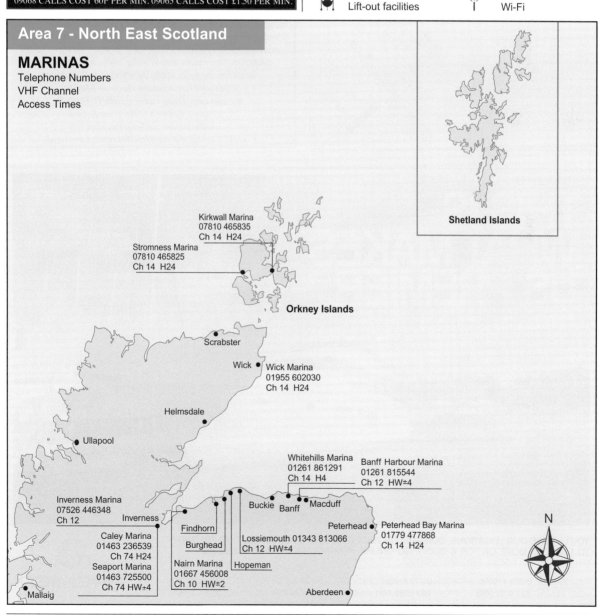

Shetland Islands

Kirkwall Marina
07810 465835
Ch 14 H24

Stromness Marina
07810 465825
Ch 14 H24

Orkney Islands

Scrabster

Wick • Wick Marina
01955 602030
Ch 14 H24

Helmsdale

Ullapool

Whitehills Marina
01261 861291
Ch 14 H4

Banff Harbour Marina
01261 815544
Ch 12 HW±4

Inverness Marina
07526 446348
Ch 12

Inverness

Buckie Banff Macduff

Findhorn

Caley Marina
01463 236539
Ch 74 H24
Seaport Marina
01463 725500
Ch 74 HW+4

Burghead

Nairn Marina
01667 456008
Ch 10 HW±2

Hopeman

Lossiemouth 01343 813066
Ch 12 HW±4

Peterhead • Peterhead Bay Marina
01779 477868
Ch 14 H24

N

Mallaig

Aberdeen •

PETERHEAD BAY MARINA

Peterhead Port Authority
Harbour Office, West Pier, Peterhead, AB42 1DW
Tel: 01779 477868/483600 Fax: 01779 478397
Email: info@peterheadport.co.uk
www.peterheadport.co.uk

| VHF | Ch 14 |
| ACCESS | H24 |

Based in the south west corner of Peterhead Bay Harbour, the marina provides one of the finest marine leisure facilities in the east of Scotland. In addition to the services on site, there are plenty of nautical businesses in the vicinity, ranging from ship chandlers and electrical servicing to boat repairs and surveying.

Due to its easterly location, Peterhead affords an ideal stopover for those yachts heading to or from Scandinavia as well as for vessels making for the Caledonian Canal.

FACILITIES AT A GLANCE

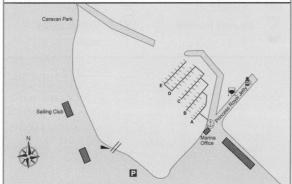

Caravan Park

Sailing Club

E D C B A

Marina Office

Princess Royal Jetty

P

N

BANFF HARBOUR MARINA

Banff Harbour Marina
Harbour Office, Quayside, Banff, Aberdeenshire, AB45 1HQ
Tel: 01261 815544 Fax: 01261 815544
Email: james.henderson@aberdeenshire.gov.uk

VHF Ch 12
ACCESS HW±4

A former fishing and cargo port now used as a recreational harbour. Banff offers excellent facilities to both regular and visiting users. The marina now provides 92 berths, of which 76 are serviced pontoon berths and 16 unserviced, traditional moorings, in one of the safest harbours on the NE coast of Scotland.

The outer basin offers adequate berthing for visitors and a tidal area for regulars.

The harbour is tidal with a sandy bottom. Movement during low water neaps is no problem for the shallow drafted boat.

FACILITIES AT A GLANCE

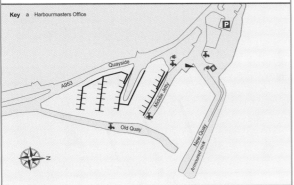

Key a Harbourmasters Office

WHITEHILLS MARINA

Whitehills Harbour Commissioners
Whitehills, Banffshire AB45 2NQ
Tel: 01261 861291 Fax: 01261 861291
www.whitehillsharbour.co.uk
Email: harbourmaster@whitehillsharbour.co.uk

VHF Ch 14
ACCESS H24

Built in 1900, Whitehills is a Trust Harbour fully maintained and run by nine commissioners elected from the village. It was a thriving fishing port up until 1999, but due to changes in the fishing industry, was converted into a marina during 2000.

Three miles west of Banff Harbour the marina benefits from full tidal access and comprises 38 serviced berths, with electricity, as well as eight non-serviced berths.

The nearby village of Whitehills boasts a selection of local stores and a couple of pubs. A coastal path leads from the marina to the top of the headland, affording striking views across the Moray Firth to the Caithness Hills.

FACILITIES AT A GLANCE

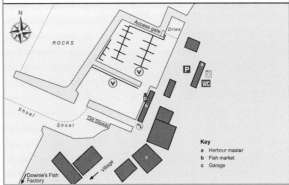

Key
a Harbour master
b Fish market
c Garage

LOSSIEMOUTH MARINA

The Harbour Office
Lossiemouth, Moray, IV31 6NT
Tel: 01343 813066 Fax: 01343 813066
Email: info@lossiemouthmarina.com

VHF | Ch 12
ACCESS | HW±4

Situated on the beautiful Moray Firth coastline, Lossiemouth Marina provides 47 berths in its East Basin and 41 berths for larger vessels in its West Basin. Although the berths are primarily taken up by residential yachts, during the summer months a certain number are allocated to visitors who can benefit from the friendly, efficient service. The marina lies within easy walking distance of the town, which has a good range of shops and restaurants and boasts an array of leisure facilities, two golf courses and acres of sandy beaches. Lossiemouth is also a great starting off point for Scotland's whisky trail.

FACILITIES AT A GLANCE

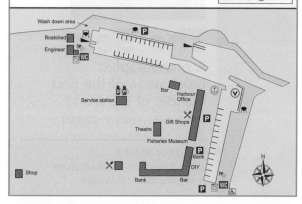

NAIRN MARINA

Nairn Marina, Nairnshire, Scotland
Tel: 01667 456008 Fax: 01667 452877
Email: nairn.harbourmaster@virgin.net

VHF | Ch 10
ACCESS | HW±2

Nairn is a small town on the coast of the Moray Firth. Formerly renowned both as a fishing port and as a holiday resort dating back to Victorian times, it boasts miles of award-winning, sandy beaches, famous castles such as Cawdor, Brodie and Castle Stuart, and two championship golf courses. Other recreational activities include horse riding or walking through spectacular countryside.

The marina lies at the mouth of the River Nairn, entry to which should be avoided in strong N to NE winds. The approach is made from the NW at or around high water as the entrance is badly silted and dries out.

FACILITIES AT A GLANCE

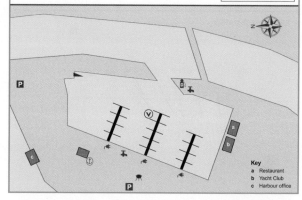

Key
a Restaurant
b Yacht Club
c Harbour office

INVERNESS MARINA

Inverness Marina
Longman Drive, Inverness, IV1 1SU
Tel: 01463 220501
Email: info@invernessmarina.com
www.invernessmarina.com

VHF | Ch 12
ACCESS | H24

Inverness Marina is a new marina (October 2008) situated in the Inverness firth just 1 mile from the city centre and half a mile from the entrance to the Caledonian Canal. The marina has a minimum depth of 3.0m, 24hr access and 150 fully serviced berths. On site are a chandlery and services including rigging, engineering, electronics and boat repair.

Inverness is the capital of the highlands with transport networks including bus, train, and flights to the rest of the UK and Europe. Inverness is the gateway to the Highlands with best possible location as a base for touring with golf courses, historic sites and the Whisky Trail. The marina is a perfect base for cruising Orkney, Shetland and Scandinavia.

FACILITIES AT A GLANCE

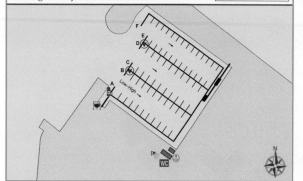

SEAPORT MARINA

Seaport Marina
Muirtown Wharf, Inverness, IV3 5LE
Tel: 01463 725500 Fax: 01463 710942
Email: enquiries.scotland@britishwaterways.co.uk
www.scottishcanals.co.uk

VHF | Ch 74
ACCESS | HW±4

Seaport Marina is based at Muirtown Basin at the eastern entrance of the Caledonian Canal; a 60 mile coast-to-coast channel slicing through the majestic Great Glen. Only a 15 minute walk from the centre of Inverness, the Marina is an ideal base for visiting the Highlands.

As well as the facilities listed, a crew lift is available at Seaport Marina as well as various locations along the canal: Caley Marina, Temple Pier, Fort Augustus and Banavie. There are shops and amenities nearby, and Caley Marina, only a short walk from Muirtown Basin, offers a chandlery, repair services, and a slipway.

FACILITIES AT A GLANCE

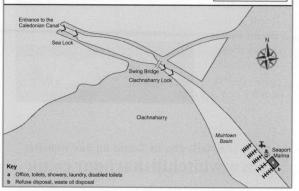

Key
a Office, toilets, showers, laundry, disabled toilets
b Refuse disposal, waste oil disposal

CALEY MARINA

Caley Marina
Canal Road, Inverness, IV3 8NF
Tel: 01463 236539 Fax: 01463 238323
Email: info@caleymarina.com
www.caleymarina.com

VHF	Ch 74
ACCESS	H24

Caley Marina is a family run business based near Inverness. With the four flight Muirtown locks and the Kessock Bridge providing a dramatic backdrop, the marina runs alongside the Caledonian Canal which, opened in 1822, is regarded as one of the most spectacular waterways in Europe. Built as a short cut between the North Sea and the Atlantic Ocean, thus avoiding the potentially dangerous Pentland Firth on the north coast of Scotland, the canal is around 60 miles long and takes about three days to cruise from east to west. With the prevailing winds behind you, it takes slightly less time to cruise in the other direction.

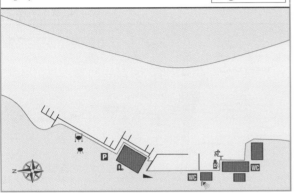

WICK MARINA

Wick Marina
Harbour Office, Wick, Caithness, KW1 5HA
Tel: 01955 602030 Fax: 01955 605936
Email: malcolm.bremner@wickharbour.co.uk

VHF	Ch 14, 16
ACCESS	H24

This is the most northerly marina on the British mainland and the last stop before the Orkney and Shetland Islands. Situated an easy five minutes walk from the town centre Wick Marina accommodates 70 fully serviced berths with all the support facilities expected in a modern marina including a boat lift.

This part of Scotland with its rugged coastline and rich history is easily accessible by air and a great starting point for cruising in the northern isles, Moray Firth, Caledonian Canal and Scandinavia, a comfortable 280-mile sail.

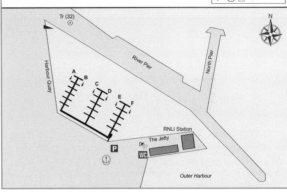

KIRKWALL MARINA

Kirkwall Marina
Harbour Street, Kirkwall, Orkney, KW15
Tel: 07810 465835 Fax: 01856 871313
Email: info@orkneymarinas.co.uk www.orkneymarinas.co.uk

VHF Ch 14
ACCESS H24

The Orkney Isles, comprising 70 islands in total, provides some of the finest cruising grounds in Northern Europe. The Main Island, incorporating the ancient port of Kirkwall, is the largest, although 16 others have lively communities and are rich in archaeological sites as well as spectacular scenery and wildlife.

Kirkwall Marina offers excellent facilities along with 24hr access and good shelter. The marina is very close to the historic Kirkwall, whose original town is one of the best preserved examples of an ancient Norse dwelling.

FACILITIES AT A GLANCE

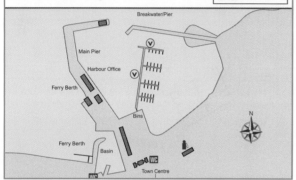

STROMNESS MARINA

Stromness Marina
Stromness, Orkney, KW16
Tel: 07810 465825 Fax: 01856 871313
Email: info@orkneymarinas.co.uk
www.orkneymarinas.co.uk

VHF Ch 14
ACCESS H24

Just 16 miles to the west of Kirkwall, Stromness lies on the south-western tip of the Orkney Isles' Mainland. Sitting beneath the rocky ridge known as Brinkie's Brae, it is considered one of Orkney's major seaports, with sailors first attracted to the fine anchorage provided by the bay of Hamnavoe.

Stromness, like Kirkwall offers comprehensive facilities including a chandlery and repair services. Also on hand are an internet café, a fitness suite and swimming pool as well as car and bike hire.

FACILITIES AT A GLANCE

Key
a   Terminal building, Harbour Master's office
b   Cafe
c   Rope centre

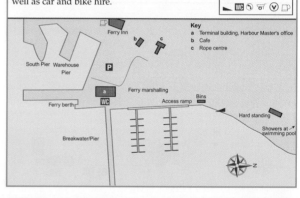

Orkney Marinas

Marinas in Kirkwall, Stromness & Westray

www.orkneymarinas.co.uk   info@orkneymarinas.co.uk

2012/MG36/k

NORTH WEST SCOTLAND - Cape Wrath to Crinan Canal

Key to Marina Plans symbols

Bottled gas		P	Parking
Chandler			Pub/Restaurant
Disabled facilities			Pump out
Electrical supply			Rigging service
Electrical repairs			Sail repairs
Engine repairs			Shipwright
First Aid			Shop/Supermarket
Fresh Water			Showers
Fuel - Diesel			Slipway
Fuel - Petrol		WC	Toilets
Hardstanding/boatyard			Telephone
Internet Café			Trolleys
Laundry facilities		V	Visitors berths
Lift-out facilities			Wi-Fi

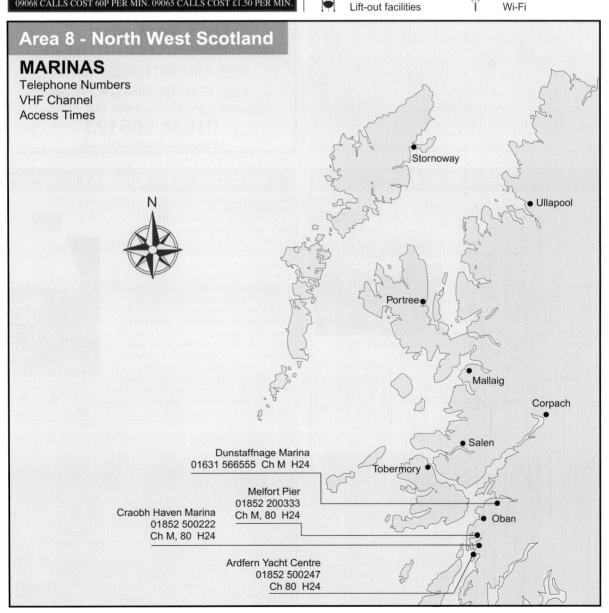

Area 8 - North West Scotland

MARINAS
Telephone Numbers
VHF Channel
Access Times

N

Stornoway

Ullapool

Portree

Mallaig

Corpach

Salen

Dunstaffnage Marina
01631 566555 Ch M H24

Melfort Pier
01852 200333
Ch M, 80 H24

Tobermory

Oban

Craobh Haven Marina
01852 500222
Ch M, 80 H24

Ardfern Yacht Centre
01852 500247
Ch 80 H24

DUNSTAFFNAGE MARINA

Dunstaffnage Marina Ltd
Dunbeg, by Oban, Argyll, PA37 1PX
Tel: 01631 566555 Fax: 01631 571044
Email: lizzy@dunstaffnage.sol.co.uk

VHF	Ch M
ACCESS	H24

Located just two to three miles north of Oban, Dunstaffnage Marina has recently been renovated to include an additional 36 fully serviced berths, a new breakwater providing shelter from NE'ly to E'ly winds and an increased amount of hard standing. Also on site is the Wide Mouthed Frog, offering a convivial bar, restaurant and accomodation with spectacular views of the 13th century Dunstaffnage Castle.

The marina is perfectly placed to explore Scotland's stunning west coast and Hebridean Islands. Only 10 miles NE up Loch Linnhe is Port Appin, while sailing 15 miles S, down the Firth of Lorne, brings you to Puldohran where you can walk to an ancient hostelry situated next to the C18 Bridge Over the Atlantic.

FACILITIES AT A GLANCE

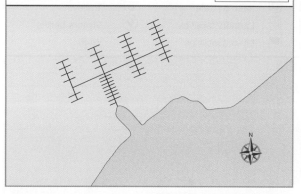

OBAN MARINA

Oban Marina
Isle of Kerrera, Oban, Argyll, PA34 4SX
Tel: 01631 565333 Fax: 01631 565888
Email: info@obanmarina.com

VHF	Ch 80
ACCESS	H24

Oban Marina is situated on the picturesque Isle of Kerrera. less than a mile from Oban town, the gateway to the western isles. This is a well-serviced marina popular with sailors and motorboats owners alike, offering one of the few facilities with all tides access on the west coast of Scotland.

For those travelling by land or sea, Kerrera is a short ride away from Oban itself in the marina's own complimentary shuttle, which can carry up to 65 people.

One of the many improvements undertaken by Oban Marina Ltd is the opening of the fully licensed Waypoint Bar & Grill serving a wide selection of island-produced seafood and meats available from start of May to the end of September.

FACILITIES AT A GLANCE

Key
a Reception
b Showers/toilets
c Bar & grill
d Shed

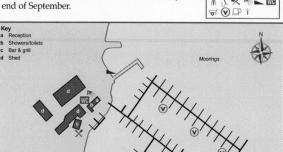

MELFORT PIER AND HARBOUR

Melfort Pier and Harbour
Kilmelford, by Oban, Argyll
Tel: 01852 200333 Fax: 01852 200329
Email: melharbour@aol.com

VHF	M, 80
ACCESS	H24

Melfort Pier & Harbour is situated on the shores of Loch Melfort, one of the most peaceful lochs on the south west coast of Scotland. Overlooked by the Pass of Melfort and the Braes of Lorn, it lies approximately 18 miles north of Lochgilphead and 16 miles south of Oban. Its onsite facilities include showers, laundry, telephone, free Wi-Fi access and parking – pets welcome. Fuel, power and water are available at nearby Kilmelford Yacht Haven. There is an onsite restaurant – The Melfort Mermaid – serving freshly cooked local food. For those who want a few nights on dry land, Melfort Pier & Harbour offers lochside houses, each one equipped with a sauna, spa bath and balcony offering stunning views over the loch - available per night.

FACILITIES AT A GLANCE

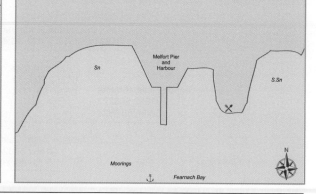

CRAOBH HAVEN MARINA

Craobh Haven Marina
By Lochgilphead, Argyll, Scotland, PA31 8UA
Tel: 01852 500222 Fax: 01852 500252
Email: info@craobhmarina.co.uk
www.craobhmarina.co.uk

| VHF | Ch M, 80 |
| ACCESS | H24 |

Craobh Marina is idyllically situated in the heart of Scotland's most sought after cruising grounds. Not only does Craobh offer ready access to a wonderful choice of scenic cruising throughout the western isles, the marina is conveniently close to Glasgow and its international transport hub.

Craobh Marina has been developed from a near perfect natural harbour, offering secure and sheltered berthing for up to 250 vessels to 22m LOA and with a draft of 4m. With an unusually deep and wide entrance Craobh Marina provides shelter and a warm welcome for all types of craft.

FACILITIES AT A GLANCE

Key
a Holiday cottages
b Village store
c Bar
d Gift shop
e Waste oil
f Boat shed
g Marina office

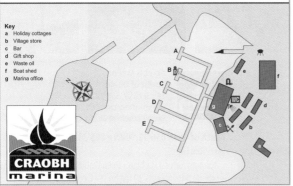

CRAOBH marina

ARDFERN YACHT CENTRE

Ardfern Yacht Centre
Ardfern, by Lochgilphead, Argyll, PA31 8QN
Tel: 01852 500247 Fax: 01852 500624
www.ardfernyacht.co.uk Email: office@ardfernyacht.co.uk

| VHF | Ch 80 |
| ACCESS | H24 |

Developed around an old pier once frequented by steamers, Ardfern Yacht Centre lies at the head of Loch Craignish, one of Scotland's most sheltered and picturesque sea lochs. With several islands and protected anchorages nearby, Ardfern is an ideal place from which to cruise the west coast of Scotland and the Outer Hebrides.

The Yacht Centre comprises pontoon berths and swinging moorings as well as a workshop, boat storage and well-stocked chandlery, while a grocery store and eating places can be found in the village. Among the onshore activities available locally are horse riding, cycling, and walking.

FACILITIES AT A GLANCE

Key
a Workshop
b Showers, toilets and launderette
c Chandlery and office

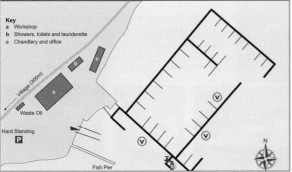

Village (300m)
Waste Oil
Hard Standing
Fish Pier

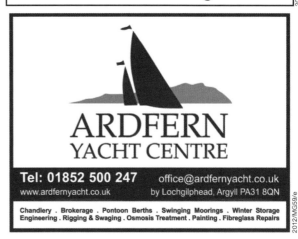
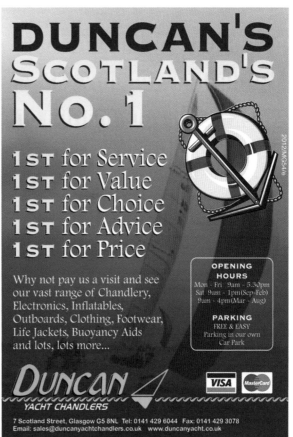
8

SOUTH WEST SCOTLAND - Crinan Canal to Mull of Galloway

Key to Marina Plans symbols

Bottled gas		Parking	
Chandler		Pub/Restaurant	
Disabled facilities		Pump out	
Electrical supply		Rigging service	
Electrical repairs		Sail repairs	
Engine repairs		Shipwright	
First Aid		Shop/Supermarket	
Fresh Water		Showers	
Fuel - Diesel		Slipway	
Fuel - Petrol		Toilets	
Hardstanding/boatyard		Telephone	
Internet Café		Trolleys	
Laundry facilities		Visitors berths	
Lift-out facilities		Wi-Fi	

Area 9 - South West Scotland

MARINAS
Telephone Numbers
VHF Channel
Access Times

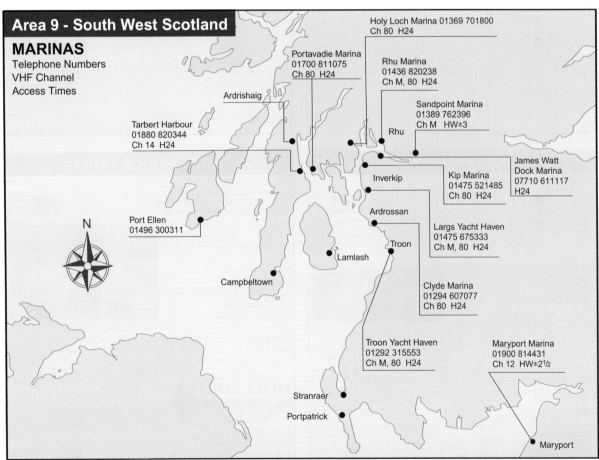

Holy Loch Marina 01369 701800
Ch 80 H24

Portavadie Marina
01700 811075
Ch 80 H24

Rhu Marina
01436 820238
Ch M, 80 H24

Ardrishaig

Sandpoint Marina
01389 762396
Ch M   HW±3

Rhu

Tarbert Harbour
01880 820344
Ch 14 H24

James Watt
Dock Marina
07710 611117
H24

Inverkip

Kip Marina
01475 521485
Ch 80 H24

Port Ellen
01496 300311

Ardrossan

Largs Yacht Haven
01475 675333
Ch M, 80 H24

Lamlash

Troon

Campbeltown

Clyde Marina
01294 607077
Ch 80 H24

N

Troon Yacht Haven
01292 315553
Ch M, 80 H24

Maryport Marina
01900 814431
Ch 12 HW±2½

Stranraer

Portpatrick

Maryport

9

PORT ELLEN MARINA

Port Ellen Marina
Port Ellen, Islay, Argyll, PA42 7DB
Tel: 01496 300301 Fax: 01496 300302
www.portellenmarina.com

VHF	
ACCESS	**H24**

A safe and relaxed marina for visitors to the *Malt Whisky Island*. There are seven classic distilleries and yet another still (private) to start production soon. If you are planning a cruise to the north then superb sailing will take you onward via Craighouse on Jura. Meeting guests or short term storage is trouble free with the excellent air and ferry services connecting to Glasgow. Once on Islay you will be tempted to extend your stay so be warned, check www.portellenmarina.com for the many reasons to visit, from golf to music.

FACILITIES AT A GLANCE

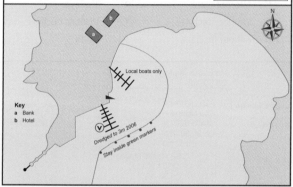

Key
a   Bank
b   Hotel

PORTAVADIE MARINA

Portavadie Marina
Portavadie, Loch Fyne, Argyll, PA21 2DA
Tel: 01700 811075 Fax: 01700 811074
Email: r.kitchin@yahoo.co.uk

VHF	Ch 80
ACCESS	**H24**

Portavadie Marina offers deep and sheltered berthing to residential and visiting yachts in an area renowned for its superb cruising waters. Situated on Loch Fyne in close proximity to several islands and the famous Kyles of Bute, Portavadie is within easy sailing distance of the Crinan Canal, giving access to the Inner and Outer Hebrides.

The marina provides 230 berths, of which 50 are reserved for visitors, plus comprehensive on-shore facilities including a bar and restaurant. Self-catering cottages, with free berthing for small craft, are also available.

This unspoiled area of Argyll is less than 2 hours from Glasgow. In nearby villages there are shops, eating places and outdoor activities including golf and horse-riding.

FACILITIES AT A GLANCE

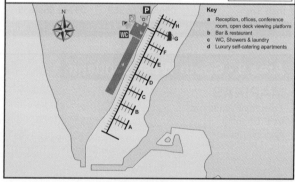

Key
a   Reception, offices, conference room, open deck viewing platform
b   Bar & restaurant
c   WC, Showers & laundry
d   Luxury self-catering apartments

TARBERT HARBOUR

Tarbert Harbour Authority
Harbour Office, Garval Road, Tarbert, Argyll, PA29 6TR
Tel: 01880 820344 Fax: 01880 820719
Email: tarbertharbour@btconnect.com

VHF	Ch 14
ACCESS	**H24**

Tarbert is situated on the west side of Loch Fyne, at 70km the longest sea loch in Scotland opening to the south into the Firth of Clyde.

The harbour is a natural amphi-theatre with an easily navigated narrow entrance at the east side opening onto Loch Fyne. Its eastern boundary is a line between Garbhaird point and Rubha Loisgte. The Harbour is accessible at all states of the tide and is one of Scotland's most sheltered harbours making it an excellent place to stay or leave a vessel unattended.

There are visiting berths for 65 – 100 sailing and motor yachts of varying sizes. Fresh water and electricity are available on the pontoons.

FACILITIES AT A GLANCE

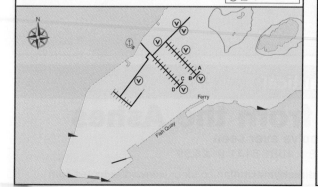

HOLY LOCH MARINA

Holy Loch Marina
Rankin's Brae, Sandbank, Dunoon, PA23 8FE
Tel: 01369 701800 Fax: 01369 704749
Email: info@holylochmarina.co.uk

VHF	Ch 80
ACCESS	**H24**

Holy Loch Marina, the marine gateway to Loch Lomond and the Trossachs National Park, lies on the south shore of the loch, roughly half a mile west of Lazaretto Point. Holy Loch is among the Clyde's most beautiful natural harbours and, besides being a peaceful location, offers an abundance of wildlife, places of local historical interest as well as excellent walking and cycling through the Argyll Forest Park. The marina can be entered in all weather conditions and is within easy sailing distance of Loch Long and Upper Firth.

FACILITIES AT A GLANCE

HOLY LOCH MARINA

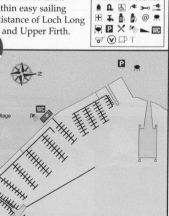

Key
a   Office/Harbourmaster
b   Boat storage
c   Holy Loch Sailing Club
d   Pier

RHU MARINA

Rhu Marina
Rhu, Dunbartonshire, G84 8LH
Tel: 01436 820238 Fax: 01436 821039
Email: dockmaster@rhumarina.co.uk

VHF | Ch M, 80
ACCESS | H24

Located on the north shore of the Clyde Estuary, Rhu Marina is accessible at all states of the tide and can accommodate yachts up to 18m in length. It also operates 60 swinging moorings in the bay adjacent to the marina, with a ferry service provided.

Within easy walking distance of the marina is Rhu village, a conservation village incorporating a few shops, a pub and the beautiful Glenarn Gardens as well as the Royal Northern & Clyde Yacht Club. A mile or two to the east lies the holiday town of Helensburgh, renowned for its attractive architecture and elegant parks and gardens, while Glasgow city is just 40 miles away and can be easily reached by train.

FACILITIES AT A GLANCE

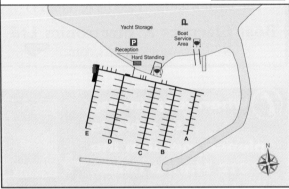

SANDPOINT MARINA

Sandpoint Marina Ltd
Sandpoint, Woodyard Road, Dumbarton, G82 4BG
Tel: 01389 762396 Fax: 01389 732605
Email: sales@sandpoint-marina.co.uk
www.sandpoint-marina.co.uk

VHF | CH M
ACCESS | HW±3

Lying on the north bank of the Clyde estuary on the opposite side of the River Leven from Dumbarton Castle, Sandpoint Marina provides easy access to some of the most stunning cruising grounds in the United Kingdom. It is an independently run marina, offering a professional yet personal service to every boat owner. Among the facilities to hand are an on site chandlery, storage areas, a 40 ton travel hoist and 20 individual workshop units.

Within a 20-minute drive of Glasgow city centre, the marina is situated close to the shores of Loch Lomond, the largest fresh water loch in Britain.

FACILITIES AT A GLANCE

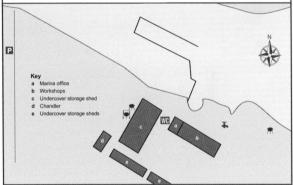

Key
a Marina office
b Workshops
c Undercover storage shed
d Chandler
e Undercover storage sheds

JAMES WATT DOCK MARINA

James Watt Dock Marina
East Hamilton Street
Greenock, Renfrewshire, PA15 2TD
Tel: 07710 611117 Fax: 01505 500064
www.csmscotland.co.uk Email: enquiries@csmscotland.co.uk

VHF |
ACCESS | H24

Based in the historic James Watt Dock alongside the stunning Victorian Sugar Shed, this new marina opened in May 2011 and is the first step in establishing an exciting new River Clyde waterfront development only 23 miles from Glasgow and 15 miles from the airport. James Watt Dock will have all the usual amenities expected of a modern marina.

Within easy reach of Greenock's cinema, pool, ice rink, restaurants and shops, and with nearby transport connections, the marina will be a great location for both visitors and regular berthers.

FACILITIES AT A GLANCE

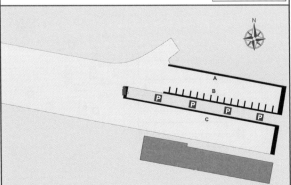

James Watt
Dock Marina
Origin 1878

James Watt Dock Marina opened in June 2011 and was host to the Tall Ships visit to Greenock in July. The marina has 65 berths with plans to develop up to 140 berths. Centred around the historic, A-listed James Watt Dock the marina benefits from the latest Varis pontoons and Rolec services. With depths of 5.0m at LWS the marina can cater for vessels up to 200ft on wall and pontoon berths. The marina is covered by HD security cameras and has secure 24hr gate access for vehicles and berth holders. Glasgow Airport is 15 minutes by car with Glasgow City Centre accessible in 30 minutes. Cartsdyke Station is a 10 minute walk from the marina and offers regular connections to Glasgow Central (40 mins) and Gourock ferries (10 mins).

- 65 pontoon berths
- Accessible at all states of tide
- Modern fuel jetty & gas supplies
- Modern showers & toilets
- Historic dock location
- Easily accessed by car and public transport
- Visitor berths always available
- VHF Ch. 80

T: +44 (0) 1475 729 838   W: jameswattdockmarina.co.uk
E: enquiries@jameswattdockmarina.co.uk

2012/MG138/d

9

KIP MARINA

Kip Marina, The Yacht Harbour
Inverkip, Renfrewshire, Scotland, PA16 0AS
Tel: 01475 521485 Fax: 01475 521298
www.kipmarina.co.uk Email: enquire@kipmarina.co.uk

VHF	Ch 80
ACCESS	H24

Inverkip is a small village which lies on the south shores of the River Kip as it enters the Firth of Clyde. Once established for fishing, smuggling and, in the 17th century, witch-hunts, it became a seaside resort in the 1860s as a result of the installation of the railway. Today it is a yachting centre, boasting a state-of-the-art marina with over 600 berths and full boatyard facilities. With the capacity to accommodate yachts of up to 23m LOA, Kip Marina offers direct road and rail access to Glasgow and its international airport, therefore making it an ideal location for either a winter lay up or crew changeover.

FACILITIES AT A GLANCE

Key
a Boat sales, chandlery and reception
b Workshop and contractors
c Chartroom bar and restaurant

LARGS YACHT HAVEN

Largs Yacht Haven Ltd
Irvine Road, Largs, Ayrshire, KA30 8EZ
Tel: 01475 675333 Fax: 01475 672245
www.yachthavens.com Email: largs@yachthavens.com

VHF	Ch 80
ACCESS	H24

Largs Yacht Haven offers a superb location among lochs and islands, with numerous fishing villages and harbours nearby. Sheltered cruising can be enjoyed in the inner Clyde, while the west coast and Ireland are only a day's sail away. With a stunning backdrop of the Scottish mountains, Largs incorporates 700 fully serviced berths and provides a range of on site facilities including chandlers, sailmakers, divers, engineers, shops, restaurants and club.

A 20-minute coastal walk brings you to the town of Largs, which has all the usual amenities as well as good road and rail connections to Glasgow.

FACILITIES AT A GLANCE

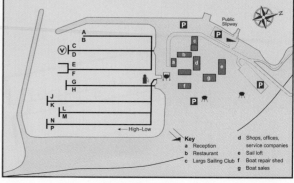

Key
a Reception
b Restaurant
c Largs Sailing Club
d Shops, offices, service companies
e Sail loft
f Boat repair shed
g Boat sales

CLYDE MARINA

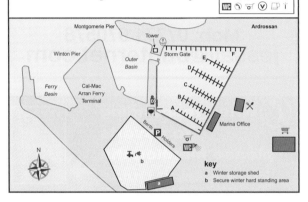

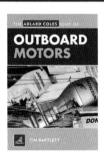
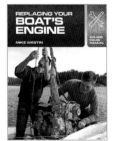
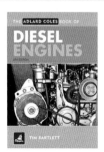

9

TROON YACHT HAVEN

Troon Yacht Haven Ltd
The Harbour, Troon, Ayrshire, KA10 6DJ
Tel: 01292 315553 Fax: 01292 312836
Email: troon@yachthavens.com
www.yachthavens.com

| VHF | Ch 80, M |
| ACCESS | H24 |

Troon Yacht Haven, situated on the Southern Clyde Estuary, benefits from deep water at all states of the tide. Tucked away in the harbour of Troon, it is well sheltered and within easy access of the town centre. There are plenty of cruising opportunities to be had from here, whether it be hopping across to the Isle of Arran, with its peaceful anchorages and mountain walks, sailing round the Mull or through the Crinan Canal to the Western Isles, or heading for the sheltered waters of the Clyde.

FACILITIES AT A GLANCE

Key
a Main building
   Toilets
   Showers
   Baths
   Laundry
b Marina office

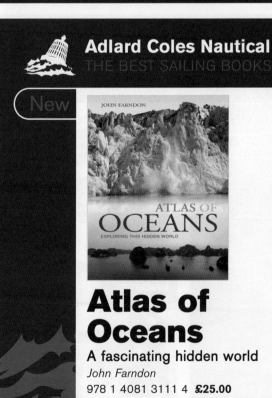

MARYPORT MARINA

Maryport Development Ltd
Marine Road, Maryport, Cumbria, CA15 8AY
Tel: 01900 814431
www.maryportmarina.com
Email: enquires@maryportmarina.com

| VHF | Ch 12,16 |
| ACCESS | HW±2.5 |

Maryport Marina is located in the historic Senhouse Dock, which was originally built for sailing clippers in the late 19th century. The old stone harbour walls provide good shelter to the 190 berths from the prevailing south westerlies.

Maryport town centre and its shops, pubs and other amenities is within easy walking distance from the marina. Maryport a perfect location from which to explore the west coast of Scotland as well as the Isle of Man and the Galloway Coast. For those who wish to venture inland, then the Lake District is only seven miles away.

FACILITIES AT A GLANCE

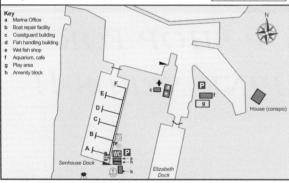

Key
a Marina Office
b Boat repair facility
c Coastguard building
d Fish handling building
e Wet fish shop
f Aquarium, cafe
g Play area
h Amenity block

MARYPORT MARINA

offers a warm and friendly welcome to all boat owners sailing the Solway Firth and Irish Sea.

For further information contact 01900 814431 or email: enquiries@maryportmarina.com
www.maryportmarina.com

2012/MG26/e

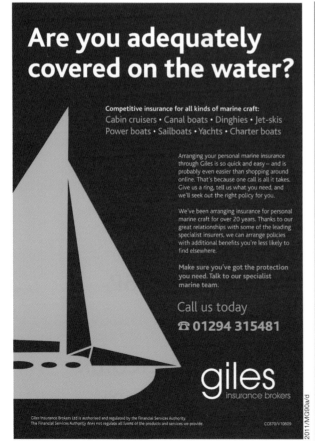

9

NW ENGLAND, ISLE OF MAN & N WALES - Mull of Galloway to Bardsey Is

ADLARD COLES NAUTICAL
WEATHER FORECASTS
BY FAX & TELEPHONE

Coastal/Inshore	2-day by Fax	5-day by Phone
Northern Ireland	09065 222 355	09068 969 655
Clyde	09065 222 352	09068 969 652
North West	09065 222 351	09068 969 651
Wales	09065 222 350	09068 969 650
National (3-5 day)	09065 222 340	09068 969 640

Offshore	2-5 day by Fax	2-5 day by Phone
Northern North Sea	09065 222 362	09068 969 662
North West Scotland	09065 222 361	09068 969 661
Irish Sea	09065 222 359	09068 969 659
English Channel	09065 222 357	09068 969 657

09068 CALLS COST 60P PER MIN. 09065 CALLS COST £1.50 PER MIN.

Key to Marina Plans symbols

🛢	Bottled gas	🅿	Parking
	Chandler	✕	Pub/Restaurant
♿	Disabled facilities		Pump out
	Electrical supply		Rigging service
	Electrical repairs		Sail repairs
	Engine repairs		Shipwright
✛	First Aid		Shop/Supermarket
	Fresh Water		Showers
	Fuel - Diesel		Slipway
	Fuel - Petrol	WC	Toilets
	Hardstanding/boatyard		Telephone
@	Internet Café		Trolleys
	Laundry facilities	Ⓥ	Visitors berths
	Lift-out facilities		Wi-Fi

Area 10 - North West England & Wales

MARINAS
Telephone Numbers
VHF Channel
Access Times

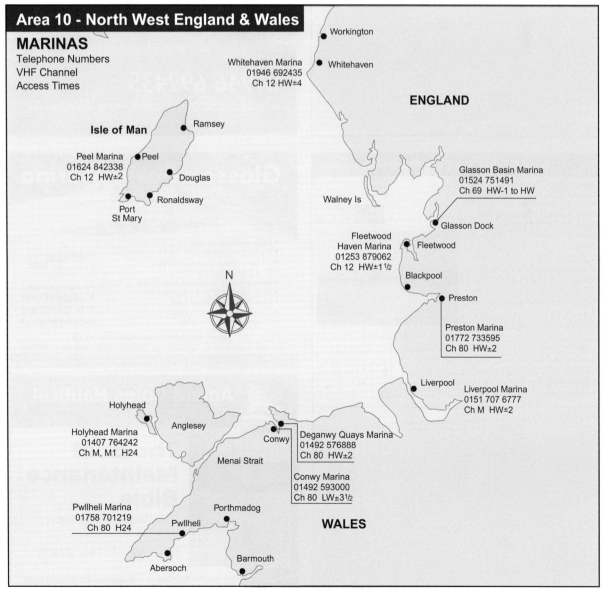

Workington

Whitehaven Marina
01946 692435
Ch 12 HW±4

Whitehaven

ENGLAND

Ramsey

Isle of Man

Peel Marina
01624 842338
Ch 12 HW±2

Peel

Douglas

Ronaldsway

Port
St Mary

Walney Is

Glasson Basin Marina
01524 751491
Ch 69 HW-1 to HW

Glasson Dock

Fleetwood
Haven Marina
01253 879062
Ch 12 HW±1½

Fleetwood

Blackpool

Preston

Preston Marina
01772 733595
Ch 80 HW±2

Liverpool

Liverpool Marina
0151 707 6777
Ch M HW±2

Holyhead

Holyhead Marina
01407 764242
Ch M, M1 H24

Anglesey

Conwy

Deganwy Quays Marina
01492 576888
Ch 80 HW±2

Menai Strait

Conwy Marina
01492 593000
Ch 80 LW±3½

Pwllheli Marina
01758 701219
Ch 80 H24

Pwllheli

Porthmadog

WALES

Abersoch

Barmouth

N

10

WHITEHAVEN MARINA

Whitehaven Marina Ltd
Harbour Office, Bulwark Quay, Whitehaven, Cumbria, CA28 7HW
Tel: 01946 692435
Email: enquiries@whitehavenmarina.co.uk
www.whitehavenmarina.co.uk

VHF	Ch 12
ACCESS	HW±4

Whitehaven Marina can be found at the south-western entrance to the Solway Firth, providing a strategic departure point for those yachts heading for the Isle of Man, Ireland or Southern Scotland. The harbour is one of the more accessible ports of refuge in NW England, affording a safe entry in most weathers. The approach channel across the outer harbour is dredged to about 1.0m above chart datum, allowing entry into the inner harbour via a sea lock at around HW±4.

Conveniently situated for visiting the Lake District, Whitehaven is an attractive Georgian town, renowned in the C18 for its rum and slave imports.

FACILITIES AT A GLANCE

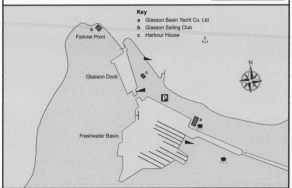

GLASSON BASIN MARINA

Glasson Basin Yacht Company Ltd
Glasson Dock, Lancaster, LA2 0AW
Tel: 01524 751491 Fax: 01524 752626
Email: info@glassonmarina.com
www.glassonmarina.com

VHF	Ch 69
ACCESS	HW-1 to HW

Glasson Dock Marina lies on the River Lune, west of Sunderland Point.   Access is via the outer dock which opens 45 minutes before H. W.Liverpool and thence via BWB lock into the inner basin. It is recommended to leave Lune No. 1 Buoy approx 11/2 hrs. before H. W.. Contact the dock on Channel 69.   The Marina can only be contacted by telephone. All the necessary requirements can be found either on site or within easy reach of Glasson Dock, including boat, rigging and sail repair services as well as a launderette, ablution facilities, shops and restaurants.

FACILITIES AT A GLANCE

Key
a   Glasson Basin Yacht Co. Ltd
b   Glasson Sailing Club
c   Harbour House

PEEL MARINA

Peel Marina
The Harbour Office, East Quay, Peel, IM5 1AR
Tel: 01624 842338 Fax: 01624 843610
www.gov.im/harbours/
Email: enquiries@harbours.dot.gov.im

| VHF | Ch 12 |
| ACCESS | HW±2 |

The Inner Harbour has recently been re-developed to provide a 120-berth marina in the southern end. Access is via a flap gate which opens approximately HW±2. A depth of 2·5m is retained at LW. Fresh water and electricity are provided on the pontoons, and a full range of facilities, including showers, laundry, chandlery, fuel and gas are available either in the marina or close by. There is no boat hoist but a mobile crane can be hired locally. Deepwater berths are available on the breakwater

Peel is the most active fishing port on the Isle of Man. The harbour is overlooked by its ancient castle, which also features the award-winning House of Manannan heritage centre. The town offers good shopping, banks, bars, a post office and chemist.

FACILITIES AT A GLANCE

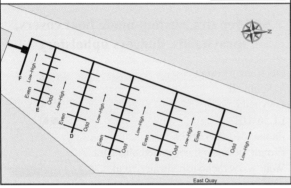

East Quay

FLEETWOOD HAVEN MARINA

Fleetwood Haven Marina
The Dock Office, Wyre Dock, Fleetwood, FY7 6PP
Tel: 01253 879062 Fax: 01253 879063
Email: fleetwoodhaven@abports.co.uk

| VHF | Ch 12 |
| ACCESS | HW±1.5 |

Fleetwood Haven Marina provides a good location from which to cruise Morecambe Bay and the Irish Sea. To the north west is the Isle of Man, to the north is the Solway Firth and the Clyde Estuary, while to the south west is Conwy, the Menai Straits and Holyhead.

Tucked away in a protected dock which dates back as far as 1835, Fleetwood Haven Marina has 450 berths and offers extensive facilities. Overlooking the marina is a 15-acre retail and leisure park laid out in a popular American style.

FACILITIES AT A GLANCE

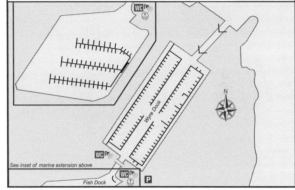

Wyre Dock

See inset of marina extension above

Fish Dock

PRESTON MARINA

Preston Marine Services Ltd
The Boathouse, Navigation Way, Preston, PR2 2YP
Tel: 01772 733595 Fax: 01772 731881
Email: info@prestonmarina.co.uk www.prestonmarina.co.uk

| VHF | Ch 80 |
| ACCESS | HW±2 |

Preston Marina forms part of the comprehensive Riversway Docklands development, meeting all the demands of modern day boat owners. With the docks' history dating back

over 100 years, today the marina comprises 40 acres of fully serviced pontoon berths sheltered behind the refurbished original lock gates.

Lying 15 miles up the River Ribble, which itself is an interesting cruising ground with an abundance of wildlife, Preston is well placed for sailing to parts of Scotland, Ireland or Wales. The Docklands development includes a wide choice of restaurants, shops and cinemas as well as being in easy reach of all the cultural and leisure facilities provided by a large town.

FACILITIES AT A GLANCE

Key
a Riverway control building
b Marina HQ
c Pub/restaurant

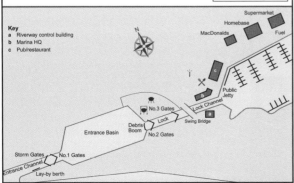

10

LIVERPOOL MARINA

Liverpool Marina
Coburg Wharf, Sefton Street, Liverpool, L3 4BP
Tel: 0151 707 6777 Fax: 0151 707 6770
Email: mail@liverpoolmarina.co.uk

VHF	Ch M
ACCESS	HW±2

Liverpool Marina is ideally situated for yachtsmen wishing to cruise the Irish Sea. Access is through a computerised lock that opens two and a half hours either side of high water between 0600 and 2200 daily. Once in the marina, you can enjoy the benefits of the facilities on offer, including a first class club bar and restaurant.

Liverpool - recently announced Capital of Culture 2008 - is now a thriving cosmopolitan city, with attractions ranging from numerous bars and restaurants to museums, art galleries and the Beatles Story.

FACILITIES AT A GLANCE

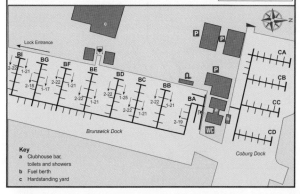

Key
a Clubhouse bar, toilets and showers
b Fuel berth
c Hardstanding yard

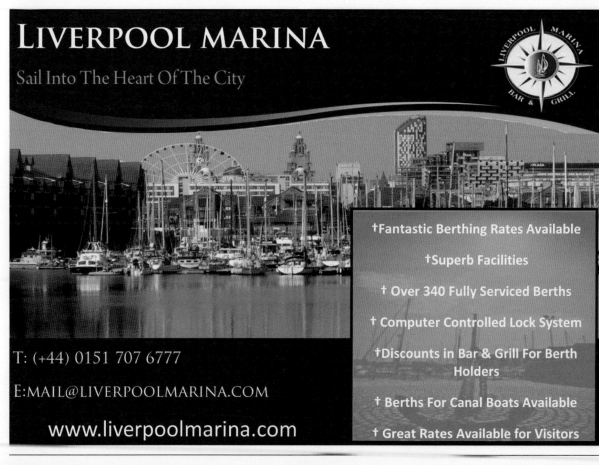

CONWY MARINA

Conwy Marina
Conwy, LL32 8EP
Tel: 01492 593000 Fax: 01492 572111
Email: jroberts@quaymarinas.com
www.quaymarinas.com

VHF Ch 80
ACCESS LW±3.5

Situated in an area of outstanding natural beauty, with the Mountains of Snowdonia National Park providing a stunning backdrop, Conwy is the first purpose-built marina to be developed on the north coast of Wales. Enjoying a unique

site next to the 13th century Conwy Castle, the third of Edward I's great castles, it provides a convenient base from which to explore the cruising grounds of the North Wales coast. The unspoilt coves of Anglesey and the beautiful Menai Straits prove a popular destination, while further afield are the Llyn Peninsula and the Islands of Bardsey and Tudwells. The marina incorporates about 500 fully serviced berths which are accessible through a barrier gate between half tide and high water.

FACILITIES AT A GLANCE

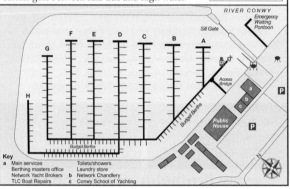

Key
a Main services
  Berthing masters office
  Network Yacht Brokers
  TLC Boat Repairs
  Toilets/showers
  Laundry store
b Network Chandlery
c Conwy School of Yachting

DEGANWY QUAYS MARINA

Deganwy Quays Marina
Deganwy, Conwy, LL31 9DJ
Tel: 01492 576888 Fax: 01492 580066
Email: jjones@quaymarinas.com www.quaymarinas.com

VHF Ch 80
ACCESS HW±2

Deganwy Quays Marina is located in the centre of the north Wales coastline on the estuary of the Conwy River and sits between the river and the small town of Deganwy with the beautiful backdrop of the Vardre hills. The views from the Marina across the

Conwy River are truly outstanding with the medieval walled town and Castle of Conwy outlined against the foothills of the Snowdonia National Park.

Deganwy Quays Marina opened in 2004 and has 165 fully serviced berths which are accessed via a tidal gate between half tide and high water.

FACILITIES AT A GLANCE

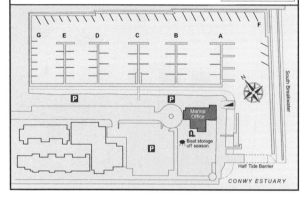

HOLYHEAD MARINA

Holyhead Marina Ltd
Newry Beach, Holyhead, Gwynedd, LL65 1YA
Tel: 01407 764242 Fax: 01407 769152
Email: info@holyheadmarina.co.uk

VHF Ch M, M1
ACCESS H24

One of the few natural deep water harbours on the Welsh coast, Anglesey is conveniently placed as a first port of call if heading to North Wales from the North, South or West. Its marina at Holyhead, accessible at all states of the tide, is sheltered by Holyhead Mountain as well as

an enormous harbour breakwater and extensive floating breakwaters, therefore offering good protection from all directions.

Anglesey boasts numerous picturesque anchorages and beaches in addition to striking views over Snowdonia, while only a tide or two away are the Isle of Man and Eire.

FACILITIES AT A GLANCE

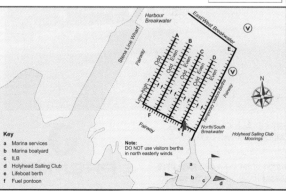

Key
a Marina services
b Marina boatyard
c ILB
d Holyhead Sailing Club
e Lifeboat berth
f Fuel pontoon

Note:
DO NOT use visitors berths in north easterly winds

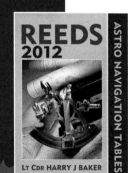

10

PWLLHELI MARINA

Pwllheli Marina
Glan Don, Pwllheli, North Wales, LL53 5YT
Tel: 01758 701219 Fax: 01758 701443
Email: hafanpwllheli@gwynedd.gov.uk

VHF	Ch 80
ACCESS	

Pwllheli is an old Welsh market town providing the gateway to the Llyn Peninsula, which stretches out as far as Bardsey Island to form an 'Area of Outstanding Natural Beauty'. Enjoying the spectacular backdrop of the Snowdonia Mountains, Pwllheli's numerous attractions include an open-air market every Wednesday, 'Neuadd Dwyfor', offering a mix of live theatre and latest films, and beautiful beaches.

Pwllheli Marina is situated on the south side of the Llyn Peninsula. One of Wales' finest marinas and sailing centres, it has over 400 pontoon berths and excellent onshore facilities.

FACILITIES AT A GLANCE

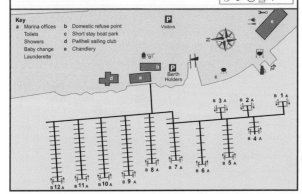

Key
a Marina offices
   Toilets
   Showers
   Baby change
   Launderette
b Domestic refuse point
c Short stay boat park
d Pwllheli sailing club
e Chandlery

SOUTH WALES & BRISTOL CHANNEL - Bardsey Island to Land's End

ADLARD COLES NAUTICAL
WEATHER FORECASTS
BY FAX & TELEPHONE

Coastal/Inshore	2-day by Fax	5-day by Phone
North West	09065 222 351	09068 969 651
Wales	09065 222 350	09068 969 650
Bristol	09065 222 349	09068 969 649
South West	09065 222 348	09068 969 648
National (3-5 day)	09065 222 340	09068 969 640

Offshore	2-5 day by Fax	2-5 day by Phone
Irish Sea	09065 222 359	09068 969 659
English Channel	09065 222 357	09068 969 657
Biscay	09065 222 360	09068 969 660
North West Scotland	09065 222 361	09068 969 661

09068 CALLS COST 60P PER MIN. 09065 CALLS COST £1.50 PER MIN.

Key to Marina Plans symbols

Bottled gas		P	Parking
Chandler			Pub/Restaurant
Disabled facilities			Pump out
Electrical supply			Rigging service
Electrical repairs			Sail repairs
Engine repairs			Shipwright
First Aid			Shop/Supermarket
Fresh Water			Showers
Fuel - Diesel			Slipway
Fuel - Petrol		WC	Toilets
Hardstanding/boatyard			Telephone
Internet Café			Trolleys
Laundry facilities		V	Visitors berths
Lift-out facilities			Wi-Fi

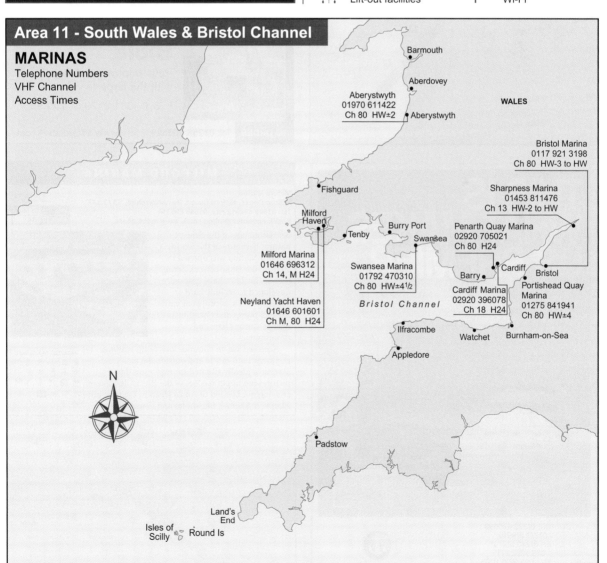

Area 11 - South Wales & Bristol Channel

MARINAS
Telephone Numbers
VHF Channel
Access Times

WALES

Barmouth

Aberdovey

Aberystwyth
01970 611422
Ch 80 HW±2 · Aberystwyth

Bristol Marina
0117 921 3198
Ch 80 HW-3 to HW

Sharpness Marina
01453 811476
Ch 13 HW-2 to HW

· Fishguard

Milford Haven

· Tenby

Burry Port

Swansea

Penarth Quay Marina
02920 705021
Ch 80 H24

Milford Marina
01646 696312
Ch 14, M H24

Swansea Marina
01792 470310
Ch 80 HW±4½

Barry ·   · Cardiff   Bristol

Cardiff Marina
02920 396078
Ch 18 H24

Portishead Quay
Marina
01275 841941
Ch 80 HW±4

Neyland Yacht Haven
01646 601601
Ch M, 80 H24

Bristol Channel

Ilfracombe
Watchet   Burnham-on-Sea

Appledore

N

Padstow

Land's
End

Isles of
Scilly   Round Is

11

ABERYSTWYTH MARINA

Aberystwyth Marina, IMP Developments
Trefechan, Aberystwyth, Ceredigion, SY23 1AS
Tel: 01970 611422 Fax: 01970 624122
Email: enquiries@aberystwythmarina.com

VHF Ch 80
ACCESS HW±2

Aberystwyth is a picturesque university seaside town on the west coast of Wales. Its £9 million marina provides over 150 permanent pontoon berths and welcomes on average between 1,500 and 2,000 visiting yachts per year. Accessible two hours either side of high water, its facilities incorporate the usual marine services as well as an on-site pub and restaurant.

A short distance away are several pretty Welsh harbours, including Fishguard, Cardigan, Porthmadog and Abersoch, while the east coast of Ireland can be reached within a day's sail.

FACILITIES AT A GLANCE

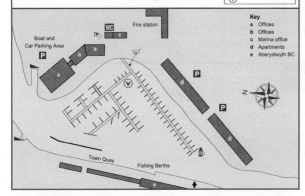

Key
a Offices
b Offices
c Marina office
d Apartments
e Aberystwyth BC

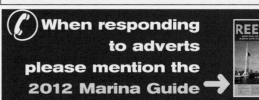

MILFORD MARINA

Milford Marina
Milford Docks, Milford Haven, Pembrokeshire, SA73 3AF
Tel: 01646 696312 Fax: 01646 696314
Email: enquiries@mhpa.co.uk www.mpha.co.uk

VHF Ch 14, M
ACCESS H24

Set within one of the deepest natural harbours in the world, Milford Marina was opened in 1991 by the Duke of York. Since then its facilities have gradually developed to include hard standing areas, secure boat yards, a diesel pump and chandlery as well as various bars and restaurants.

Accessed via an entrance lock (with waiting pontoons both inside and outside the lock), the marina is ideally situated for exploring the picturesque upper reaches of the River Cleddau or cruising out beyond St Ann's Head to the unspoilt islands of Skomer, Skokholm and Grassholm.

FACILITIES AT A GLANCE

Key
a Neil Hart Joinery
b Milford Haven Ship Repairers
c Neyland Marine Services
d Fish Processing
e Fish Markets
f Galley Café
g MPSC
h Cosalt
i MITEC Building
j Seal Hospital
k Engineering Division
l Charterhouse Restaurant
m Norrad Electrics
n Mortgage Broker
o Locks on Line
p Museum
q Marina Control
   Martha's Vs Vineyard
   Dyfed Electronics
r Phoenix Bowl
s Windjammer Marine

NEYLAND YACHT HAVEN

Neyland Yacht Haven Ltd
Brunel Quay, Neyland, Pembrokeshire, SA73 1PY
Tel: 01646 601601 Fax: 01646 600713
Email: neyland@yachthavens.com

VHF	Ch M, 80
ACCESS	H24

Approximately 10 miles from the entrance to Milford Haven lies Neyland Yacht Haven. Tucked away in a well protected inlet just before the Cleddau Bridge, this marina has 420 berths and can accommodate yachts up to 25m LOA with draughts of up to

2.5m. The marina is divided into two basins, with the lower one enjoying full tidal access, while entry to the upper one is restricted by a tidal sill. Visitor and annual berthing enquiries welcome.

Offering a comprehensive range of services, Neyland Yacht Haven is within a five minute walk of the town centre where the various shops and takeaways cater for most everyday needs.

FACILITIES AT A GLANCE

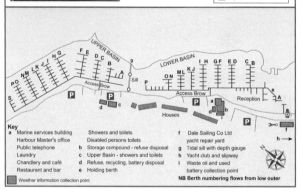

Key

a   Marine services building
    Harbour Master's office
    Public telephone
    Laundry
    Chandlery and café
    Restaurant and bar

b   Showers and toilets
    Disabled persons toilets
    Storage compound - refuse disposal
c   Upper Basin - showers and toilets
d   Refuse, recycling, battery disposal
e   Holding berth

f   Dale Sailing Co Ltd
    yacht repair yard
g   Tidal sill with depth gauge
h   Yacht club and slipway
i   Waste oil and used
    battery collection point
NB Berth numbering flows from low outer

   Weather information collection point

NEYLAND MARINE SERVICES
Tel: 01646 600358
Fax: 01646 600323
e-mail: neylandmarine@aol.com
www.neylandmarine.co.uk

We provide unequalled sales and service to the pleasure boating, fishing and shipping industry. Your complete repair and supply service for electrical and electronic equipment, engineering installations and components. Supply, service dealers for most manufacturers.

2012/MG13/k

11

SWANSEA MARINA

Swansea Marina
Lockside, Maritime Quarter, Swansea, SA1 1WG
Tel: 01792 470310 Fax: 01792 463948
www.swansea.gov.uk/swanseamarina
Email: swanmar@swansea.gov.uk

⚓⚓⚓⚓

| VHF | Ch 80 |
| ACCESS | HW±4.5 |

At the hub of the city's recently redeveloped and award winning Maritime Quarter, Swansea Marina can be accessed HW±4½ hrs via a lock. Surrounded by a plethora of shops, restaurants and marine businesses to cater for most yachtsmen's needs, the marina is in close proximity to the picturesque Gower coast, where there is no shortage of quiet sandy beaches off which to anchor. It also provides the perfect starting point for cruising to Ilfracombe, Lundy Island, the North Cornish coast or West Wales.

Within easy walking distance of the marina is the city centre, boasting a covered shopping centre and market. For those who prefer walking or cycling, take the long promenade to the Mumbles fishing village from where there are plenty of coastal walks.

FACILITIES AT A GLANCE

Key
a Leisure Centre
b Maritime Museum
c Pumphouse Restaurant
d Yacht Club
e Repair shed
f Mariott Hotel

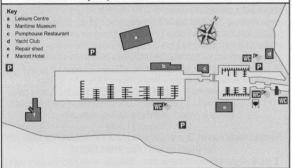
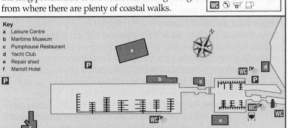

PENARTH QUAYS MARINA

Penarth Quays Marina
Penarth, Vale of Glamorgan, CF64 1TQ
Tel: 02920 705021 Fax: 02920 712170
www.quaymarinas.com
Email: sjones@quaymarinas.com

⚓⚓⚓⚓

| VHF | Ch 80 |
| ACCESS | H24 |

Penarth Quays Marina has been established in the historic basins of Penarth Docks for over 20 years and is the premier boating facility in the region. The marina is Cardiff Bay's only 5 Gold Anchor marina and provides an ideal base for those using the Bay and the Bristol Channel. With 24hr access there is always water available for boating. Penarth and Cardiff boast an extensive range of leisure facilities, shops and restaurants making this marina an ideal base or destination. The marina has a blue flag and is a member of the TransEurope Group.

FACILITIES AT A GLANCE

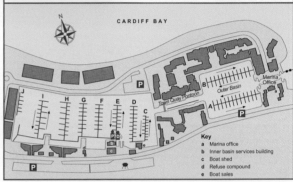

CARDIFF BAY

Key
a Marina office
b Inner basin services building
c Boat shed
d Refuse compound
e Boat sales

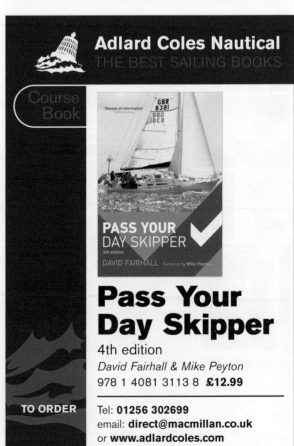

CARDIFF MARINA

Cardiff Marina
Watkiss Way, Cardiff, CF11 0JL
Tel: 02920 396078   Fax: 02920 345116
Email: info@cardiffmarina.com
www.cardiffmarina.com

VHF	Ch 18
ACCESS	H24

Cardiff Marina every facility one would expect from a first class marina, providing safe, secure and sheltered mooring in the heart of Cardiff Bay.

This is an attractive and pproachable environment for boat users and has a fast growing boating community. With 24hr access to the Bristol Channel, affordable moorings and superb road links, Cardiff Marina is perfect for boat owners. The marina does not have its own VHF channel but call up barrage control on channel 18 to enter Cardiff Bay through the barrage. Access – is 24 hours through Cardiff Bay Barrage.

FACILITIES AT A GLANCE

Key
a Marina Office
b Showers, toilets
c Workshop

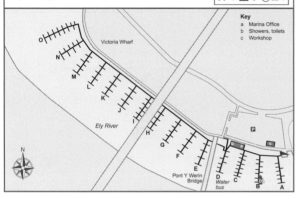

SHARPNESS MARINA

Sharpness Marina
Berkeley, Gloucestershire GL13 9UN
Tel & fax: 01453 811476
Email: sharpness@f2s.com

VHF	Ch 13
ACCESS	HW-2

Sharpness is a small port on the River Severn lying at the entrance to the Gloucester and Sharpness Canal. At the time of its completion in 1827, the canal was the largest and deepest ship canal in the world. However, although once an important commercial waterway, it is now primarily used by pleasure boats. Yachts approaching the marina from seaward can do so via a lock two hours before high water, but note that the final arrival should be timed as late as possible to avoid strong tides in the entrance. From the lock, a passage under two swing bridges and a turn to port brings you to the marina, where pontoon berths are equipped with electricity and water supplies.

FACILITIES AT A GLANCE

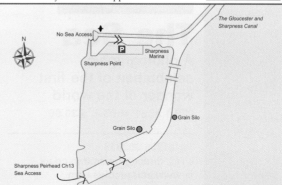

11

BRISTOL MARINA

Bristol Marina Ltd
Hanover Place, Bristol, BS1 6TZ
Tel: 0117 921 3198 Fax: 0117 929 7672
Email: info@bristolmarina.co.uk

⚓⚓⚓⚓

VHF	Ch 80
ACCESS	HW-3 to HW

Situated in the heart of the city, Bristol is a fully serviced marina providing over 100 pontoon berths for vessels up to 20m LOA. Among the facilities are a new fuelling berth and pump out station as well as an on site chandler and sailmaker. It is situated on the south side of the Floating Harbour, about eight miles from the mouth of the River Avon. Accessible from seaward via the Cumberland Basin, passing through both Entrance Lock and Junction Lock, it can be reached approximately three hours before HW.

Shops, restaurants, theatres and cinemas are all within easy reach of the marina, while local attractions include the SS *Great Britain*, designed by Isambard Kingdom Brunel, and the famous Clifton Suspension Bridge, which has an excellent visitors' centre depicting its fascinating story.

FACILITIES AT A GLANCE

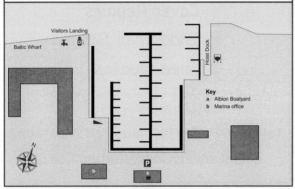

Key
a Albion Boatyard
b Marina office

PORTISHEAD QUAYS MARINA

Portishead Quays Marina
Newfoundland Way, Portishead, North Somerset, BS20 7DF
Tel: 01275 841941 Fax: 01275 841942
Email: portisheadmarina@quaymarinas.com
www.quaymarinas.com

⚓⚓⚓⚓⚓

VHF	Ch 80
ACCESS	HW±3.5

Portishead Marina is a popular destination for cruising in the Bristol Channel. Providing an excellent link between the inland waterways at Bristol and Sharpness and offering access to the open water and marinas down channel. The entrance to the Marina is via a lock, with a minimum access of HW+/-3.5hrs. Contact the Marina on VHF Ch 80 ahead of time for next available lock. The Marina provides 250 fully serviced berths and can accommodate vessels up to 40m LOA, draft up to 5.5m. The marina has a 35 tonnes boat hoist and the boatyard offers all the facilities you would expect from a Quay Marinas site.

FACILITIES AT A GLANCE

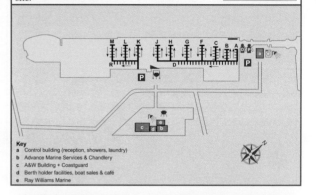

Key
a Control building (reception, showers, laundry)
b Advance Marine Services & Chandlery
c A&W Building + Coastguard
d Berth holder facilities, boat sales & café
e Ray Williams Marine

SOUTH IRELAND - Malahide, clockwise to Liscannor Bay

ADLARD COLES NAUTICAL
WEATHER FORECASTS
BY FAX & TELEPHONE

Coastal/Inshore	2-day by Fax	5-day by Phone
Northern Ireland	09065 222 355	09068 969 655
Wales	09065 222 350	09068 969 650
Bristol	09065 222 349	09068 969 649
South West	09065 222 348	09068 969 648
National (3-5 day)	09065 222 340	09068 969 640

Offshore	2-5 day by Fax	2-5 day by Phone
Irish Sea	09065 222 359	09068 969 659
English Channel	09065 222 357	09068 969 657
Biscay	09065 222 360	09068 969 660
North West Scotland	09065 222 361	09068 969 661

09068 CALLS COST 60P PER MIN. 09065 CALLS COST £1.50 PER MIN.

Key to Marina Plans symbols

Bottled gas		P	Parking
Chandler			Pub/Restaurant
Disabled facilities			Pump out
Electrical supply			Rigging service
Electrical repairs			Sail repairs
Engine repairs			Shipwright
First Aid			Shop/Supermarket
Fresh Water			Showers
Fuel - Diesel			Slipway
Fuel - Petrol		WC	Toilets
Hardstanding/boatyard			Telephone
Internet Café			Trolleys
Laundry facilities		V	Visitors berths
Lift-out facilities			Wi-Fi

Area 12 - South Ireland

MARINAS
Telephone Numbers
VHF Channel
Access Times

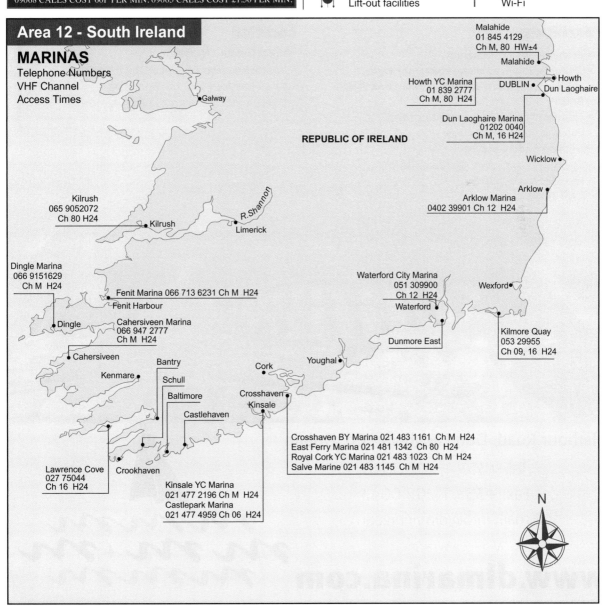

REPUBLIC OF IRELAND

Malahide
01 845 4129
Ch M, 80 HW±4
Malahide

Howth YC Marina
01 839 2777
Ch M, 80 H24

DUBLIN
Howth
Dun Laoghaire

Dun Laoghaire Marina
01202 0040
Ch M, 16 H24

Wicklow

Arklow Marina
0402 39901 Ch 12 H24
Arklow

Galway

Kilrush
065 9052072
Ch 80 H24
Kilrush
Limerick
R. Shannon

Dingle Marina
066 9151629
Ch M H24

Fenit Marina 066 713 6231 Ch M H24
Fenit Harbour

Cahersiveen Marina
066 947 2777
Ch M H24

Dingle

Cahersiveen

Kenmare

Bantry

Schull

Baltimore

Castlehaven

Lawrence Cove
027 75044
Ch 16 H24

Crookhaven

Crosshaven
Kinsale

Cork

Youghal

Waterford City Marina
051 309900
Ch 12 H24
Waterford

Dunmore East

Wexford

Kilmore Quay
053 29955
Ch 09, 16 H24

Crosshaven BY Marina 021 483 1161 Ch M H24
East Ferry Marina 021 481 1342 Ch 80 H24
Royal Cork YC Marina 021 483 1023 Ch M H24
Salve Marine 021 483 1145 Ch M H24

Kinsale YC Marina
021 477 2196 Ch M H24
Castlepark Marina
021 477 4959 Ch 06 H24

N

12

MALAHIDE MARINA

Malahide Marina
Malahide, Co. Dublin
Tel: +353 1 845 4129 Fax: +353 1 845 4255
Email: info@malahidemarina.net
www.malahidemarina.net

| VHF | Ch M, 80 |
| ACCESS | HW±4 |

Malahide Marina, situated just 10 minutes from Dublin Airport and 20 minutes north of Dublin's city centre, is a fully serviced marina accommodating up to 350 yachts. Capable of taking vessels of up to 75m in length, its first class facilities include a boatyard with hard standing for approximately 170 boats and a 30-ton mobile hoist. Its on site restaurant, Cruzzo, provides a large seating area in convivial surroundings. The village of Malahide has plenty to offer the visiting yachtsmen, with a wide variety of eating places, nearby golf courses and tennis courts as well as a historic castle and botanical gardens.

FACILITIES AT A GLANCE

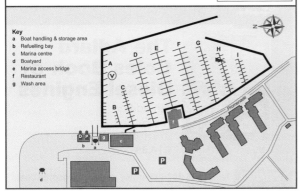

Key
a Boat handling & storage area
b Refuelling bay
c Marina centre
d Boatyard
e Marina access bridge
f Restaurant
g Wash area

HOWTH MARINA

Howth Marina
Howth Marina, Harbour Road, Howth, Co. Dublin
Tel: +353 1 8392777 Fax: +353 1 8392430
Email: marina@hyc.ie
www.hyc.ie

| VHF | Ch M, 80 |
| ACCESS | H24 |

Based on the north coast of the rugged peninsula that forms the northern side of Dublin Bay, Howth Marina is ideally situated for north or south-bound traffic in the Irish Sea. Well sheltered in all winds, it can be entered at any state of the tide. Overlooking the marina is Howth Yacht Club, which has in recent years been expanded and is now said to be the largest yacht club in Ireland. With good road and rail links, Howth is in easy reach of Dublin's airport and ferry terminal, making it an obvious choice for crew changeovers.

FACILITIES AT A GLANCE

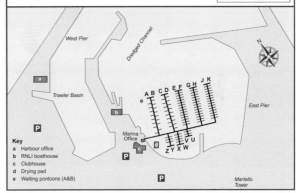

Key
a Harbour office
b RNLI boathouse
c Clubhouse
d Drying pad
e Waiting pontoons (A&B)

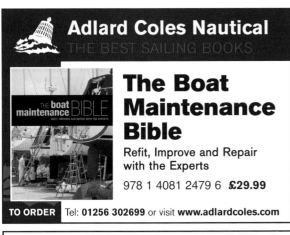

Howth Marina

The marina is owned and managed by Howth Yacht Club. It is a perfect stopping off point being situated just north of Dublin Bay, mid way through the Irish Sea; it is 30 minutes from Dublin city centre and from Dublin International Airport, both accessible by public transport.

The marina is extremely safe in all weather conditions and there is access at all stages of the tide. Facilities include water and electricity to all berths, diesel pump, 24 hour reception and security, a drying out pad and 15 ton crane. Overnight rates are exceptionally good value. The full facilities of Howth Yacht Club are available to the crews of visiting boats including changing rooms, showers, laundry, bar and catering.

2012/MG53/e

12

DUN LAOGHAIRE MARINA

Dun Laoghaire Marina
Harbour Road, Dun Laoghaire, Co Dublin, Eire
Tel: +353 1 202 0040 Fax: +353 1 202 0043
Email: info@dlmarina.com   www.dlmarina.com

VHF | Ch M, 16
ACCESS | H24

Dun Laoghaire Marina – the first marina in the Republic of Ireland to be awarded five Gold Anchors by TYHA is also recognised by the ICOMIA as maintaining standards to qualify as a 'Clean Marina' also holding an ISO 14001 rating – is the largest marina in Ireland. The town centre is within 400m. Serviced berthing for 820 boats from 8m to 23m with visitors mainly on the hammerheads. Larger vessels up to 70 metres and 120 tonnes can be accommodated alongside breakwater pontoons. Minimum draught is 3.6m LWS. With nearby HS ferry terminal and rail station, Dublin 12 kms, and airport 35kms, the marina is an ideal location for crew change. Easy access to Dublin Bay, home to the biennial Dun Laoghaire Regatta Championships and location for the 2012 ISAF Youth World Championships.

FACILITIES AT A GLANCE

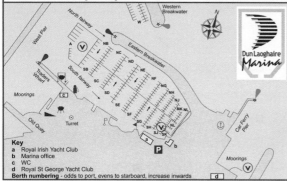

Key
a   Royal Irish Yacht Club
b   Marina office
c   WC
d   Royal St George Yacht Club
Berth numbering - odds to port, evens to starboard, increase inwards

ARKLOW MARINA

Arklow Marina
North Quay, Arklow, Co. Wicklow, Eire
Tel: +353 402 39901 Fax: +353 402 39902
Mobiles: 087 2375189 or 087 2588078
Email: technical@asl.ie
www.arklowmarina.com

VHF | Ch12
ACCESS | H24

Arklow is a popular fishing port and seaside town situated at the mouth of the River Avoca, 16 miles south of Wicklow and 11 miles north east of Gorey. The town is ideally placed for visiting the many beauty spots of County Wicklow including Glenmalure, Glendalough and Clara Lara, Avoca (Ballykissangel).

Arklow Marina is on the north bank of the river, just upstream of the commercial quays, with 42 berths in an inner harbour and 30 berths on pontoons outside the marina entrance. Vessels over 14m LOA should moor on the river pontoons.

FACILITIES AT A GLANCE

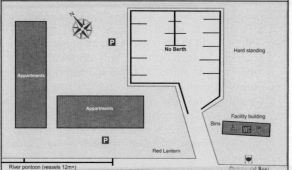

River pontoon (vessels 12m+)

KILMORE QUAY

Kilmore Quay
Wexford, Ireland
Tel: +353 53 9129955 Fax: +353 53 9129915
Email: harbourmaster@wexfordcoco.ie   www.wexford.ie

VHF | Ch 09, 16
ACCESS | H24

Located in the SE corner of Ireland, Kilmore Quay is a small rural fishing village situated approximately 14 miles from the town of Wexford and 12 miles from Rosslare ferry port.

Its 55-berthed marina, offering shelter from the elements as well as various on shore facilities, has become a regular port of call for many cruising yachtsmen. With several nearby areas of either historical or natural significance accessible using local bike hire, Kilmore is renowned for its 'green' approach to the environment.

FACILITIES AT A GLANCE

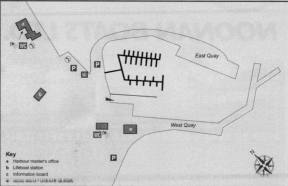

Key
a   Harbour master's office
b   Lifeboat station
c   Information board

WATERFORD CITY MARINA

Waterford City Marina
Waterford, Ireland
Tel: +353 87 238 4944 Fax: +353 51 849763
Email: olabros@waterfordcity.ie

VHF | Ch 12
ACCESS | H24

Famous for its connections with Waterford Crystal, manufactured in the city centre, Waterford is the capital of the SE region of Ireland. As a major city, it benefits from good rail links with Dublin, and Limerick, a regional airport with daily flights to Britain and an extensive bus service to

surrounding towns and villages. The marina is found on the banks of the River Suir, in the heart of this historic Viking city dating back to the ninth century. Yachtsmen can make the most of Waterford's wide range of shops, restaurants and bars without having to walk too far from their boats. With 150 fully serviced berths and first rate security, Waterford City Marina now provides shower, toilet and laundry facilities in its new reception building.

FACILITIES AT A GLANCE

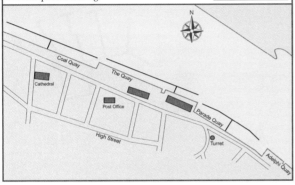

CROSSHAVEN BOATYARD MARINA

Crosshaven Boatyard Marina
Crosshaven, Co Cork, Ireland
Tel: +353 214 831161 Fax: +353 214 831603
Email: cby@eircom.net

VHF | Ch M
ACCESS | H24

One of three marinas at Crosshaven, Crosshaven Boatyard was founded in 1950 and originally made its name from the construction of some of the most world-renowned yachts, including *Gypsy Moth* and Denis Doyle's *Moonduster*. Nowadays, however, the yard

has diversified to provide a wide range of services to both the marine leisure and professional industries. Situated on a safe and sheltered river only 12 miles from Cork City Centre, the marina boasts 100 fully-serviced berths along with the capacity to accommodate yachts up to 35m LOA with a 4m draught. In addition, it is ideally situated for cruising the stunning south west coast of Ireland.

FACILITIES AT A GLANCE

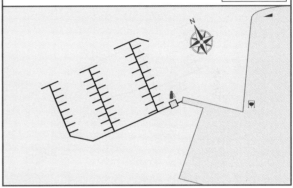

SALVE MARINE

Salve Marine
Crosshaven, Co Cork, Ireland
Tel: +353 214 831 145 Fax: +353 214 831 747
Email: salvemarine@eircom.net

VHF | Ch M
ACCESS | H24

Crosshaven is a picturesque seaside resort providing a gateway to Ireland's south and south west coasts. Offering a variety of activities to suit all types, its rocky coves and quiet sandy beaches stretch from Graball to Church Bay and from

Fennell's Bay to nearby Myrtleville. Besides a selection of craft shops selling locally produced arts and crafts, there are plenty of pubs, restaurants and takeaways to suit even the most discerning of tastes. Lying within a few hundred metres of the village centre is Salve Marine, accommodating yachts up to 43m LOA with draughts of up to 4m. Its comprehensive services range from engineering and welding facilities to hull and rigging repairs.

FACILITIES AT A GLANCE

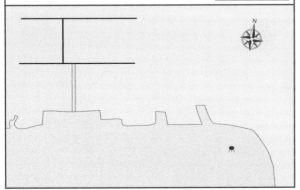

ROYAL CORK YACHT CLUB

Royal Cork Yacht Club Marina
Crosshaven, Co Cork, Ireland
Tel: +353 21 483 1023 Fax: +353 21 483 1586
Email: office@royalcork.com   www.royalcork.com

VHF | Ch M
ACCESS | H24

Founded in 1720, the Royal Cork Yacht Club is one of the oldest and most prominent yacht clubs in the world. Organising, among many other events, the prestigious biennial Ford Cork Week, it boasts a number of World, European and National sailors among its membership.

The Yacht Club's marina is situated at Crosshaven, which nestles on the hillside at the mouth of the Owenabue River just inside the entrance to Cork Harbour. The harbour is popular with yachtsmen as it is accessible and well sheltered in all weather conditions. It also benefits from the Gulf Stream producing a temperate climate practically all year round.

FACILITIES AT A GLANCE
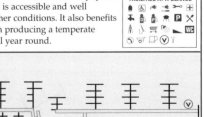

12

EAST FERRY MARINA

East Ferry Marina
Cobh, Co Cork, Ireland
Tel: +353 21 481 1342 Fax: +353 21 481 1342

VHF Ch 80
ACCESS H24

East Ferry Marina lies on the east side of Great Island, one of three large islands in Cork Harbour which are now all joined by roads and bridges. Despite its remote, tranquil setting, it offers all the fundamental facilities including showers, water, fuel, electricity and that all important pub. The nearest town is Cobh, which is a good five mile walk away, albeit a pleasant one.

Formerly known as Queenstown, Cobh (pronounced 'cove') reverted back to its original Irish name in 1922 and is renowned for being the place from where thousands of Irish men and women set off to America to build a new life for themselves, particularly during the famine years of 1844–48.

FACILITIES AT A GLANCE

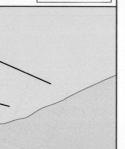

KINSALE YACHT CLUB MARINA

Kinsale Yacht Club Marina
Kinsale, Co Cork, Ireland
Tel: +353 21 4772196 Fax: +353 21 4774455
Email: kyc@iol.ie

VHF Ch M
ACCESS H24

Kinsale is a natural, virtually land-locked harbour on the estuary of the Bandon River, approximately 12 miles south west of Cork harbour entrance. Home to a thriving fishing fleet as well as frequented by commercial shipping, it boasts two fully serviced marinas, with the Kinsale Yacht Club & Marina being the closest to the town. Visitors to this marina automatically become temporary members of the club and are therefore entitled to make full use of the facilities, which include a fully licensed bar and restaurant serving evening meals on Wednesdays, Thursdays and Saturdays. Fuel, water and repair services are also available.

FACILITIES AT A GLANCE

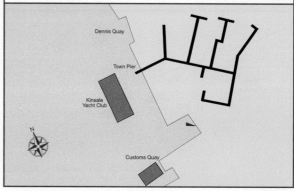

Dennis Quay
Town Pier
Kinsale Yacht Club
Customs Quay

CASTLEPARK MARINA

Castlepark Marina Centre
Kinsale, Co Cork, Ireland
Tel: +353 21 4774959 Fax: +353 21 4773894
Email: maritime@indigo.ie

VHF Ch 06
ACCESS H24

Situated on the south side of Kinsale Harbour, Castlepark is a small marina with deep water pontoon berths that are accessible at all states of the tide. Surrounded by rolling hills, it boasts its own beach as well as being in close proximity to the parklands of James Fort and a traditional Irish pub. The attractive town of Kinsale, with its narrow streets and slate-clad houses, lies just 1.5 miles by road or five minutes away by ferry. Known as Ireland's 'fine food centre', it incorporates a number of gourmet food shops and high quality restaurants as well as a wine museum.

FACILITIES AT A GLANCE

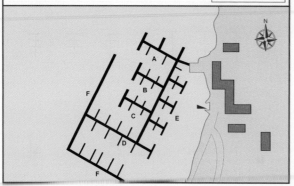

LAWRENCE COVE MARINA

Lawrence Cove Marina
Lawrence Cove, Bere Island, Co Cork, Ireland
Tel: +353 27 75044 Fax: +353 27 75044
Email: lcm@iol.ie
www.lawrencecovemarina.com

VHF Ch 16
ACCESS H24

Lawrence Cove enjoys a peaceful location on an island at the entrance to Bantry Bay. Privately owned and run, it offers sheltered and secluded waters as well as excellent facilities and fully serviced pontoon berths. A few hundred yards from the marina you will find a shop, pub and restaurant, while the mainland, with its various attractions, can be easily reached by ferry. Lawrence Cove lies at the heart of the wonderful cruising grounds of Ireland's south west coast and, just two hours from Cork airport, is an ideal place to leave your boat for long or short periods.

FACILITIES AT A GLANCE

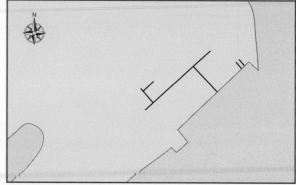

CAHERSIVEEN MARINA

Cahersiveen Marina
The Pier, Cahersiveen, Co. Kerry, Ireland
Tel: +353 66 9472777 Fax: +353 66 9472993
Email: info@cahersiveenmarina.ie
www.cahersiveenmarina.ie

VHF Ch M
ACCESS H24

Situated two miles up Valentia River from Valentia Harbour, Cahersiveen Marina is well protected in all wind directions and is convenient for sailing to Valentia Island and Dingle Bay as well as for visiting some of the spectacular uninhabited islands in the surrounding area. Boasting a host of sheltered sandy beaches, the region is renowned for salt and fresh water fishing as well as being good for scuba diving.

Within easy walking distance of the marina lies the historic town of Cahersiveen, incorporating an array of convivial pubs and restaurants.

FACILITIES AT A GLANCE

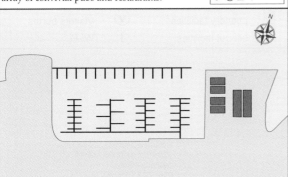

DINGLE MARINA

Dingle Marina
Strand Street, Dingle, Co Kerry, Ireland
Tel: +353 66 9151629 Fax: +353 69 5152546
Email:1dingle@eircom.net   www.dinglemarina.com

VHF Ch M
ACCESS H24

Dingle is Ireland's most westerly marina, lying at the heart of the sheltered Dingle Harbour, and is easily reached both day and night via a well buoyed approach channel. The surrounding area is an interesting and unfrequented cruising ground, with several islands, bays and beaches for the yachtsman to explore.

The marina lies in the heart of the old market town, renowned for its hospitality and traditional Irish pub music. Besides enjoying the excellent seafood restaurants and 52 pubs, other recreational pastimes include horse riding, golf, climbing and diving.

FACILITIES AT A GLANCE

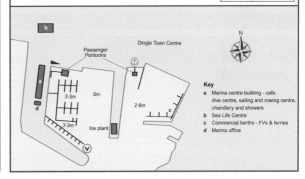

Key
a Marina centre building - cafe, dive centre, sailing and rowing centre, chandlery and showers
b Sea Life Centre
c Commercial berths - FVs & ferries
d Marina office

FENIT HARBOUR MARINA

Fenit Harbour
Fenit, Tralee, Co. Kerry, Republic of Ireland
Tel: +353 66 7136231 Fax: +353 66 7136473
Email: fenitmarina@eircom.net

VHF Ch M
ACCESS H24

Fenit Harbour Marina is tucked away in Tralee Bay, not far south of the Shannon Estuary. Besides offering a superb cruising ground, being within a day's sail of Dingle and Kilrush, the marina also provides a convenient base from which to visit inland attractions such as the picturesque tourist towns of Tralee and Killarney. This 120-berth marina accommodates boats up to 15m LOA and benefits from deep water at all states of tide.

The small village of Fenit incorporates a grocery shop as well a several pubs and restaurants, while among the local activities are horse riding, swimming from one of the nearby sandy beaches and golfing.

FACILITIES AT A GLANCE

Key
a Fenit Seaworld
b Fish store
c Warehouse
d Marina services, harbour office, lifeboat station

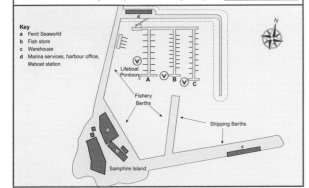

KILRUSH MARINA

Kilrush Marina Ltd
Kilrush, Co. Clare, Ireland
Tel: +353 65 9052072 Mobile: +353 86 2313870
Fax: +353 65 9051692 Email: hehirj@shannondevelopment.ie

VHF Ch 80
ACCESS H24

Kilrush Marina and boatyard is strategically placed for exploring the unspoilt west coast of Ireland, including Galway Bay, Dingle, W Cork and Kerry. It also provides a gateway to over 150 miles of cruising on Lough Derg, the R. Shannon and the Irish canal system. Accessed via lock gates, the marina lies at one end of the main street in Kilrush, the marina centre provides all the facilities for the visiting sailor. Kilrush is a vibrant market town with a long maritime history. A 15-minute ferry ride from the marina takes you to Scattery Is, once a 6th century monastic settlement but now only inhabited by wildlife. The Shannon Estuary is reputed for being the country's first marine Special Area of Conservation (SAC) and is home to Ireland's only known resident group of bottlenose dolphins.

FACILITIES AT A GLANCE

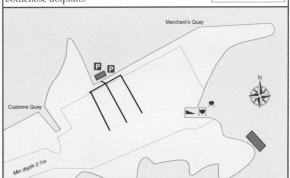

12

NORTH IRELAND - Liscannor Bay, clockwise to Lambay Island

ADLARD COLES NAUTICAL
WEATHER FORECASTS
BY FAX & TELEPHONE

Coastal/Inshore	2-day by Fax	5-day by Phone
Caledonia	09065 222 353	09068 969 653
Northern Ireland	09065 222 355	09068 969 655
Clyde	09065 222 352	09068 969 652
North West	09065 222 341	09068 969 641
National (3-5 day)	09065 222 340	09068 969 640

Offshore	2-5 day by Fax	2-5 day by Phone
Irish Sea	09065 222 359	09068 969 659
English Channel	09065 222 357	09068 969 657
Biscay	09065 222 360	09068 969 660
North West Scotland	09065 222 361	09068 969 661

09068 CALLS COST 60P PER MIN. 09065 CALLS COST £1.50 PER MIN.

Key to Marina Plans symbols

	Bottled gas	P	Parking
	Chandler		Pub/Restaurant
	Disabled facilities		Pump out
	Electrical supply		Rigging service
	Electrical repairs		Sail repairs
	Engine repairs		Shipwright
	First Aid		Shop/Supermarket
	Fresh Water		Showers
D	Fuel - Diesel		Slipway
P	Fuel - Petrol	WC	Toilets
	Hardstanding/boatyard		Telephone
@	Internet Café		Trolleys
	Laundry facilities	V	Visitors berths
	Lift-out facilities		Wi-Fi

Area 13 - North Ireland

MARINAS
Telephone Numbers
VHF Channel
Access Times

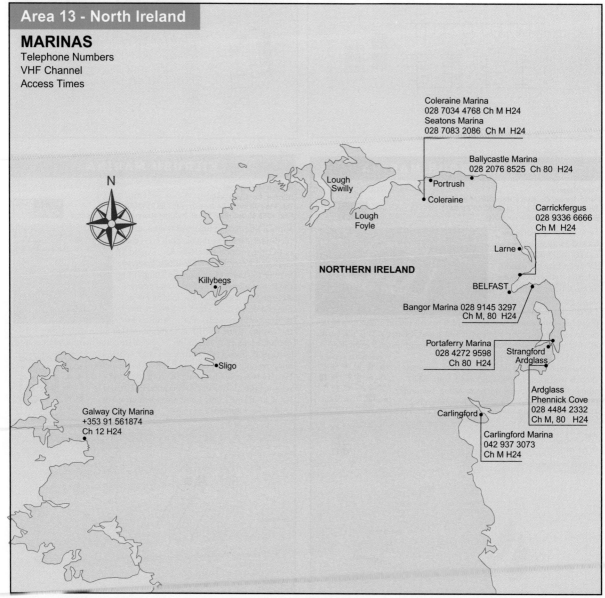

Coleraine Marina
028 7034 4768 Ch M H24
Seatons Marina
028 7083 2086 Ch M H24

Ballycastle Marina
028 2076 8525 Ch 80 H24

Lough Swilly

Lough Foyle

Portrush

Coleraine

Carrickfergus
028 9336 6666
Ch M H24

Larne

NORTHERN IRELAND

Killybegs

BELFAST

Bangor Marina 028 9145 3297
Ch M, 80 H24

Portaferry Marina
028 4272 9598
Ch 80 H24

Strangford
Ardglass

Sligo

Ardglass
Phennick Cove
028 4484 2332
Ch M, 80   H24

Galway City Marina
+353 91 561874
Ch 12 H24

Carlingford

Carlingford Marina
042 937 3073
Ch M H24

GALWAY CITY MARINA

Galway City Marina
Galway Harbour Co, Harbour Office, Galway, Ireland
Tel: +353 91 561874 Fax: +353 91 563738
Email: info@galwayharbour.com

VHF	Ch 12, 16
ACCESS	HW-2 to HW

The Galway harbour Company operates a small marina in the confines of Galway Harbour with an additional 60m of pontoon-walkway. Freshwater and electrical power is available at the pontoons. Power cars can be purchased from the harbour office during the days and also from a local pub 'Bar 8' on dock located on dock road. A number of visitors pontoons are available for hire during the summer and for winter layup. Sailors intending to call to Galway Harbour should first make contact with the Harbour office to determine if a berth is available — advisable as demand is high in this quiet and beautiful part of Ireland.

FACILITIES AT A GLANCE

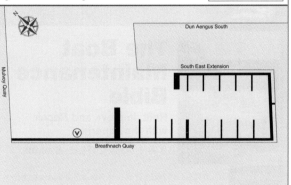

COLERAINE MARINA

Coleraine Marina
64 Portstewart Road, Coleraine,
Co Londonderry, BT52 1RS
Tel: 028 7034 4768

VHF	Ch M
ACCESS	H24

Coleraine Marina complex enjoys a superb location in sheltered waters just one mile north of the town of Coleraine and four and a half miles south of the River Bann Estuary and the open sea. Besides accommodating vessels up to 18m LOA, this modern marina with 105 berths offers hard standing, fuel, a chandlery and shower facilities.

Among one of the oldest known settlements in Ireland, Coleraine is renowned for its linen, whiskey and salmon. Its thriving commercial centre includes numerous shops, a four-screen cinema and a state-of-the-art leisure complex.

FACILITIES AT A GLANCE

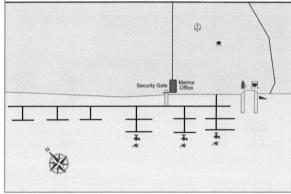

SEATONS MARINA

Seatons Marina
Drumslade Rd, Coleraine, Londonderry, BT52 1SE
Tel: 028 7083 2086
Email: ssp@seatonsmarina.co.uk www.seatonsmarina.co.uk

VHF	Ch M
ACCESS	H24

Seatons Marina is a privately owned business on the north coast of Ireland, which was established by Eric Seaton in 1962. It lies on the east bank of the River Bann, approximately two miles downstream from Coleraine and three miles from the sea. Long term pontoon berths are available for yachts up to 11.5 with a maximum draft of 2.4m; fore and aft moorings are available for larger vessels. Lift out and mast stepping facilities are provided by a 14 tonne trailer hoist.

FACILITIES AT A GLANCE

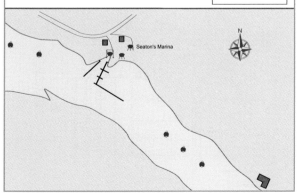

BALLYCASTLE MARINA

Ballycastle Marina
Bayview Road, Ballycastle, Northern Ireland
Tel: 028 2076 8525/07803 505084 Fax: 028 2076 6215
Email: info@moyle-council.org

VHF	Ch 80
ACCESS	H24

Ballycastle is a traditional seaside town situated on Northern Ireland's North Antrim coast. The 74-berthed, sheltered marina provides a perfect base from which to explore the well known local attractions such as the Giant's Causeway world heritage site, the spectacular Nine Glens of Antrim, and Rathlin, the only inhabited island in Northern Ireland. The most northern coastal marina in Ireland, Ballycastle is accessible at all states of the tide, although yachts are required to contact the marina on VHF Ch 80 before entering the harbour. Along the seafront are a selection of restaurants, bars and shops, while the town centre is only about a five-minute walk away.

FACILITIES AT A GLANCE

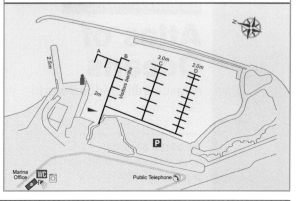

CARRICKFERGUS MARINA

Carrickferus Marina
3 Quayside, Carrickfergus, Co. Antrim, BT38 8BJ
Tel: 028 9336 6666 Fax: 028 9335 0505
Email: marinarec@carrickfergus.org
www.carrickfergus.org

VHF | Ch M
ACCESS | H24

Located on the north shore of Belfast Lough, Carrickfergus Marina and harbour incorporates two sheltered areas suitable for leisure craft. The harbour is dominated by a magnificent 12th century Norman Castle which, recently renovated, includes a film theatre, banqueting room and outdoor models depicting the castle's chequered history.

The marina is located 250 metres west of the harbour and has become increasingly popular since its opening in 1985. A range of shops and restaurants along the waterfront caters for most yachtsmen's needs.

FACILITIES AT A GLANCE

Key
a Development site
b Hotel/bar/restaurant
c Marina office
d Cinema/café/restaurant
e Retail superstore

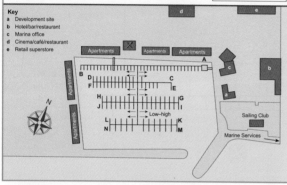

BANGOR MARINA

Quay Marinas Limited
Bangor Marina, Bangor, Co. Down, BT20 5ED
Tel: 028 9145 3297 Fax: 028 9145 3450
Email: ajaggers@quaymarinas.com
www.quaymarinas.com

VHF | Ch 80
ACCESS | H24

Situated on the south shore of Belfast Lough, Bangor is located close to the Irish Sea cruising routes. The Marina is right at the town's centre, within walking distance of shops, restaurants, hotels and bars. The Tourist information centre is across the road from marina reception and there are numerous visitors' attractions in the Borough. The Royal Ulster Yacht Club and the Ballyholme Yacht Club are both nearby and welcome visitors.

transeurope

FACILITIES AT A GLANCE

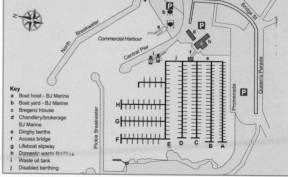

Key
a Boat hoist - BJ Marine
b Boat yard - BJ Marine
c Bregenz House
d Chandlery/brokerage
   BJ Marine
e Dinghy berths
f Access bridge
g Lifeboat slipway
h Domestic waste facility
i Waste oil tank
j Disabled berthing

CARLINGFORD MARINA

Carlingford Marina
Co. Louth, Ireland
Tel: +353 (0)42 937 3073   Fax: +353 (0)42 937 3075
Email: cmarina@iol.ie
www.carlingfordmarina.ie

VHF | Ch M
ACCESS | H24

Carlingford Lough is an eight-mile sheltered haven between the Cooley Mountains to the south and the Mourne Mountains to the north. The marina is situated on the southern shore, about four miles from Haulbowline Lighthouse, and can be easily reached via a deep water shipping channel. Among the most attractive destinations in the Irish Sea, Carlingford is only 60 miles from the Isle of Man and within a day's sail from Strangford Lough and Ardglass. Full facilities in the marina include a first class bar and restaurant offering superb views across the water.

FACILITIES AT A GLANCE

Key
a Bar and restaurant
b Toilets, showers and laundry
c Refuse
d Office
e Chandlery
f Marina office
g Waiting pontoon

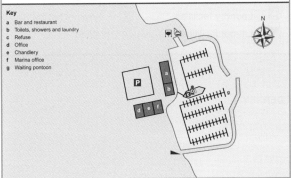

ARDGLASS MARINA

Ardglass Marina
19 Quay Street, Ardglass, BT30 7SA
Tel & fax: 028 4484 2332
Email: ardglassmarina@tiscali.co.uk
www.ardglassmarina.co.uk

VHF | Ch M, 80
ACCESS | H24

Situated just south of Strangford, Ardglass has the capacity to accommodate up to 33 yachts as well as space for small craft. Despite being relatively small in size, the marina boasts an extensive array of facilities, either on site or close at hand. Most of the necessary shops, including grocery stores, a post office, chemist and off-licence, are all within a five-minute walk from the marina. Among the local onshore activities are golf, mountain climbing in Newcastle, which is 18 miles south, as well as scenic walks at Ardglass and Delamont Park.

FACILITIES AT A GLANCE

Key
a Administration building
b Boat storage

North Dock

Additional Facilities
Reception car park - 60 vehicles
Waste oil tanks
Local charts for Strangford Lough
Heavy duty battery charging
High pressure water washing
Internet and email access
Barbeque facilities
Car hire
Weather fax

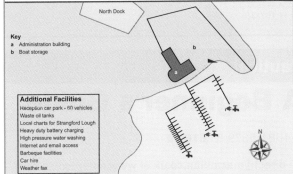

PORTAFERRY MARINA

Portaferry Marina
11 The Strand, Portaferry, BT22 1PF
Mobile: 07703 209780 Fax: 028 4272 9784
Email: info@portaferrymarina.co.uk

VHF | Ch 80
ACCESS | H24

Portaferry Marina lies on the east shore of the Narrows, the gateway to Strangford Lough on the north east coast of Ireland. A marine nature reserve of outstanding natural beauty, the Lough offers plenty of recreational activities. The marina, which caters for draughts of up to 2.5m, is fairly small, accommodating around 30 yachts. The office is situated about 200m from the marina itself, where you will find ablution facilities along with a launderette.

Portaferry incorporates several pubs and restaurants as well as a few convenience stores, while one of its prime attractions is the Exploris Aquarium. Places of historic interest in the vicinity include Castleward, an 18th century mansion in Strangford, and Mount Stewart House & Garden in Newtownards.

FACILITIES AT A GLANCE

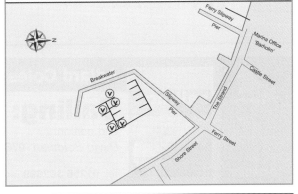

Ferry Slipway
Pier
Marina Office 'Bartholm'
Castle Street
Breakwater
Slipway
Pier
The Strand
Shore Street
Ferry Street

CHANNEL ISLANDS - Guernsey & Jersey

Key to Marina Plans symbols

Bottled gas		Parking	
Chandler		Pub/Restaurant	
Disabled facilities		Pump out	
Electrical supply		Rigging service	
Electrical repairs		Sail repairs	
Engine repairs		Shipwright	
First Aid		Shop/Supermarket	
Fresh Water		Showers	
Fuel - Diesel		Slipway	
Fuel - Petrol		Toilets	
Hardstanding/boatyard		Telephone	
Internet Café		Trolleys	
Laundry facilities		Visitors berths	
Lift-out facilities		Wi-Fi	

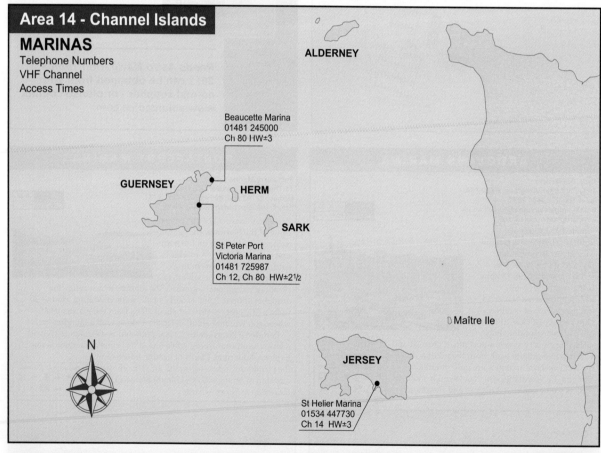

Area 14 - Channel Islands

MARINAS
Telephone Numbers
VHF Channel
Access Times

ALDERNEY

GUERNSEY

HERM

SARK

Beaucette Marina
01481 245000
Ch 80 HW±3

St Peter Port
Victoria Marina
01481 725987
Ch 12, Ch 80 HW±2½

Maître Ile

JERSEY

St Helier Marina
01534 447730
Ch 14 HW±3

N

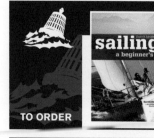

On an island paradise...

BEAUCETTE
M A R I N A

... one gem shines above all else

Accesible 3 hours either side of high water at St Peter Port, Beaucette Marina, situated on the North East of Guernsey, is the perfect base to discover the island.

All the services you would expect from a modern facility are on-hand to make your stay easy and ejoyable. Our staff are highly experienced and ready to help, so you can feel safe in the knowledge that your boat and your crew are in good hands.

Contact us by using the details below or call us on VHF 80 - call sign 'Beaucette Marina'. If you are unsure of the buoyed channel or the entrance to Beaucette, please call on VHF 80 and we will send a boat out to assist you.

For more information, please visit our website at: www.beaucettemarina.com

We look forward to welcoming you.

**BEAUCETTE MARINA LTD,
VALE, GUERNSEY,
CHANNEL ISLANDS GY3 5BQ
T: +44 (0)1481 245000
F: +44 (0)1481 247071
E: INFO@BEAUCETTEMARINA.COM
M: +44 (0)7781 102302
W: WWW.BEAUCETTEMARINA.COM
VHF CHANNEL 80**

VISITING & ANNUAL BERTHS | WATER & ELECTRICITY ON ALL BERTHS | FUEL & GAS | LAUNDERETTE RESTAURANT | SHOWERS & TOILETS | WEATHER FORECAST | FREE WIFI ACCESS | CAR HIRE

BEAUCETTE MARINA

Beaucette Marina
Vale, Guernsey, GY3 5BQ
Tel: 01481 245000 Fax: 01481 247071
Mobile: 07781 102302
Email: info@beaucettemarina.com

VHF	Ch 80
ACCESS	HW±3

Situated on the north east tip of Guernsey, Beaucette enjoys a peaceful, rural setting in contrast to the more vibrant atmosphere of Victoria Marina. Now owned by a private individual and offering a high standard of service, the site was originally formed from an old quarry.

There is a general store close by, while the bustling town of St Peter Port is only 20 minutes away by bus.

FACILITIES AT A GLANCE

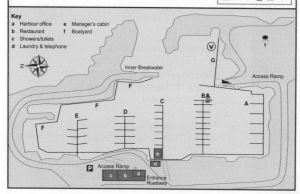

Key
a Harbour office e Manager's cabin
b Restaurant f Boatyard
c Showers/toilets
d Laundry & telephone

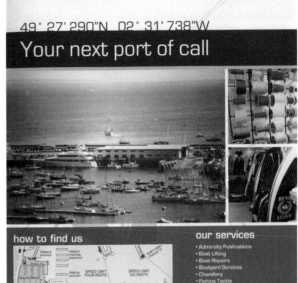

49° 27′290″N 02° 31′738″W

Your next port of call

14

ST PETER PORT

Harbour Authority
PO Box 631, St Julian's Emplacement, St Peter Port
Tel: 01481 720229 Fax: 01481 714177
Email: guernsey.harbour@gov.gg

| VHF | Ch 12, 80 |
| ACCESS | HW±2.5 |

The harbour of St Peter Port comprises the Queen Elizabeth II Marina to the N and Victoria and Albert Marinas to the S, with visiting yachtsmen usually accommodated in Victoria Marina.

Renowned for being an international financial centre and tax haven, St Peter Port is the capital of Guernsey. Its regency architecture and picturesque cobbled streets filled with restaurants and boutiques help to make it one of the most attractive harbours in Europe. Among the places of interest are Hauteville House, home of the writer Victor Hugo, and Castle Cornet.

FACILITIES AT A GLANCE

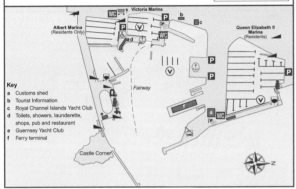

Key
a   Customs shed
b   Tourist Information
c   Royal Channel Islands Yacht Club
d   Toilets, showers, launderette, shops, pub and restaurant
e   Guernsey Yacht Club
f   Ferry terminal

how to find us

our services
• Admiralty Publications
• Boat Lifting
• Boat Repairs
• Boatyard Services
• Chandlery
• Fishing Tackle
• Gas
• Leisure Clothing
• Marine Diesel
• Marine Petrol
• Nautical Publications
• Osmosis Treatment
• Provisions
• Rigging
• Slipping
• Technical Clothing

Havelet Bay

Boatworks+
Castle Emplacement
St Peter Port, Guernsey, GY1 1AU
Tel: +44 [0]1481 726071
Email: boatworks@cwgsy.net
Web: www.boatworksguernsey.com

BOATWORKS+
GUERNSEY

2012/MG30/e

ST PETER PORT VICTORIA MARINA

Harbour Authority
PO Box 631, St Julian's Emplacement, St Peter Port
Tel: 01481 720229 Fax: 01481 714177
Email: guernsey.harbour@gov.gg

VHF | Ch 80
ACCESS | HW±2.5

Victoria Marina in St Peter Port accommodates some 300 visiting yachts. In the height of the season it gets extremely busy, but when full visitors can berth on 5 other pontoons in the Pool or pre-arrange a berth in the QE II or Albert marinas. There are no visitor moorings in the Pool. Depending on draught, the marina is accessible approximately two and a half hours either side of HW, with yachts crossing over a sill drying to 4.2m. The marina dory will direct you to a berth on arrival or else will instruct you to moor on one of the waiting pontoons just outside.

Guernsey is well placed for exploring the rest of the Channel Islands and nearby French ports.

FACILITIES AT A GLANCE

Key
a Toilets, showers, launderette and shops
b Royal Channel Islands Yacht Club
c Refuse skip
d Marina control, port office
e Dinghy/tender landing pontoon
f Pub/restaurant
g Tourist information

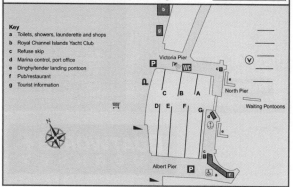

ST HELIER HARBOUR

St Helier Harbour
Maritime House, La Route du Port Elizabeth
St Helier, Jersey, JE1 1HB
Tel: 01534 447708
www.portofjersey.je Email: s.marina@gov.je

VHF | Ch 14
ACCESS | HW±3

Jersey is the largest of the Channel Islands, attracting the most number of tourists per year. Although St Helier can get very crowded in the height of the summer, if you hire a car and head out to the north coast in particular you will soon find isolated bays and pretty little fishing villages.

All visiting craft are directed to St Helier Marina, which may be entered three hours either side of HW via a sill. There is a long holding pontoon to port of the entrance accessible at any state of the tide. La Collette Yacht Basin is not for visitors but Elizabeth Marina may accept larger craft by prior arrangement.

FACILITIES AT A GLANCE

Key
a Marina office
b Water/toilets/ public phone
c Tourism
d Harbour office and Customs
e Maritime house
f Waiting pontoon
g Passenger Terminal
h Trailer park
i Port control
j Marina shop
k Cafe

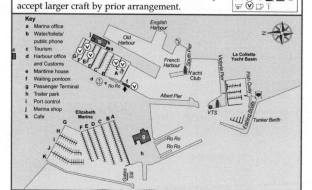

49° 27' 290"N 02° 31' 738"W
Your next port of call

how to find us

our services
• Admiralty Publications
• Boat Lifting
• Boat Repairs
• Boatyard Services
• Chandlery
• Fishing Tackle
• Gas
• Leisure Clothing
• Marine Diesel
• Marine Petrol
• Nautical Publications
• Osmosis Treatment
• Provisions
• Rigging
• Slipping
• Technical Clothing

Boatworks+
Castle Emplacement
St Peter Port, Guernsey, GY1 1AU
Tel: +44 (0)1481 726071
Email: boatworks@cwgsy.net
Web: www.boatworksguernsey.com

BOATWORKS+ GUERNSEY

2012/MG3/e

Your perfect base for exploring the Channel Islands...

TYHA 5 ANCHOR

Adhesives 128
Associations 128
Berths & Moorings 128
Boatbuilders & Repairs 128
Boatyard Services & Supplies 130
Boat Deliveries & Storage 132
Books & Charts/Publishers 133
Bow Thrusters 133
Breakdown 133
Chandlers 133
Chart Agents 139
Clothing 140
Code of Practice Examiners 140
Computers & Software 140
Deck Equipment 140
Diesel marina/Fuel Additives 140
Divers 140
Electrical & Electronic Engineers ...141
Electronic Devices & Equipment 141

Engines & Accessories 142
Foul Weather Gear 143
General Marine Equipment & Spares 143
Harbour Masters 143
Harbours 145
Insurance & Finance 145
Liferaft & Inflatables 145
Marinas 145
Marine Consultants & Surveyors ...148
Marine Engineers 148
Masts/Spars & Rigging 150
Navigational Equipment - General ...151
Paint & Osmosis 151
Propellers & Sterngear/Repairs 151
Radio Courses/Schools 151
Reefing Systems 151
Repair Materials & Accessories 151
Rope & Wire 151
Safety Equipment 151

Sailmakers & Repairs 152
Solar Power 153
Sprayhoods & Dodgers 153
Surveyors & Naval Architects 153
Tape Technology 153
Transport/Sailing Schools 153
Waterside Accommodation &
Restaurants 154
Weather Info......................155
Wood Fittings 155
Yacht Brokers 155
Yacht Charters & Holidays 155
Yacht Clubs 156
Yacht Deliveries 159
Yacht Designers 159
Yacht management 159
Yacht Valeting 159

SECTION 2
MARINE SUPPLIES AND SERVICES GUIDE

ADHESIVES

Bettabond Adhesives
Leeds   0113 278 5088

Casco Adhesives
Darwen   07710 546899

CC Marine Services Ltd
West Mersea   07751 734510

Industrial Self Adhesives Ltd
Nottingham   0115 9681895

Sika Ltd Garden City   01707 394444

Technix Rubber & Plastics Ltd
Southampton   01489 789944

Tiflex Liskeard   01579 320808

Trade Grade Products Ltd
Poole   01202 820177

UK Epoxy Resins
Burscough   01704 892364

Wessex Resins & Adhesives Ltd
Romsey   01794 521111

3M United Kingdom plc
Bracknell   01344 858315

ASSOCIATIONS/ AGENCIES

Cruising Association
London   020 7537 2828

Fishermans Mutual Association (Eyemouth) Ltd
Eyemouth   01890 750373

Maritime and Coastguard Agency
Southampton   0870 6006505

Royal Institute of Navigation
London   020 7591 3130

Royal National Lifeboat Institution
Poole   01202 663000

Royal Yachting Association (RYA)
Southampton   0845 345 0400

BERTHS & MOORINGS

ABC Powermarine
Beaumaris   01248 811413

Aqua Bell Ltd Norwich 01603 713013

Ardfern Yacht Centre
Lochgilphead   01852 500247/500636

Ardmair Boat Centre
Ullapool   01854 612054

Arisaig Marine Ltd
Inverness-shire   01687 450224

Bristol Boat Ltd Bristol 01225 872032

British Waterways Argyll
                         01546 603210

Burgh Castle Marine
Norfolk   01493 780331

Cambrian Marine Services Ltd
Cardiff   029 2034 3459

Chelsea Harbour Ltd
London   020 7225 9108

Clapson & Son (Shipbuilders) Ltd
Barton-on-Humber   01652 635620

Crinan Boatyard
Crinan   01546 830232

Dartside Quay Brixham 01803 845445

ANODES

BERTHS & MOORINGS

Douglas Marine Preston
                         01772 812462

Dublin City Moorings
Dublin   +353 1 8183300

Emsworth Yacht Harbour
Emsworth   01243 377727

Exeter Ship Canal   01392 274306

HAFAN PWLLHELI
Glan Don, Pwllheli, Gwynedd
LL53 5YT
Tel: (01758) 701219
Fax: (01758) 701443 VHF Ch80
Hafan Pwllheli has over 400 pontoon
berths and offers access at virtually all
states of the tide. Ashore, its modern
purpose-built facilities include luxury
toilets, showers, launderette, a secure
boat park for winter storage, 40-ton travel
hoist, mobile crane and plenty of space
for car parking. Open 24-hours a day, 7
days a week.   2012/MG60/e

Highway Marine
Sandwich   01304 613925

Iron Wharf Boatyard
Faversham   01795 537122

Jalsea Marine Services Ltd
Northwich   01606 77870

Jersey Harbours
St Helier   01534 447788

Jones (Boatbuilders), David
Chester   01244 390363

Lawrenny Yacht Station
Kilgetty   01646 651212

MacFarlane & Son
Glasgow   01360 870214

NEPTUNE MARINA LTD
Neptune Quay, Ipswich, Suffolk
IP4 1AX
Tel: (01473) 215204
Fax: (01473) 215206
e-mail:
enquiries@neptune-marina.com
www.neptune-marina.com
The quay to the heart of Ipswich! Call
Ipswich lock gates on Channel 68 and
Neptune Marina on Channel 80. Bring
your crew to the wonderful Ipswich
waterfront, with plenty of watering holes
and town centre activities. You won't want
to leave!   2012/MG45/e

Orkney Marinas Ltd
Kirkwall   07810 465835

V Marine
Shoreham-by-Sea   01273 461491

Sutton Harbour Marina Plymouth
                         01752 204186

Wicor Marine Fareham   01329 237112

Winters Marine Ltd
Salcombe   01548 843580

Yarmouth Marine Service
Yarmouth   01983 760521

Youngboats Faversham   01795 536176

BOAT BUILDERS & REPAIRS

ABC Hayling Island   023 9246 1968

ABC Powermarine
Beaumaris   01248 811413

Advance Yacht Systems
Southampton   023 8033 7722

Aqua-Star Ltd
St Sampsons   01481 244550

Ardoran Marine
Oban   01631 566123

Baumbach Bros Boatbuilders
Hayle   01736 753228

BB Marine Restoration Services Ltd
Southampton   023 8045 4145

Beacon Boatyard
Rochester   01634 841320

Bedwell & Co
Walton on the Naze   01255 675873

Black Dog
Falmouth   01326 318058

Blackwell, Craig
Co Meath   +353 87 677 9605

Bluewater Horizons
Weymouth   01305 782080

Boatcraft
Ardrossan   01294 603047

Brennan, John
Dun Laoghaire   +353 1 280 5308

Burghead Boat Centre
Findhorn   01309 690099

Carrick Marine Projects
Co Antrim   02893 355884

Chicks Marine Ltd
Guernsey   01481 723716

Cooks Maritime Craftsmen - Poliglow
Lymington   01590 675521

Creekside Boatyard (Old Mill Creek)
Dartmouth   01803 832649

CTC Marine & Leisure
Middlesbrough   01642 372600

Davies Marine Services
Ramsgate   01843 586172

Dickie International
Bangor   01248 363400

Dickie International
Pwllheli   01758 701828

East & Co, Robin - Frogmore BY
Kingsbridge   01548 531257

East Llanion Marine Ltd
Pembroke Dock   01646 686866

Emblem Enterprises
East Cowes   01983 294243

Fairlie Quay Fairlie   01475 568267

Fairweather Marine
Fareham   01329 283500

Farrow & Chambers Yacht Builders
Humberston   01472 362424

Fast Tack Plymouth   01752 255171

Fergulsea Engineering
Ayr   01292 262978

Ferrypoint Boat Co
Youghal   +353 24 94232

Floetree Ltd (Loch Lomond Marina)
Balloch   01389 752069

Freshwater Boatyard
Truro   01326 270443

Furniss Boat Building
Falmouth   01326 311766

Gallichan Marine Ltd
Jersey   01534 746387

Goodchild Marine Services
Great Yarmouth   01493 782301

Gosport Boatyard
Gosport   023 9252 6534

Gweek Quay Boatyard
Helston   01326 221657

Halls
Walton on the Naze   01255 675596

Hardway Marine
Gosport   023 9258 0420

Harris Pye Marine
Barry   01446 720066

Haven Boatyard
Lymington   01590 677073

Hayling Yacht Company
Hayling Island   023 9246 3592

Hoare Ltd, Bob
Poole   01202 736704

Holyhead Boatyard
Holyhead   01407 760111

International Marine Designs
Aberdyfi   01654 767572

Jackson Marine
Whitehaven   01946 699332

Jackson Yacht Services
Jersey   01534 743819

JEP Marine
Canterbury   01227 710102

Jones (Boatbuilders), David
Chester   01244 390363

JWS Marine Services
Southsea   023 9275 5155

KG McColl Oban   01852 200248

Kimelford Yacht Haven
Oban   01852 200248

Kingfisher Marine
Weymouth   01305 766595

Kingfisher Ultraclean UK Ltd
Tarporley   0800 085 7039

King's Boatyard
Pin Mill   01473 780258

Kippford Slipway Ltd
Dalbeattie   01556 620249

Langley Marine Services Ltd
Eastbourne   01323 470244

Lavis & Son, CH
Exmouth   01395 263095

Lawrenny Yacht Station
Lawrenny   01646 651212

Lencraft Boats Ltd
Dungarvan   +353 58 682220

Mackay Boatbuilders
Arbroath   01241 872879

Marine Services
Norwich   01692 582239

Mashford Brothers
Torpoint   01752 822232

Mayor & Co Ltd, J
Preston   01772 812250

McKellar's Slipway Ltd
Helensburgh   01436 842334

Mears, HJ Axmouth   01297 23344

Mill, Dan
Galway   +353 86 3379304

Miller Marine
Tyne & Wear   01207 542149

Moody Yachts International Ltd
Swanwick   01489 885000

Morrison, A Killyleagh   028 44828215

Moss (Boatbuilders), David
Thornton-Cleveleys   01253 893830

Multi Marine Composites Ltd
Torpoint   01752 823513

Newing, Roy E
Canterbury   01227 860345

Noble and Sons, Alexander
Girvan   01465 712223

Northney Marine Services
Hayling Island   023 9246 9246

Northshore Sport & Leisure
King's Lynn   01485 210236

O'Sullivans Marine Ltd
Tralee   +353 66 7124524

Oulton Manufacturing Ltd
Lowestoft   01502 585631

Oyster Marine Ltd
Ipswich   01473 688888

Pachol, Terry Brighton   01273 682724

Partington Marine Ltd, William
Pwllheli   01758 612808

Pasco's Boatyard
Truro   01326 270269

Penrhos Marine
Aberdovey   01654 767478

Penzance Marine Services
Penzance   01736 361081

PJ Bespoke Boat Fitters Ltd
Crewe   01270 812244

Preston Marine Services Ltd
Preston   01772 733595

Red Bay Boats Ltd
Cushendall   028 2177 1331

Reliance Marine
Wirral   0151 625 5219

Retreat Boatyard Ltd
Exeter   01392 874720/875934

Richardson Boatbuilders, Ian
Stromness   01856 850321

Richardson Yacht Services Ltd
Newport   01983 821095

River Tees Engineering & Welding Ltd
Middlesbrough   01642 226226

Roberts Marine Ltd, S
Liverpool   0151 707 8300

Rothman Pantall & Co
Fareham   01329 280221

Rustler Yachts Falmouth 01326 310210

Salterns Boatyard
Poole   01202 707391

Sea & Shore Ship Chandler
Dundee   01382 450666

SEAFIT MARINE SERVICES LTD
Falmouth Marina, North Parade,
Falmouth, Cornwall TR11 2TD
Tel: (01326) 313713
Fax: (01326) 313713
Mob: 07971 196175
Email:
mary.townsend@homecall.co.uk
For installation maintenance and repair
work - electrical, plumbing, hulls, rigs etc.

2012/MG32/e

Seamark-Nunn & Co
Felixstowe   01394 275327

Seapower
Woolverstone   01473 780090

Searanger Yachts
Peterborough   01832 274199

Slipway Cooperative Ltd
Bristol   0117 907 9938

Spencer Sailing Services, Jim
Brightlingsea   01206 302911

Spicer Boatbuilder, Nick
Weymouth Marina   01305 767118

Storrar Marine Store
Newcastle upon Tyne   0191 266 1037

Tarquin Boat Co
Emsworth   01243 375211

Trio Mouldings Marine
Southampton   01489 787887

Troon Marine Services
Troon   01292 316180

TT Marine Ashwell   01462 742449

WA Simpson Marine Ltd
Dundee   01382 566670

Waterfront Marine
Bangor   01248 352513

Way, A&R, Boat Building
Tarbert, Loch Fyne   01546 606657

WestCoast Marine
Troon   01292 318121

Western Marine
Dublin   +353 1 280 0321

Wigmore Wright Marine Services
Penarth   029 2070 9983

Williams, Peter
Fowey   01726 870987

WQI Ltd
Bournemouth   01202 771292

Yarmouth Marine Service
                                    01983 760521

Youngboats Faversham   01795 536176

A & P Ship Care
Ramsgate   01843 593140

ABC Marine
Hayling Island   023 9246 1968

Abersoch Boatyard Services Ltd
Abersoch   01758 713900

Amble Boat Co Ltd
Amble   01665 710267

Amsbrisbeg Ltd
Port Bannatyne   01700 502719

Ardmair Boat Centre
Ullapool   01854 612054

Ardmaleish Boat Building Co
Rothesay   01700 502007

www.ardoran.co.uk
West coast Scotland. All marine facilities.

Ardrishaig Boatyard
Lochgilphead   01546 603280

Arklow Slipway
Arklow   +353 402 33233

Baltic Wharf Boatyard
Totnes   01803 867922

Baltimore Boatyard
Baltimore   +353 28 20444

Bedwell and Co
Walton-on-the-Naze   01255 675873

Berthon Boat Co
Lymington   01590 673312

Birch Boatbuilders, ER 01268 696094

Birdham Shipyard
Chichester   01243 512310

BJ Marine Ltd Bangor   028 91271434

Blagdon, A Plymouth   01752 561830

Bluewater Horizons
Weymouth   01305 781518

Boatcraft
Ardrossan   01294 603047

Boatworks + Ltd
St Peter Port   01481 726071

Booth W Kelly Ltd
Ramsey   01624 812322

Brennan, John
Dun Laoghaire   +353 1 280 5308

Brighton Marina Boatyard
Brighton   01273 819919

Bristol Marina (Yard)
Bristol   0117 921 3198

Buchan & Son Ltd, J
Peterhead   01779 475395

Buckie Shipyard Ltd
Buckie   01542 831245

Bucklers Hard Boat Builders Ltd
Brockenhurst   01590 616214

C & J Marine Services
Newcastle Upon Tyne   0191 295 0072

Caley Marina Inverness   01463 236539

Cambrian Boat Centre
Swansea   01792 467263

Cambrian Marine Services Ltd
Cardiff   029 2034 3459

Cantell and Son Ltd
Newhaven   01273 514118

Carroll's Ballyhack Boatyard
New Ross   +353 51 389164

Castlepoint Boatyard
Crosshaven   +353 21 4832154

Chabot, Gary Newhaven   07702 006767

Chapman & Hewitt Boatbuilders
Wadebridge   01208 813487

Chippendale Craft Rye   01797 227707

Clapson & Son (Shipbuilders) Ltd
Barton on Humber   01652 635620

Coastal Marine Boatbuilders
(Berwick upon Tweed)
Eyemouth   01890 750328

Coastcraft Ltd
Cockenzie   01875 812150

Coates Marine Ltd
Whitby   01947 604486

Coombes, AA
Bembridge   01983 872296

Corpach Boatbuilding Company
Fort William   01397 772861

Craobh Marina
By Lochgilphead   01852 500222

Creekside Boatyard (Old Mill Creek)
Dartmouth   01803 832649

Crinan Boatyard
By Lochgilphead   01546 830232

Crosshaven Boatyard Co Ltd
Crosshaven   +353 21 831161

Dale Sailing Co Ltd
Neyland   01646 603110

Darthaven Marina
Kingswear   01803 752242

Dartside Quay Brixham   01803 845445

Dauntless Boatyard Ltd
Canvey Island   01268 793782

Davis's Boatyard Poole   01202 674349

Dinas Boat Yard Ltd
Y Felinheli   01248 671642

Dorset Yachts Poole   01202 674531

Douglas Boatyard
Preston   01772 812462

Dover Yacht Co Dover   01304 201073

Dun Laoghaire Marina
Dun Laoghaire   +353 1 2020040

Elephant Boatyard
Southampton   023 8040 3268

Elton Boatbuilding Ltd
Kirkcudbright   01557 330177

Farrow & Chambers Yacht Builders
Humberston   01472 362424

Felixstowe Ferry Boatyard
Felixstowe   01394 282173

Ferguson Engineering
Wexford   +353 6568 66822133

Ferry Marine South
Queensferry   0131 331 1233

Findhorn Boatyard
Findhorn   01309 690099

Firmhelm Ltd Pwllheli   01758 612251

Fleming Engineering, J
Stornoway   01851 703488

Forrest Marine Ltd
Exeter   08452 308335

Fowey Boatyard Fowey   01726 832194

Fox's Marina Ipswich   01473 689111

Frank Halls & Son
Walton on the Naze   01255 675596

Freeport Marine Jersey   01534 888100

Furniss Boat Building
Falmouth 01326 311766

Goodchild Marine Services
Great Yarmouth 01493 782301

Gosport Boatyard
Gosport 023 9252 6534

Gweek Quay Boatyard
Helston 01326 221657

Haines Boatyard
Chichester 01243 512228

Harbour Marine
Plymouth 01752 204691

Harbour Marine Services Ltd
Southwold 01502 724721

Harris Pye Marine
Barry 01446 720066

Hartlepool Marine Engineering
Hartlepool 01429 867883

Hayles, Harold Yarmouth 01983 760373

Henderson, J Shiskine 01770 860259

Heron Marine
Whitstable 01227 361255

Hewitt, George Binham 01328 830078

Holyhead Marina & Trinity Marine Ltd
Holyhead 01407 764242

Instow Marine Services
Bideford 01271 861081

Ipswich Haven Marina
Ipswich 01473 236644

Iron Wharf Boatyard
Faversham 01795 537122

Island Boat Services
Port of St Mary 01624 832073

Isle of Skye Yachts
Ardvasar 01471 844216

Jalsea Marine Services Ltd Weaver
Shipyard, Northwich 01606 77870

J B Timber Ltd
North Ferriby 01482 631765

Jersey Harbours Dept
St Helier 01534 885588

Kilnsale Boatyard
Kinsale +353 21 4774774

Kilrush Marina & Boatyard – Ireland
+353 65 9052072

Kingfisher Ultraclean UK Ltd
Tarporley 01928 787878

KPB Beaucette 07781 152581

Lake Yard Poole 01202 674531
Lallow, C Isle of Wight 01983 292112

Latham's Boatyard
Poole 01202 748029

Leonard Marine, Peter
Newhaven 01273 515987

Lincombe Marine
Salcombe 01548 843580

Lomax Boatbuilders
Cliffony +353 71 66124

Lymington Yacht Haven
Lymington 01590 677071

MacDougalls Marine Services
Isle of Mull 01681 700294

Macduff Shipyard Ltd
Macduff 01261 832234

Madog Boatyard
Porthmadog 01766 514205/513435

Mainbrayce Marine
Alderney 01481 822772

Malakoff and Moore
Lerwick 01595 695544

**Mallaig Boat Building and
Engineering** Mallaig 01687 462304

Maramarine
Helensburgh 01436 810971

Marindus Engineering
Kilmore Quay +353 53 29794

Marine Gleam
New Milton 01425 611566

Mariners Farm Boatyard
Gillingham 01634 233179

McCallum & Co Boat Builders, A
Tarbert 01880 820209

McCaughty (Boatbuilders), J
Wick 01955 602858

McGruar and Co Ltd
Helensburgh 01436 831313

Mill, Dan
Galway +353 86 3379304

Mitchell's Boatyard
Poole 01202 747857

Mooney Boats
Killybegs +353 73 31152/31388

Moore & Son, J
St Austell 01726 842964

Morrison, A Killyleagh 028 44828215

Moss (Boatbuilders), David
Thornton-Cleveleys 01253 893830

New Horizons Rhu 01436 821555

Noble and Sons, Alexander
Girvan 01465 712223

North Pier (Oban) Oban 01631 562892

North Wales Boat Centre
Conwy 01492 580740

Northam Marine
Brightlingsea 01206 302003

Northshore Yacht Yard
Chichester 01243 512611

Oban Yachts and Marine Services
By Oban 01631 565333

Parker Yachts and Dinghys Ltd
Nr Boston 01205 722697

Pearn and Co, Norman
Looe 01503 262244

Penrhos Marine
Aberdovey 01654 767478

**Penzance Dry Dock and Engineering
Co Ltd** Penzance 01736 363838

Philip & Son Dartmouth 01803 833351

Phillips, HJ Rye 01797 223234

Ponsharden Boatyard
Penryn 01326 372215

Powersail and Island Chandlers Ltd
East Cowes Marina 01983 299800

Priors Boatyard
Burnham-on-Crouch 01621 782160

R K Marine Ltd
Swanwick 01489 583572

Rat Island Sailboat Company (Yard)
St Mary's 01720 423399

Retreat Boatyard Ltd
Exeter 01392 874720/875934

Rice and Cole Ltd
Burnham-on-Crouch 01621 782063

Richardson Boatbuilders, Ian
Stromness 01856 850321

Richardsons Boatbuilders
Binfield 01983 821095

Riverside Yard
Shoreham Beach 01273 592456

Robertsons Boatyard
Woodbridge 01394 382305

Rossbrin Boatyard
Schull +353 28 37352

Rossiter Yachts Ltd
Christchurch 01202 483250

Rossreagh Boatyard
Rathmullan +353 74 9150182

Rudders Boatyard & Moorings
Milford Haven 01646 600288

Ryan & Roberts Marine Services
Askeaton +353 61 392198

Rye Harbour Marina Rye
01797 227667

Rynn Engineering, Pat
Galway +353 91 562568

Salterns Boatyard
Poole 01202 707391

Sandbanks Yacht Company
Poole 01202 707500

Scarborough Marine Engineering Ltd
Scarborough 01723 375199

Severn Valley Cruisers Ltd (Boatyard)
Stourport-on-Severn 01299 871165

Shepards Wharf Boatyard Ltd
Cowes 01983 297821

Shipshape
King's Lynn 01553 764058

Shotley Marina Ltd
Ipswich 01473 788982

Shotley Marine Services Ltd
Ipswich 01473 788913

Silvers Marina Ltd
Helensburgh 01436 831222

Skinners Boat Yard
Baltimore +353 28 20114

Smith & Gibbs
Eastbourne 01323 833830

**South Dock (Seaham Harbour Dock
Co)** Seaham 0191 581 3877

Sparkes Boatyard
Hayling Island 023 92463572

Spencer Sailing Services, Jim
Brightlingsea 01206 302911

Standard House Boatyard
Wells-next-the-Sea 01328 710593

Storrar Marine Store
Newcastle upon Tyne 0191 266 1037

Strand Shipyard Rye 01797 222070

Surry Boatyard
Shoreham-by-Sea 01273 461491

The Shipyard
Littlehampton 01903 713327

Titchmarsh Marina
Walton-on-the-Naze   01255 672185

Tollesbury Marina
Tollesbury   01621 869202

T J Rigging Conwy   07780 972411

Toms and Son Ltd, C
Fowey   01726 870232

Tony's Marine Service
Coleraine   028 7035 6422

Torquay Marina
Torquay   01803 200210

Trinity Marine & Holyhead Marina
Holyhead   01407 763855

Trouts Boatyard (River Exe)
Topsham   01392 873044

Upson and Co, RF
Aldeburgh   01728 453047

Versatility Workboats
Rye   01797 224422

Weir Quay Boatyard
Bere Alston   01822 840474

West Solent Boatbuilders
Lymington   01590 642080

Wicor Marine Fareham 01329 237112

Woodrolfe Boatyard
Maldon   01621 869202

BOAT DELIVERIES & STORAGE

ABC Marine
Hayling Island   023 9246 1968

Abersoch Boatyard Services Ltd
Pwllheli   01758 713900

Ambrisbeg Ltd
Port Bannatyne   01700 502719

Arisaig Marine
Inverness-shire   01687 450224

Bedwell and Co
Walton-on-the-Naze   01255 675873

Bembridge Boatyard Marine Works
Bembridge   01983 872911

Berthon Boat Company
Lymington   01590 673312

Bluewater Horizons
Weymouth   01305 782080

C & J Marine Services
Newcastle upon Tyne   0191 295 0072

Caley Marine
Inverness   01463 233437

Carrick Marine Projects
Co Antrim   02893 355884

Challenger Marine
Penryn   01326 377222

Coates Marine Ltd
Whitby   01947 604486

Creekside Boatyard (Old Mill Creek)
Dartmouth   01803 832649

Crinan Boatyard Ltd
Crinan   01546 830232

Dale Sailing Co Ltd
Neyland   01646 603110

Dartside Quay
Brixham   01803 845445

Dauntless Boatyard Ltd
Canvey Island   01268 793782

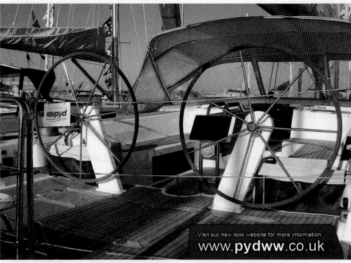

OUTSTANDING CUSTOMER SERVICE SINCE 1995

Tel: +44 (0) 1539 552130 Fax: +44 (0) 1539 552131
Email: pyd@pydww.com

2012/MGB/d

Debbage Yachting
Ipswich   01473 601169

Douglas Marine Preston 01772 812462

East & Co, Robin
Kingsbridge   01548 531257

Emsworth Yacht Harbour
Emsworth   01243 377727

Exeter Ship Canal   01392 274306

Exmouth Marina   01395 269314

Firmhelm Ltd Pwllheli 01758 612244

Fowey Boatyard Fowey 01726 832194

Freshwater Boatyard
Truro   01326 270443

Hafan Pwllheli Pwllheli 01758 701219

Gweek Quay Boatyard
Helston   01326 221657

Iron Wharf Boatyard
Faversham   01795 537122

Jalsea Marine Services Ltd
Northwich   01606 77870

KG McColl Oban   01852 200248

Latham's Boatyard
Poole   01202 748029

Lavis & Son, CH
Exmouth   01395 263095

Lincombe Boat Yard
Salcombe   01548 843580

Marine Resource Centre Ltd
Oban   01631 720291

Marine & General Engineers
Guernsey   01481 245808

Milford Marina
Milford Haven   01646 696312/3

Southerly
Chichester   01243 512611

Oulton Manufacturing Ltd
Lowestoft   01502 585631

Pasco's Boatyard
Truro   01326 270269

Pearn and Co, Norman
Looe   01503 262244

Philip Leisure Group
Dartmouth   01803 833351

Ponsharden Boatyard
Penryn   01326 372215

Portsmouth Marine Engineering
Fareham 01329 232854

Priors Boatyard
Burnham-on-Crouch 01621 782160

Rossiter Yachts
Christchurch 01202 483250

**Shepards Wharf Boatyard
Cowes Harbour Commission**
Cowes 01983 297821

Silvers Marina Ltd
Helensburgh 01436 831222

Waterfront Marine
Bangor 01248 352513

Wicor Marine Fareham 01329 237112

Winters Marine Ltd
Salcombe 01548 843580

Yacht Solutions Ltd
Portsmouth 023 9275 5155

Yarmouth Marine Service
Yarmouth 01983 760521

Youngboats Faversham 01795 536176

BOOKS, CHARTS & PUBLISHERS

Adlard Coles Nautical
London 0207 7580200

Brown Son & Ferguson Ltd
Glasgow 0141 429 1234

Chattan Security Ltd
Edinburgh 0131 555 3155

Cooke & Son Ltd, B Hull 01482 223454

Dubois Phillips & McCallum Ltd
Liverpool 0151 236 2776

Imray, Laurie, Norie & Wilson
Huntingdon 01480 462114

Kelvin Hughes
Southampton 023 8063 4911

Lilley & Gillie Ltd, John 0191 257 2217

Marine Chart Services
Wellingborough 01933 441629

Price & Co Ltd, WF
Bristol 0117 929 2229

QPC
Fareham 01329 287880

Stanford Charts
Bristol 0117 929 9966

Stanford Charts
London 020 7836 1321

Stanford Charts 0845 880 3730
Manchester 0870 890 3730

Wiley Nautical
Chichester 01243 779777

BOW THRUSTERS

ARS Anglian Diesels Ltd
Wakefield 01924 332492

Buckler's Hard Boat Builders Ltd
Beaulieu 01590 616214

JS Mouldings International
Bursledon 023 8063 4400

BREAKDOWN

BJ Marine Ltd
Bangor, Ireland 028 9127 1434

Seafit Marine Services
Falmouth 01326 313713

CHANDLERS

ABC Powermarine
Beaumaris 01248 811413

**Acamar Marine Services/Sirius Yacht
Training** Christchurch 01202 488030

Admiral Marine Supplies
Bootle 01469 575909

Alderney Boating Centre
Alderney 01481 823725

Allgadgets.co.uk
Exmouth 01395 227727

Alpine Room & Yacht Equipment
Chelmsford 01245 223563

Aquatogs Cowes 01983 247891

Arbroath Fishermen's Association
Arbroath 01241 873132

Ardfern Yacht Centre Ltd
Argyll 01852 500247

Ardoran Marine Oban 01631 566123

Arthurs Chandlery
Gosport 023 9252 6522

Arun Aquasports
Littlehampton 01903 713553

Arun Canvas and Rigging Ltd
Littlehampton 01903 732561

Aruncraft Chandlers
Littlehampton 01903 713327

**ASAP Supplies – Equipment &
Spares Worldwide**
Beccles 0845 1300870

Auto Marine Sales
Southsea 023 9281 2263

Bayside Marine
Brixham 01803 856771

Bedwell and Co
Walton on the Naze 01255 675873

BJ Marine Ltd Bangor 028 9127 1434

Bluecastle Chandlers
Portland 01305 822298

Bluewater Horizons
Weymouth 01305 782080

Blue Water Marine Ltd
Pwllheli 01758 614600

Boatshop Chandlery
Brixham 01803 882055

Boatacs
Westcliffe on Sea 01702 475057

Boathouse, The Penryn 01326 374177

Boston Marina 01205 364420

Bosun's Locker, The
Falmouth 01326 312212

Bosun's Locker, The
Ramsgate 01843 597158

Bosuns Locker, The
South Queensferry 0131 331 3875/4496

Bridger Marine, John
Exeter 01392 216420

Brigantine Teignmouth 01626 872400

Bristol Boat Ltd Bristol 01225 872032

Brixham Chandlers
Brixham 01803 882055

Brixham Yacht Supplies Ltd
Brixham 01803 882290

Brunel Chandlery Ltd
Neyland 01646 601667

Bucklers Hard Boat Builders
Beaulieu 01590 616214

Burghead Boat Centre
Findhorn 01309 690099

Bussell & Co, WL
Weymouth 01305 785633

Buzzard Marine
Yarmouth 01983 760707

C & M Marine
Bridlington 01262 672212

Cabin Yacht Stores
Rochester 01634 718020

Caley Marina Inverness 01463 236539

Cambrian Boat Centre
Swansea 01792 467263

Cantell & Son Ltd
Newhaven 01273 514118

Carne (Sales) Ltd, David
Penryn 01326 374177

Carrickcraft
Malahide +353 1 845 5438

Caters Carrick Ltd
Carrickfergus 028 93351919

CH Marine (Cork)
Cork +353 21 4315700

CH Marine Skibbereen +353 28 23190

Charity & Taylor Ltd
Lowestoft 01502 581529

Chertsey Marine Ltd
Penton Hook Marina 01932 565195

Chicks Marine Ltd
Guernsey 01481 723716

Christchurch Boat Shop
Christchurch 01202 482751

Churcher Marine
Worthing 01903 230523

Clapson & Son (Shipbuilders) Ltd
South Ferriby Marina 01652 635620

Clarke, Albert
Newtownards 01247 872325

Clyde Chandlers
Ardrossan 01294 471444

Coastal Marine Boatbuilders Ltd
(Dunbar) Eyemouth 01890 750328

Coates Marine Ltd
Whitby 01947 604486

Collins Marine St Helier 01534 732415

Compass Marine
Lancing 01903 761773

Cosalt International Ltd
Aberdeen 01224 588327

Cosalt International Ltd
Southampton 023 8063 2824

Cotter, Kieran
Baltimore +353 28 20106

Cox Yacht Charter Ltd, Nick
Lymington 01590 673489

C Q Chandlers Ltd
Poole   01202 682095

Crinan Boats Ltd
Lochgilphead   01546 830232

CTC Marine & Leisure
Middlesbrough   01642 372600

Dale Sailing Co Ltd
Milford Haven   01646 603110

Danson Marine Sidcup 0208 304 5678

Dartside Quay
Brixham   01803 845445

Dauntless Boatyard Ltd
Canvey Island   01268 793782

Davis's Yacht Chandler
Littlehampton   01903 722778

Denholm Fishselling
Scrabster   01847 896968

Denney & Son, EL
Redcar   01642 483507

Deva Marine
Conwy   01492 572777

Dickie & Sons Ltd, AM
Bangor   01248 363400

Dickie & Sons Ltd, AM
Pwllheli   01758 701828

**Dinghy Supplies Ltd/Sutton Marine
Ltd** Sutton   +353 1 832 2312

Diverse Yacht Services
Hamble   023 80453399

Dixon Chandlery, Peter
Exmouth   01395 273248

Doling & Son, GW
Barrow In Furness   01229 823708

Dovey Marine Aberdovey 01654 767581

Down Marine Co Ltd
Belfast   028 9048 0247

Douglas Marine Preston 01772 812462

Dubois Phillips & McCallum Ltd
Liverpool   0151 236 2776

Duncan Ltd, JS Wick   01955 602689

Duncan Yacht Chandlers
Ely   01353 663095

East Anglian Sea School
Ipswich   01473 659992

Eccles Marine Co
Middlesbrough   01642 372600

Ely Boat Chandlers
Hayling Island   023 9246 1968

Emsworth Chandlery
Emsworth   01243 375500

Endeavour Chandlery
Gosport   023 9252 9333

Exe Leisure Exeter   01392 879055

Express Marine Services
Chichester   01243 773788

Fairways Chandlery
Burnham-on-Crouch   01621 782659

Fairweather Marine
Fareham   01329 283500

Fal Chandlers
Falmouth Marina   01326 212411

Ferrypoint Boat Co
Youghal   +353 24 94232

Findhorn Marina & Boatyard
Findhorn   01309 690099

Firmhelm Ltd Pwllheli   01758 612244

**Fisherman's Mutual Asssociation
(Eyemouth) Ltd**
Eyemouth   01890 750373

**Fleetwood Trawlers' Supply Co Ltd,
The** Fleetwood   01253 873476

Floetree Ltd (Loch Lomond Marina)
Balloch   01389 752069

Force 4 (Deacons)
Bursledon   023 8040 2182

Force 4 Chichester   01243 773788

Force 4 (Hamble Point)
Southampton   023 80455 058

Force 4 (Mercury)
Southampton   023 8045 4849

Force 4 (Port Hamble)
Southampton   023 8045 4858

Force 4 (Swanwick)
Swanwick   01489 881825

Freeport Marine Jersey 01534 888100

French Marine Motors Ltd
Brightlingsea   01206 302133

Furneaux Riddall & Co Ltd
Portsmouth   023 9266 8621

Gallichan Marine Ltd
Jersey   01534 746387

Galway Marine Chandlers Ltd
Galway   +353 91 566568

GB Attfield & Company
Dursley   01453 547185

Gibbons Ship Chandlers Ltd
Sunderland   0191 567 2101

Gibbs Marine
Shepperton   01932 242977

Glaslyn Marine Supplies Ltd
Porthmadog   01766 513545

Goodwick Marine
Fishguard   01348 873955

Gorleston Marine Ltd
Great Yarmouth   01493 661883

GP Barnes Ltd
Shoreham   01273 591705/596680

Great Outdoors
Clarenbridge, Galway +353 87 2793821

Green Marine, Jimmy
Fore St Beer   01297 20744

Gunn Navigation Services, Thomas
Aberdeen   01224 595045

Hale Marine, Ron
Portsmouth   023 92732985

Harbour Marine Services Ltd (HMS)
Southwold   01502 724721

Hardware & Marine Supplies
Wexford   +353 53 29791

Hardway Marine
Gosport   023 9258 0420

Harris Marine (1984) Ltd, Ray
Barry   01446 740924

Hartlepool Marine Supplies
Hartlepool   01429 862932

Harwich Chandlers Ltd
Harwich   01255 504061

Harwoods Yarmouth   01983 760258

Hawkins Marine Shipstores, John
Rochester   01634 840812

Hayles, Harold
Yarmouth   01983 760373

Herm Seaway Marine Ltd
St Peter Port   01481 726829

Highway Marine
Sandwich   01304 613925

Hoare Ltd, Bob
Poole   01202 736704

Hornsey (Chandlery) Ltd, Chris
Southsea   023 9273 4728

Hunter & Combes
Cowes   01983 299599

Iron Stores Marine
St Helier   01534 877755

Isles of Scilly Steamship Co
St Mary's   01720 422710

Jackson Yacht Services
Jersey   01534 743819

Jamison and Green Ltd
Belfast   028 9032 2444

Jeckells and Son Ltd
Lowestoft   01502 565007

JF Marine Chandlery
Rhu   01436 820584

JNW Services Aberdeen 01224 594050

JNW Services Peterhead 01779 477346

JSB Ltd
Tarbert, Loch Fyne   01880 820180

Johnston Brothers
Mallaig   01687 462215

Johnstons Marine Stores
Lamlash   01770 600333

Kearon Ltd, George
Arklow   +353 402 32319

Kelpie Boats
Pembroke Dock   01646 683661

Kelvin Hughes Ltd
Southampton   023 80634911

Kildale Marine Hull   01482 227464

Kingfisher Marine
Weymouth   01305 766595

Kings Lock Chandlery
Middlewich   01606 737564

Kip Chandlery Inverkip
Greenock   01475 521485

Kirkcudbright Scallop Gear Ltd
Kirkcudbright   01557 330399

Kyle Chandlers Troon 01292 311880

Landon Marine, Reg
Truro   01872 272668

Largs Chandlers Largs 01475 686026

Lencraft Boats Ltd
Dungarvan   +353 58 68220

Lincoln Marina Lincoln 01522 526896

Looe Chandlery
West Looe   01503 264355

Lynch Ltd, PA Morpeth 01670 512291

Mackay Boatbuilders (Arbroath) Ltd
Aberdeen   01241 872879

Mackay Marine Services
Aberdeen   01224 575772

Mailspeed Marine
Burnham-on-Crouch   01342 710618

Mailspeed Marine
Essex Marina   01342 710618

Mailspeed Marine
Warrington   01342 710618

Mainbrace Chandlers
Braye, Alderney   01481 822772

Manx Marine Ltd
Douglas   01624 674842

Marine & Leisure Europe Ltd
Plymouth   01752 268826

Marine Instruments
Falmouth   01326 312414

Marine Scene Cardiff   029 2070 5780

Marine Services Jersey   01534 626930

Marine Store Wyatts
West Mersea   01206 384745

Marine Store Maldon   01621 854380

Marine Store
Walton on the Naze   01255 679028

Marine Superstore Port Solent
Chandlery Portsmouth   023 9221 9843

MarineCo Looe   01503 265444

Maryport Harbour and Marina
Maryport   01900 814431

Matchett Ltd, HC
Widnes   0151 423 4420

Matthews Ltd, D
Cork   +353 214 277633

Mayflower Chandlery
Plymouth   01752 500121

McCready Sailboats Ltd
Holywood   028 9042 1821

Moore & Son, J
Mevagissey   01726 842964

Morgan & Sons Marine, LH
Brightlingsea   01206 302003

Mount Batten Boathouse
Plymouth   01752 482666

Murphy, Nicholas
Dunmore East   +353 51 383259

Mylor Chandlery & Rigging
Falmouth   01326 375482

Nancy Black Oban   01631 562550

Nautical World Bangor   028 91460330

New World Yacht Care
Helensburgh   01436 820586

Newhaven Chandlery
Newhaven   01273 612612

Nifpo Ardglass   028 4484 2144

Norfolk Marine
Great Yarmouth   01692 670272

Norfolk Marine Chandlery Shop
Norwich   01603 783150

Northshore Sport & Leisure
Brancaster Staithe   01485 210236

Ocean Leisure Ltd
London   020 7930 5050

One Stop Chandlery
Maldon   01621 853558

Partington Marine Ltd, William
Pwllheli   01758 612808

Pascall Atkey & Sons Ltd
Isle of Wight   01983 292381

Peculiar's Chandlery
Gosport   023 9258 9953

Pennine Marine Ltd
Skipton   01756 792335

Penrhos Marine
Aberdovey   01654 767478

Penzance Marine Services
Penzance   01736 361081

Perry Marine, Rob
Axminster   01297 631314

Pepe Boatyard
Hayling Island   023 9246 1968

Peters PLC Chichester   01243 511033

Pinnell & Bax
Northampton   01604 592808

Piplers of Poole Poole   01202 673056

Pirate's Cave, The
Rochester   01634 295233

Powersail Island Chandlers Ltd
East Cowes Marina   01983 299800

Preston Marine Services Ltd
Preston   01772 733595

Price & Co Ltd, WF
Bristol   0117 929 2229

PSM Ltd Alderney   07781 106635

Purple Sails & Marine
Walsall   01922 614787

Quay West Chandlers
Poole   01202 742488

Quayside Marine
Salcombe   01548 844300

Racecourse Yacht Basin (Windsor)
Ltd Windsor   01753 851501

Rat Rigs Water Sports
Cardiff   029 2062 1309

Reliance Marine Wirral   0151 625 5219

RHP Marine Cowes   01983 290421

RNS Marine Northam   01237 474167

Sail Loft Bideford   01271 860001

Sailaway St Anthony   01326 231357

Salcombe Boatstore
Salcombe   01548 843708

Salterns Chandlery
Poole   01202 701556

Sand & Surf Chandlery
Salcombe   01548 844555

Sandrock Marine Rye   01797 222679

Schull Watersports Centre
Schull   +353 28 28554

Sea & Shore Ship Chandler
Dundee   01382 450666

Sea Cruisers of Rye Rye 01797 222070

Sea Span Edinburgh   0131 552 2224

Sea Teach Ltd Emsworth 01243 375774

Seafare Tobermory   01688 302277

Seahog Boats Preston   01772 633016

Seamark-Nunn & Co
Felixstowe   01394 451000

Seaquest Marine Ltd
St Peter Port   01481 721773

Seaware Ltd Penryn   01326 377948

Seaway Marine Macduff 01261 832877

Severn Valley Boat Centre
Stourport-on-Severn   01299 871165

Shamrock Chandlery
Southampton   023 8063 2725

Sharp & Enright Dover   01304 206295

Shearwater Engineering Services Ltd
Dunoon   01369 706666

Shipmates Chandlery
Dartmouth   01803 839292

Shipshape Marine
King's Lynn   01553 764058

Ship Shape
Ramsgate   01843 597000

Shipsides Marine Ltd
Preston   01772 797079

Shorewater Sports
Chichester   01243 672315

Simpson Marine Ltd
Newhaven   01273 612612

Simpson Marine Ltd, WA
Dundee   01382 566670

Sketrick Marine Centre
Killinchy   028 9754 1400

Smith & Gibbs
Eastbourne   01323 723824

Smith AM (Marine) Ltd
London   020 8529 6988

Solent Marine Chandlery Ltd
Gosport   023 9258 4622

South Coast Marine
Christchurch   01202 482695

South Pier Shipyard
St Helier   01534 711000

Southampton Yacht Services Ltd
Southampton   023 803 35266

Southern Masts & Rigging
Brighton   01273 668900

Sparkes Chandlery
Hayling Island   02392 463572

S Roberts Marine Ltd
Liverpool   0151 707 8300

Standard House Chandlery
Wells-next-the-Sea   01328 710593

Stornoway Fishermen's Co-op
Stornoway   01851 702563

Sunset Marine & Watersports
Sligo   +353 71 9162792

Sussex Marine
St Leonards on Sea   01424 425882

Sussex Marine Centre
Shoreham   01273 454737

Sutton Marine (Dublin)
Sutton   +353 1 832 2312

SW Nets Newlyn   01736 360254

Tarbert Ltd, JSB Tarbert 01880 820180

TCS Chandlery
Essex Marina   01702 258094
TCS Chandlery Grays   01375 374702

TCS Chandlery
Southend   01702 444423

Thulecraft Ltd Lerwick   01595 693192

Torbay Boating Centre
Paignton   01803 558760

Torquay Chandlers
Torquay   01803 211854

Trafalgar Yacht Services
Fareham   01329 822445

Trident UK N Shields   0191 490 1736

Union Chandlery
Cork   +353 21 4554334

Uphill Boat Services
Weston-Super-Mare   01934 418617

Upper Deck Marine and Outriggers
Fowey   01726 832287

V Ships (Isle of Man)
Douglas   01624 688886

V F Marine Rhu   01436 820584

Viking Marine Ltd
Dun Laoghaire   +353 1 280 6654

Waterfront Marine
Bangor   01248 352513

Watersport and Leisure
Kings Lynn   01485 210236

Wayne Maddox Marine
Margate   01843 297157

Western Marine
Dalkey   +353 1280 0321

Whitstable Marine
Whitstable   01227 274168

Williams Ltd, TJ Cardiff 029 20 487676

Work & Leisure
Arbroath   01241 431134

XM Yachting
Southampton   0870 751 4666

Yacht & Boat Chandlery
Faversham   01795 531777
Yacht Parts Plymouth   01752 252489
Yacht Shop, The
Fleetwood   01253 879238
Yachtmail Ltd
Lymington   01590 672784

CHART AGENTS

Brown Son & Ferguson Ltd
Glasgow   0141 429 1234
Chattan Security Ltd
Edinburgh   0131 554 7527
Cooke & Son Ltd, B
Hull   01482 223454
Dubois Phillips & McCallum Ltd
Liverpool   0151 236 2776
Imray Laurie Norie and Wilson Ltd
Huntingdon   01480 462114
Kelvin Hughes
Southampton   023 8063 4911

Lilley & Gillie Ltd, John
North Shields   0191 257 2217

MARINE CHART SERVICES
Maritime House, 32 Denington
Rd, Wellingborough NN8 2QH
Tel: 01933 441629
Fax: 01933 442662
www.chartsales.co.uk
Access to many thousands of Navigation
Charts & publications in different format.
2012/MG33/e

Morgan Mapping
Exeter   01392 255788
Price & Co, WF Bristol 0117 929 2229
Sea Chest Nautical Bookshop
Plymouth   01752 222012
Seath Instruments (1992) Ltd
Lowestoft   01502 573811
Small Craft Deliveries
Woodbridge   01394 382655

Smith (Marine) Ltd, AM
London 020 8529 6988

South Bank Marine Charts Ltd
Grimsby 01472 361137

Stanford Charts
Bristol 0117 929 9966

Stanford Charts
London 020 7836 1321

Todd Chart Agency Ltd
County Down 028 9146 6640

UK Hydrographics Office
Taunton 01823 337900

Warsash Nautical Bookshop
Warsash 01489 572384

CLOTHING

Absolute
Gorleston on Sea 01493 442259

Aquatogs Cowes 01493 247890

Crew Clothing London 020 8875 2300

Crewsaver Gosport 023 9252 8621

Douglas Gill Nottingham 0115 9460844

Fat Face fatface.com

Gul International Ltd
Bodmin 01208 262400

Guy Cotten UK Ltd
Liskeard 01579 347115

Harwoods Yarmouth 01983 760258

Helly Hansen
Nottingham 0115 979 5997

Henri Lloyd Manchester 0161 799 1212

Joules 0845 6066871

Mad Cowes Clothing Co
Cowes 0845 456 5158

Matthews Ltd, D
Cork +353 214 277633

Mountain & Marine
Poynton 01625 859863

Musto Ltd Laindon 01268 491555

Ocean World Ltd Cowes 01983 291744

Purple Sails & Marine Walsall
01922 614787

Quba Sails Cowes 01983 299004

Quba Sails Lymington 01590 689362

Quba Sails Salcombe 01548 844599

Ravenspring Ltd Totnes 01803 867092

Shorewater Sports
Chichester 01243 672315

Splashdown Leeds 0113 270 7000

Yacht Parts Plymouth 01752 252489

CODE OF PRACTICE EXAMINERS

Booth Marine Surveys, Graham
Birchington-on-Sea 01843 843793

Cannell & Associates, David M
Wivenhoe 01206 823337

COMPUTERS & SOFTWARE

Dolphin Maritime Software
White Cross 01524 841946

Forum Software Ltd
Nr Haverfordwest 01646 636363

Kelvin Hughes Ltd
Southampton 023 8063 4911

Memory-Map
Aldermaston 0844 8110950

PC Maritime Plymouth 01752 254205

Sea Information Systems Ltd
Aberdeen 01224 621326

DECK EQUIPMENT

Aries Van Gear Spares
Penryn 01326 377467

Frederiksen Boat Fittings (UK) Ltd
Gosport 023 9252 5377

Harken UK Lymington 01590 689122

Kearon Ltd George +353 402 32319

Nauquip Warsash 01489 885336

Pro-Boat Ltd
Burnham-on-Crouch 01621 785455

Ryland, Kenneth
Stanton 01386 584270

Smith, EC & Son Ltd
Luton 01582 729721

Timage & Co Ltd
Braintree 01376 343087

DIESEL MARINE/ FUEL ADDITIVES

Corralls Poole 01202 674551

Cotters Marine & General Supplies
Baltimore +353 28 20106

Expresslube Henfield 01444 254115

Gorey Marine Fuel Supplies
Gorey 07797 742384

Hammond Motorboats
Dover 01304 206809

Iron Wharf Boatyard
Faversham 01795 536296

Lallow, Clare Cowes 01983 760707

Marine Support & Towage
Cowes 01983 200716/07860 297633

Quayside Fuel
Weymouth 07747 182181

Rossiter Yachts
Christchurch 01202 483250

Sleeman & Hawken
Shaldon 01626 778266

DIVERS

Abco Divers Belfast 028 90610492

Andark Diving
So' 01489 581755

Argonaut Marine
Aberdeen 01224 706526

Baltimore Diving and Watersports Centre West Cork +353 28 20300

C & C Marine Services
Largs 01475 687180

Cardiff Commercial Boat Operators Ltd Cardiff 029 2037 7872

Clyde Diving Centre
Inverkip 01475 521281

Divetech UK King's Lynn 01485 572323

Diving & Marine Engineering
Barry 01446 721553

Donnelly, R South Shields 07973 119455

DV Diving 028 9146 4671

Falmouth Divers Ltd
Penryn 01326 374736

Fathom Diving (Chislehurst)
Chislehurst 020 8289 8237

Fathoms Ltd Wick 01955 605956

Felixarc Marine Ltd
Felixstowe 01394 676497

Grampian Diving Services
New Deer 01771 644206

Higgins, Noel +353 872027650

Hudson, Dave
Trearddur Bay 01407 860628

Hunt, Kevin
Tralee +353 6671 25979

Kaymac Diving Services
Swansea 01792 301818

Keller, Hilary
Buncrana +353 77 62146

Kilkee Diving Centre
Kilkee +353 6590 56707

Leask Marine Kirkwall 01856 874725

Looe Divers Hannafore 01503 262727

MacDonald, D Nairn 01667 455661

Medway Diving Contractors Ltd
Gillingham 01634 851902

MMC Diving Services
Lake, Isle of Wight 07966 579965

Mojo Maritime Penzance 01736 762771

Murray, Alex Stornoway 01851 704978

New Dawn Dive Centre
Lymington 01590 675656

New Tec Diving Services
Blackpool 01253 691665

Northern Divers (Engineering) Ltd
Hull 01482 227276

Offshore Marine Services Ltd
Bembridge 01983 873125

Parkinson (Sinbad Marine Services), J Killybegs +353 73 31417

Port of London Authority
Gravesend 01474 560311

Purcell, D – Crouch Sailing School
Burnham 01621 784140/0585 33

Salvesen UK Ltd
Liverpool 0151 933 6038

Sea-Lift Diving Dover 01304 829956

Southern Cylinder Services
Fareham 01329 221125

Sub Aqua Services
North Ormesby 01642 230209

Teign Diving Centre
Teignmouth 01626 773965

Thorpe, Norman Portree 01478 612274

Tuskar Rock Marine
Rosslare +353 53 33376

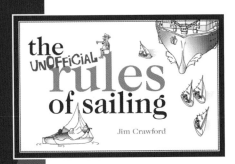

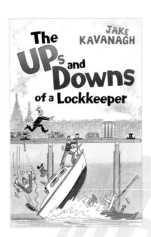
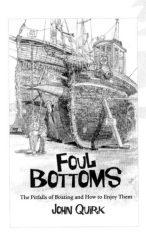

Underwater Services
Dyffryn Arbwy   01341 247702

Wilson Alan c/o Portrush Yacht Club
Portrush   028 2076 2225

Woolford, William
Bridlington   01262 671710

ELECTRICAL AND ELECTRONIC ENGINEERS

AAS Marine
Aberystwyth   01970 631090

Allworth Riverside Services, Adrian
Chelsea Harbour Marina   07831 574774

Belson Design Ltd, Nick
Southampton   077 6835 1330

Biggs, John Weymouth Marina,
Weymouth   01305 778445

BJ Marine Ltd Bangor   028 9127 1434

Boat Electrics
Troon   01292 315355

Calibra Marine
Dartmouth   01803 833094

Campbell & McHardy Lossiemouth
Marina, Lossiemouth   01343 812137

CES Sandown Sparkes Marina,
Hayling Island   023 9246 6005

Colin Coady Marine
Malahide   +353 87 265 6496

Contact Electrical
Arbroath   01241 874528

DDZ Marine Ardossan   01294 607077

EC Leisure Craft
Essex Marina   01702 257090

Energy Solutions
Rochester   01634 290772

Enterprise Marine Electronic & Technical Services Ltd
Aberdeen   01224 593281

Eurotex Brighton   01273 818990

Floetree Ltd (Loch Lomond Marina)
Balloch   01389 752069

Hamble Marine
Hamble   02380 001088

HNP Engineers (Lerwick) Ltd
Lerwick   01595 692493

Index Marine
Bournemouth   01202 470149

Jackson Yacht Services
Jersey   01534 743819

Jedynak, A Salcombe   01548 843321

Kippford Slipway Ltd
Dalbeattie   01556 620249

Lifeline Marine Services
Dolphin Haven, Poole   01202 669676

Lynch Ltd, PA
Morpeth   01670 512291

Mackay Boatbuilders (Arbroath) Ltd
Aberdeen   01241 872879

Marine, AW
Gosport   023 9250 1207

Marine Electrical Repair Service
London   020 7228 1336

MB Marine Troon   01292 311944

MES Falmouth Marina,
Falmouth   01326 378497

Mount Batten Boathouse
Plymouth   01752 482666

New World Yacht Care
Rhu   01436 820586

Neyland Marine Services Ltd
Milford Haven   01646 600358

Powell, Martin Shamrock Quay,
Southampton   023 8033 2123

R & J Marine Electricians Suffolk Yacht
Harbour Ltd, Ipswich   01473 659737

Radio & Electronic Services Beaucette
Marina, Guernsey   01481 728837

Redcar Fish Company
Stockton-on-Tees   01642 633638

RHP Marine Cowes   01983 290421

Rothwell, Chris
Torquay Marina   01803 850960

Ruddy Marine
Galway   +353 86 8492888

Rutherford, Jeff Largs   01475 568026

Sea Electric Hamble   023 8045 6255

SM International
Plymouth   01752 662129

Sussex Fishing Services
Rye   01797 223895

Ultra Marine Systems
Mayflower International Marina, Plymouth
                             07989 941020

Upham, Roger
Chichester   01243 528299

Volspec Ipswich   01473 780144

Waypoint Marine
Plymouth   01752 661913

Weyland Marine Services
Milford Haven   01646 600358

ELECTRONIC DEVICES AND EQUIPMENT

Anchorwatch UK
Edinburgh   0131 447 5057

Aquascan International Ltd
Newport   01633 841117

Atlantis Marine Power Ltd
Plymouth   01752 225679

Autosound Marine
Bradford   01274 688990

B&G Romsey   01794 518448

Brookes & Gatehouse
Romsey   01794 518448

Boat Electrics & Electronics Ltd
Troon   01292 315355

Cactus Navigation & Communication
London   020 7833 3435

CDL Aberdeen   01224 706655

Charity & Taylor Ltd
Lowestoft   01502 581529

Diverse Yacht Services
Hamble   023 8045 3399

Dyfed Electronics Ltd
Milford Haven   01646 694572

Echopilot Marine Electronics Ltd
Ringwood   01425 476211

Enterprise Marine
Aberdeen   01224 593281

Euronav Ltd
Portsmouth   023 9237 3855

Furuno UK
Fraserburgh   01346 518300

Furuno UK
Havant   023 9244 1000

Garmin (Europe) Ltd
Romsey   0870 850 1242

Golden Arrow Marine Ltd
Southampton   023 8071 0371

Greenham Regis Marine Electronics
Lymington   01590 671144

Greenham Regis Marine Electronics
Poole   01202 676363

Greenham Regis Marine Electronics
Southampton   023 8063 6555

ICS Electronics Arundel 01903 731101

JG Technologies Ltd
Weymouth   0845 458 9616

KM Electronics
Lowestoft   01502 569079

Kongsberg Simrad Ltd
Aberdeen   01224 226500

Kongsberg Simrad Ltd
Wick   01955 603606

Landau UK Ltd Hamble 02380 454040

Enterprise Marine
Aberdeen   01224 593281

Marathon Leisure
Hayling Island   023 9263 7711

Marine Instruments
Falmouth   01326 375483

MB Marine Troon   01292 311944

Microcustom Ltd Ipswich 01473 215777

Nasa Marine Instruments
Stevenage   01438 354033

Navcom Chichester   01243 776625

Navionics UK Plymouth 01752 204735

Ocean Leisure Ltd
London   020 7930 5050

Plymouth Marine Electronics
Plymouth   01752 227711

Radio & Electronic Services Ltd
St Peter Port   01481 728837

Raymarine Ltd
Portsmouth   02392 714700

Redfish Car Company
Stockton-on-Tees   01642 633638

Robertson, MK Oban   01631 563836

Satcom Distribution Ltd
Salisbury   01722 410800

Stowe Marine
Lymington   01590 610072

STN Atlas Marine UK Ltd
Peterhead   01779 478233

Tacktick Ltd Havant   02392 484194

Transas Nautic
Portsmouth   023 9267 4016

Veripos Precise Navigation
Fraserburgh   01346 511411

Wema (UK) Honiton   01404 881810

Western Battery Service
Mallaig   01687 462044

Wilson & Co Ltd, DB
Glasgow   0141 647 0161

Woodsons of Aberdeen Ltd
Aberdeen   01224 722884

ENGINES AND ACCESSORIES

Airylea Motors
Aberdeen   01224 872891

Amble Boat Co Ltd
Amble   01665 710267

Anchor Marine Products
Benfleet   01268 566666

Aquafac Ltd Luton   01582 568700

Attfield & Company, GB
Dursley   01453 547185

Barrus Ltd, EP Bicester 01869 363636

Brigantine
Teignmouth   01626 872400

British Polar Engines Ltd
Glasgow   0141 445 2455

Bukh Diesel UK Ltd
Poole   01202 668840

CJ Marine Mechanical
Troon   01292 313400

Cleghorn Waring Ltd
Letchworth   01462 480380

Cook's Diesel Service Ltd
Faversham   01795 538553

Felton Marine Engineering
Brighton   01273 601779

Felton Marine Engineering
Eastbourne   01323 470211

Fender-Fix Maidstone   01622 751518

Fettes & Rankine Engineering
Aberdeen   01224 573343

Fleetwood & Sons Ltd, Henry
Lossiemouth   01343 813015

Gorleston Marine Ltd
Great Yarmouth   01493 661883

Halyard Salisbury   01722 710922

Interseals (Guernsey) Ltd
Guernsey   01481 246364

Kelpie Boats
Pembroke Dock   01646 683661

Keypart Watford   01923 330570

Lancing Marine Brighton 01273 410025

Lencraft Boats Ltd
Dungarvan   +353 58 68220

Lewmar Ltd Havant   023 9247 1841

Seaquest Marine Ltd
Guernsey   01481 721773

Seatronics Aberdeen   01224 853100

Selex Communications
Aberdeen   01224 890316

Selex Communications
Bristol   0117 931 3550

Selex Communications
Brixham   01803 882716

Selex Communications
Fraserburgh   01346 518187

Selex Communications
Glasgow   0141 882 6909

Selex Communications
Hull   01482 326144

Selex Communications
Kilkeel   028 4176 9009

Selex Communications
Liverpool   0151 647 6222

Selex Communications
Lowestoft   01502 572365

Selex Communications
Newcastle upon Tyne   0191 265 0374

Selex Communications
Newlyn   01736 361320

Selex Communications
Penryn   01326 378031

Selex Communications
Plymouth   01752 222878

Selex Communications
Rosyth   01383 419606

Selex Communications
Southampton   023 8051 1868

Silva Ltd Livingston   01506 419555

SM International
Plymouth   01752 662129

Sperry Marine Ltd
Peterhead   01779 473475

Stenmar Ltd Aberdeen 01224 827288

Liverpool Power Boats
Bootle   0151 944 1163

Lynch Ltd, PA Morpeth   01670 512291

MacDonald & Co Ltd, JN
Glasgow   0141 810 3400

Mariners Weigh
Shaldon   01626 873698

MMS Ardrossan   01294 604831

Mooring Mate Ltd
Bournemouth   01202 421199

Newens Marine, Chas
Putney   020 8788 4587

Ocean Safety
Southampton   023 8072 0800

Outboard Centre
Fareham   01329 234277

Riley Marine Dover   01304 214544

RK Marine Ltd Hamble   01489 583585

RK Marine Ltd Swanwick 01489 583572

Rule – ITT Industries
Hoddesdon   01992 450145

Sillette Sonic Ltd
Sutton   020 8337 7543

Smith & Son Ltd, EC
Luton   01582 729721

Sowester Simpson-Lawrence Ltd
Poole   01202 667700

Timage & Co Ltd
Braintree   01376 343087

Vetus Den Ouden Ltd
Totton   023 8045 4507

Western Marine
Dublin   +353 1 280 0321

Whitstable Marine
Whitstable   01227 262525

Yates Marine, Martin
Galgate   01524 751750

Ynys Marine Cardigan   01239 613179

FOUL-WEATHER GEAR

Aquatogs Cowes   01983 295071

Century Finchampstead   0118 9731616

Crewsaver Gosport   023 9252 8621

Douglas Gill
Nottingham   0115 9460844

FBI Leeds   0113 270 7000

Gul International Ltd
Bodmin   01208 262400

Helly Hansen
Nottingham   0115 979 5997

Henri Lloyd Manchester 0161 799 1212

Musto Ltd Laindon   01268 491555

Pro Rainer Windsor   07752 903882

GENERAL MARINE EQUIPMENT & SPARES

Ampair Ringwood   01425 480780

Aries Vane Gear Spares
Penryn   01326 377467

Arthurs Chandlery, R
Gosport   023 9252 6522

Barden UK Ltd Fareham 01489 570770

Calibra Marine International Ltd
Southampton   08702 400358

CH Marine (Cork)
Cork   +353 21 4315700

Chris Hornsey (Chandlery) Ltd
Southsea   023 9273 4728

Compass Marine (Dartmouth)
Dartmouth   01803 835915

Cox Yacht Charter Ltd, Nick
Lymington   01590 673489

CTC Marine & Leisure
Middlesbrough   01642 372600

Docksafe Ltd Bangor   028 9147 0453

Frederiksen Boat Fittings (UK) Ltd
Gosport   023 9252 5377

Furneaux Riddall & Co Ltd
Portsmouth   023 9266 8621

Hardware & Marine Supplies
Co Wexford   +353 (53) 29791

Index Marine
Bournemouth   01202 470149

Kearon Ltd, George
Arklow   +353 402 32319

Marathon Leisure
Hayling Island   023 9263 7711

Pro-Boat Ltd
Burnham-on-Crouch   01621 785455

Pump International Ltd
Cornwall   01209 831937

Quay West Chandlers
Poole   01202 742488

Rogers, Angie Bristol 0117 973 8276

Ryland, Kenneth
Stanton   01386 584270

Tiflex Liskeard   01579 320808

Vetus Boating Equipment
Southampton   02380 454507

Western Marine Power Ltd
Plymouth   01752 408804

Whitstable Marine
Whitstable   01227 262525

Yacht Parts Plymouth   01752 252489

HARBOUR MASTERS

Aberaeron   01545 571645

Aberdeen   01224 597000

Aberdovey   01654 767626

Aberystwyth   01970 611433

Alderney & Burhou   01481 822620

Amble   01665 710306

Anstruther   01333 310836

Appledore   01237 474569

Arbroath   01241 872166

Ardglass   028 4484 1291

Ardrossan Control Tower   01294 463972

Arinagour Piermaster   01879 230347

Arklow   +353 402 32466

Baltimore   +353 28 22145

Banff   01261 815544

Bantry Bay   +353 27 53277

Barmouth   01341 280671

Barry   01446 732665

Beaucette   01481 245000

Beaulieu River   01590 616200

Belfast Lough   028 90 553012

Belfast River Manager 028 90 328507

Bembridge   01983 872828

Berwick-upon-Tweed   01289 307404

Bideford   01237 346131

Blyth   01670 352678

Boston   01205 362328

Bridlington   01262 670148/9

Bridport   01308 423222

Brighton   01273 819919

Bristol   0117 926 4797

Brixham   01803 853321

Buckie   01542 831700
                            07842 532360

Bude   01288 353111

Burghead   01343 835337

Burnham-on-Crouch   01621 783602

Burnham-on-Sea   01278 782180

Burtonport   +353 075 42155

Caernarfon   01286 672118

Caernarfon   07786 730865

Camber Berthing Offices –
Portsmouth   023 92297395

Campbeltown   01586 552552
                            07825 732862

Caledonian Canal Off.
(Inverness)   01463 725500

Cardiff   029 20400500

Carnlough Harbour   07703 606763

Castletown Bay   01624 823549

Charlestown   01726 67526

Chichester Harbour   01243 512301

Conwy   01492 596253

Cork   +353 21 4273125

Corpach Canal Sea Lock   01397 772249

Courtmacsherry
                    +353 23 46311/46600
                    +353 8610 40812

Coverack   01326 380679

Cowes   01983 293952

Crail   01333 450820

Craobh Haven   01852 502222

Crinan Canal Office   01546 603210

Cromarty Firth	01381 600479	Kettletoft Bay	01857 600227	Poole	01202 440233
Cromarty Harbour	01381 600493	Killybegs	+353 73 31032	Port Isaac	01208 880321
Crookhaven	+353 28 35319	Kilmore Quay	+353 53 912 9955		07855 429422
Cullen	01542 831700	Kinlochbervie	01971 521235	Port St Mary	01624 833205
Dingle	+353 66 9151629		07901 514350	Porth Dinllaen	01758 720276
Douglas	01624 686628	Kinsale	+353 21 4772503	Porthleven	01326 574207
Dover	01304 240400 Ext 4520	Kirkcudbright	01557 331135	Porthmadog	01766 512927
Dublin	+353 1 874871	Kirkwall	01856 872292	Portknockie	01542 840833
Dun Laoghaire		Langstone Harbour	023 9246 3419	Portland	01305 824044
	+353 1 280 1130/8074	Larne	02828 872100	Portpatrick	01776 810355
Dunbar	01368 863206	Lerwick	01595 692991	Portree	01478 612926
Dundee	01382 224121	Littlehampton	01903 721215	Portrush	028 70822307
Dunmore East	+353 51 383166	Liverpool	0151 949 6134/5	Portsmouth Harbour Commercial Docks	023 92297395
East Loch Tarbert	01859 502444	Loch Gairloch	01445 712140	Portsmouth Harbour Control	
Eastbourne	01323 470099	Loch Inver	01571 844267		023 92723694
Eigg Harbour	01687 482428		07958 734610	Portsmouth Harbour	023 92723124
Elie	01333 330051	Looe	01503 262839	Preston	01772 726711
Estuary Control - Dumbarton	01389 726211		07918 728955	Pwllheli	01758 704081
Exe	01392 274306	Lossiemouth (Marina)	07969 213513	Queenborough	01795 662051
Eyemouth	01890 750223		07969213521	Queens Gareloch/Rhu	01436 674321
Falmouth	01326 312285	Lough Foyle	028 7186 0555	Ramsey	01624 812245
Felixstowe	07803 476621	Lowestoft	01502 572286	Ramsgate	01843 572100
Findochty	01542 831700	Lyme Regis	01297 442137	River Bann & Coleraine	
Fisherrow	0131 665 5900	Lymington	01590 672014		028 7034 2012
Fishguard (Lower Hbr)	01348 874726	Lyness	01856 791387	River Blackwater	01621 856487
Fishguard	01348 404425	Macduff	01261 832236	River Colne (Brightlingsea)	01206 302200
Fleetwood	01253 872323	Maryport	01900 814431	River Dart	01803 832337
Flotta	01856 701411	Menai Strait	01248 712312	River Deben	01394 283785
Folkestone	01303 715354	Methil	01333 462725	River Exe Dockmaster	01392 274306
Fowey	01726 832471/2.	Mevagissey	01726 843305	River Humber	01482 327171
Fraserburgh	01346 515858	Milford Haven	01646 696100	River Medway	01795 596593
Galway Bay	+353 91 561874	Minehead (Mon-Fri)	01643 702566	River Orwell	01473 231010
Garlieston	01988 600274	Montrose	01674 672302	River Roach	01621 783602
Glasson Dock	01524 751724	Mousehole	01736 731511	River Stour	01255 243000
Gorey Port Control	01534 447788	Mullion Cove	01326 240222	River Tyne/North Shields	0191 257 2080
Gourdon	01569 762741	Nairn Harbour Office	01667 452453	River Yealm	01752 872533
Great Yarmouth	01493 335501	Newhaven Harbour Admin		Rivers Alde & Ore	07528 092635
Grimsby Dockmaster	01472 359181		01273 612872/612926	Rosslare Europort	+353 53 915 7921
Groomsport Bay	028 91 278040	Newlyn	01736 731897	Rothesay	01700 503842
Hamble River	01489 576387	Newquay	01637 872809		07799 724225
Hayle	01736 754043		07737 387217	Ryde	01983 613879
Helford River	01326 250749	Newport Harbour Office	01983 525994	Salcombe	01548 843791
Helmsdale	01431 821692	North Berwick	00776 467373	Sark	01481 832323
Holy Island	01289 389217	Oban	01631 562892	Scalloway	01595 880574
Holyhead	01407 763071	Padstow	01841 532239	Scarborough	01723 373530
Hopeman	01343 835337	Peel	01624 842338	Scrabster	01847 892779
Howth	+353 1 832 2252	Penrhyn Bangor	01248 352525	Seaham	07786 565205
Ilfracombe	01271 862108	Penzance	01736 366113	Sharpness	01453 811862/64
Inverness	01463 715715	Peterhead	01779 483630	Shoreham	01273 598100
Irvine	01294 487286	Pierowall	01857 677216	Silloth	016973 31358
Johnshaven	01561 362262	Pittenweem	01333 312591		
		Plockton	01599 534589		
		Polperro	01503 272809		

Sligo	+353 91 53819
	+353 86 0870767
Southampton	023 8033 9733
Southend-on-Sea	01702 611889
Southwold	01502 724712
St Helier	01534 447788
St Ives	01736 795018
St Margaret's Hope	01856 831454
St Mary's	01720 422768
St Michael's Mount	07870 400282
St Monans (part-time)	07930 869538
St Peter Port	01481 720229
Stonehaven	01569 762741
Stornoway	01851 702688
Strangford Lough	028 44 881637
Stromness	01856 850744
Stronsay	01857 616317
Sullom Voe	01806 242551
Sunderland	0191 567 2626
Swale	01795 561234
Swansea	01792 653787
Tayport Hbr Trust	01382 553799
Tees & Hartlepool Port Authority	01429 277205
Teignmouth	01626 773165
Tenby	01834 842717
Thames Estuary	01474 562200
Tobermory Moorings Officer	07917 832497
Torquay	01803 292429
Troon	01292 281687
Truro	01872 272130
Ullapool	01854 612091
Waldringfield	01394 276004
Walton-on-the-Naze	01255 851899
Watchet	07739 958441
Waterford	+353 51 874907

Wells-next-the-Sea	01328 711646
West Bay (Bridport)	01308 423222
	07870 240636
Wexford	+353 53 912 2039
Weymouth	01305 206423
Whitby	01947 602354
Whitehaven	01946 692435
Whitehills	01261 861291
Whitstable	01227 274086
Wick	01955 602030
Wicklow	+353 404 67455
Workington	01900 602301
Yarmouth	01983 760321
Youghal	+353 24 92626

HARBOURS

Bristol Harbour	0117 903 1484
Clyde Marina – Ardrossan	
	01294 607077
Jersey Harbours	
St Helier	01534 885588
Maryport Harbour and Marina	
Maryport	01900 818447/4431
Peterhead Bay Authority	
Peterhead	01779 474020
Sark Moorings – Channel Islands	
	01481 832260

INSURANCE/FINANCE

Admiral Marine Ltd	
Salisbury	01722 416106
Bigfish London	020 8651 4096
Bishop Skinner Boat Insurance	
London	0800 7838057
Bluefin London	0800 074 5200
Bristol Channel Marine	
Cardiff	029 2063 1163
Castlemain Ltd	
St Peter Port	01481 721319
Clark Insurance, Graham	
Tyneside	0191 455 8089
Craven Hodgson Associates	
Leeds	0113 243 8443
Giles Insurance Brokers	
Irvine	01294 315481

GJW Direct Liverpool	0151 473 8000
Haven Knox-Johnston	
West Malling	01732 223600
Lombard	
Southampton	023 8024 2171
Mardon Insurance	
Shrewsbury	0800 515629
Marine & General Insurance Services Ltd Maidstone	01622 201106
Mercia Marine Malvern	01684 564457
Nautical Insurance Services Ltd	
Leigh-on-Sea	01702 470811
Navigators & General	
Brighton	01273 863400
Pantaenius UK Ltd	
Plymouth	01752 223656
Porthcawl Insurance Consultants	
Porthcawl	01656 784866
Saga Boat Insurance Folkestone	
	01303 771135
St Margarets Insurances	
London	020 8778 6161

LIFERAFTS & INFLATABLES

Adec Marine Ltd	
Croydon 020 8686 9717	
Avon Inflatables Llanelli 01554 882000	
Cosalt International Ltd	
Aberdeen	01224 588327
Glaslyn Marine Supplies Ltd	
Porthmadog	01766 513545
Hale Marine, Ron	
Portsmouth	023 9273 2985
Herm Seaway Marine Ltd	
St Peter Port	01481 722838
IBS Boats South Woodham Ferrers	
	01245 323211/425551
KTS Seasafety Kilkeel 028 918 28405	
Nationwide Marine Hire	
Warrington	01925 245788
Norwest Marine Ltd	
Liverpool	0151 207 2860
Ocean Safety	
Southampton	023 8072 0800
Polymarine Ltd Conwy 01492 583322	
Premium Liferaft Services	
Burnham-on-Crouch	0800 243673
Ribeye Dartmouth	01803 832060
Secumar Swansea	01792 280545
South Eastern Marine Services Ltd	
Basildon	01268 534427
Suffolk Sailing Ipswich 01473 833010	
Whitstable Marine	
Whitstable	01227 262525

MARINAS

Aberystwyth Marina	01970 611422
Amble Marina	01665 712168
Arbroath Harbour	01241 872166
Ardfern Yacht Centre	
	01852 500247
Ardglass Marina	028 4484233
Arklow Marina	+353 402 39901

Ballycastle Marina	028 2076 8525	
Banff Harbour Marina	01261 815544	
Bangor Marina	028 91 453297	
Beaucette Marina	01481 245000	
Bembridge Harbour	01983 872828	
Berthon Lymington Marina		
	01590 647405	
Birdham Pool Marina	01243 512310	
Blackwater Marina	01621 740264	
Boston Marina	01205 364420	
Bradwell Marina	01621 776235	
Bray Marina	01628 623654	
Brentford Dock Marina		
	020 8232 8941	
Bridgemarsh Marine	01621 740414	
Brighton Marina	01273 819919	
Bristol Marina	0117 9213198	
Brixham Marina	01803 882929	
Bucklers Hard Marina	01590 616200	
Burnham Yacht Harbour Marina		
	01621 782150	
Cahersiveen Marina		
	+353 66 947 2777	
Caley Marina	01463 236539	
Cardiff Marina	02920 396078	
Carlingford Marina	+353 42 9373073	
Carrickfergus Marina	028 9336 6666	
Castlepark Marina	+353 21 477 4959	
Chatham Maritime Marina		
	01634 899200	
Chelsea Harbour Marina		
	07770 542783	
Chichester Marina	01243 512731	
Clyde Marina Ltd	01294 607077	
Cobbs Quay Marina	01202 674299	
Coleraine Marina	028 703 44768	
Conwy Marina	01492 593000	
Cowes Yacht Haven	01983 299975	
Craobh Marina	01852 500222	
Crosshaven Boatyard Marina		
	+353 21 483 1161	
Dart Marina Yacht Harbour		
	01803 837161	

Darthaven Marina	01803 752242	
Dartside Quay	01803 845445	
Deganwy Quays Marina		
	01492 576888	
Dingle Marina	+353 66 915 1629	
Dover Marina	01304 241663	
Dun Laoghaire Marina		
	+353 1 202 0040	
Dunstaffnage Marina	01631 566555	
East Cowes Marina	01983 293983	
East Ferry Marina	+353 21 483 1342	
Emsworth Yacht Harbour		
	01243 377727	
Essex Marina	01702 258531	
Falmouth Marina	01326 316620	
Falmouth Visitors Yacht Haven		
	01326 310991	
Fambridge Yacht Haven		
	01621 740370	
Fenit Harbour Marina		
	+353 66 7136231	
Fleetwood Haven Marina		
	01253 879062	
Fox's Marina & Boatyard		
	01473 689111	
Gallions Point Marina		
	0207 476 7054	
Galway Harbour Marina		
	+353 91 561874	
Gillingham Marina	01634 280022	
Glasson Dock Marina	01524 751491	
Gosport Marina	023 9252 4811	
Gunwharf Quays	02392 836732	
Hafan Pwllheli	01758 701219	
Hamble Point Marina	02380 452464	
Hamilton Dock	01502 580300	
Harbour of Rye	01797 225225	
Hartlepool Marina	01429 865744	
Haslar Marina	023 9260 1201	
Heybridge Basin	01621 853506	
Holy Loch Marina	01369 701800	
Holyhead Marina	01407 764242	
Hoo Marina	01634 250311	

Howth Marina	+353 1839 2777	
Hull Marina	01482 609960	
Hythe Marina Village	02380 207073	
Inverness Marina	01463 220501	
Ipswich Haven Marina	01473 236644	
Island Harbour Marina	01983 539994	
James Watt Dock Marina		
	07710 611117	
Kemps Shipyard	023 8063 2323	
Kilmore Quay Marina		
	+353 5391 29955	
Kilrush Marina	+353 65 9052072	
Kinsale Yacht Club Marina		
	+353 21 477 2196	
Kip Marina	01475 521485	
Kirkwall Marina	07810 465835	
Lady Bee Marina	01273 593801	
Lake Yard Marina	01202 674531	
Largs Yacht Haven	01475 675333	
Lawrence Cove Marina		
	+353 27 75044	
Limehouse Marina	020 7308 9930	
Littlehampton Marina	01903 713553	
Liverpool Marina Bar & Grill		
	0151 707 6777	
Lossiemouth Marina	01343 813066	
Lowestoft Cruising Club		
	07913 391950	
Lowestoft Haven Marina		
	01502 580300	
Lymington Yacht Haven		
	01590 677071	
Malahide Marina	+353 1 845 4129	
Maryport Harbour and Marina		
	01900 814431	
Mayflower International Marina		
	01752 556633	
Melfort Pier & Harbour		
	01852 200333	
Mercury Yacht Harbour		
	023 8045 5994	
Meridian Quay Marina	01472 268424	
Milford Marina	01646 696312	
Mylor Yacht Harbour	01326 372121	
Nairn Marina	01667 456008	

DEAN & REDDYHOFF
M A R I N A S

*Premium quality berthing, accessed at all states of tide, excellent washroom
facilities, value for money and unsurpassed customer service…
… the hallmark of all Dean & Reddyhoff Marinas.*

Portland Marina
Superb facilities including bar/restaurant, hoist
dock, extensive boatyard and fuel berth.
Annual berths from just £402 per metre incl. VAT

Tel: 08454 30 2012

Weymouth Marina
Ideal stop off whilst cruising the South Coast.
Annual berths £414 per metre incl. VAT

Tel: 01305 767576

Haslar Marina
Only minutes from open water in the Solent.
Annual berths £453 per metre incl. VAT

Tel: 023 9260 1201

East Cowes Marina
Sheltered pontoon berths with all
the Isle of Wight has to offer.
Annual berths £371 per metre incl. VAT

Tel: 01983 293983

www.deanreddyhoff.co.uk

Oban Marina	01631 565333
Ocean Village Marina	023 8022 9385
Parkstone Yacht Club Haven	01202 738824
Peel Marina	01624 842338
Penarth Quays Marina	02920 705021
Penton Hook	01932 568681
Peterhead Bay Marina	01779 477868
Plymouth Yacht Haven	01752 404231
Poole Quay Boat Haven	01202 649488
Port Edgar Marina & Sailing School	0131 331 3330
Port Ellen Marina	01496 302458
Port Falmouth Marina	01326 212100
Port Hamble Marina	023 8045 2741
Port Pendennis Marina	01326 211211
Port Solent Marina	02392 210765
Portaferry Marina	07703 209780
Portavadie Marina	01700 811075
Portishead Quays Marina	01275 841941
Portland Marina	08454 30 2012
Preston Marina	01772 733595
Quay Marinas Rhu	01436 820296
Queen Anne's Battery	01752 671142
Ridge Wharf Yacht Centre	01929 552650
Royal Clarence Marina	02392 523523
Royal Cork Yacht Club Marina	+353 21 483 1023
Royal Harbour Marina, Ramsgate	01843 572105
Royal Harwich Yacht Club Marina	01473 780319
Royal Norfolk and Suffolk Yacht Club	01502 566726
Royal Northumberland Yacht Club	01670 353636
Royal Quays Marina	0191 272 8282
Ryde Leisure Harbour	01983 613879
Salterns Marina Ltd	01202 709971
Salve Engineering Marina	+353 21 483 1145
Sandpoint Marina (Dumbarton)	01389 762396
Saxon Wharf	023 8033 9490
Seaport Marina	01463 725500
Seaton's Marina	028 703 832086
Shamrock Quay	023 8022 9461
Sharpness Marine	01453 811476
Shepards Wharf Boatyard	01983 297821

Shotley Marina	01473 788982
South Dock Marina	020 7252 2244
South Ferriby Marina	01652 635620
Southsea Marina	02392 822719
Sovereign Harbour Marina	01323 470099
Sparkes Marina	023 92463572
St Helier Marina	01534 447708
St Katharine Marina Ltd	0207 264 5312
St Peter Port Marinas	01481 720229
St Peter's Marina	0191 265 4472
Stromness Marina	07810 465825
Suffolk Yacht Harbour Ltd	01473 659240
Sunderland Marina	0191 514 4721
Sutton Harbour	01752 204702
Swansea Marina	01792 470310
Swanwick Marina	01489 884081
Tarbert Harbour	01880 820344
The Shipyard	01903 713327
Titchmarsh Marina	01255 672185
Tollesbury Marina	01621 869202
Torquay Marina	01803 200210
Troon Yacht Haven	01292 315553
Universal Marina	01489 574272
Victoria Marina	01481 720229
Walton Yacht Basin	01255 675873
Waterford City Marina	+353 87 238 4944
Weymouth Harbour	01305 838423
Weymouth Marina	01305 767576
Whitby Marina	01947 602354
Whitehaven Marina	01946 692435
Whitehills Marina	01261 861291
Wick Marina	01955 602030
Windsor Marina	01753 853911
Wisbech Yacht Harbour	01945 588059
Woolverstone Marina	01473 780206
Yarmouth Harbour	01983 760321

MARINE CONSULTANTS AND SURVEYORS

Amble Boat Company Ltd Amble	01665 710267
Ark Surveys East Anglia/South Coast	01621 857065/01794 521957
Atkin and Associates Lymington	01590 688633
Barbican Yacht Agency Ltd Plymouth	01752 228855
Booth Marine Surveys, Graham Birchington-on-Sea	01843 843793

Bureau Maritime Ltd Maldon	01621 859181
Byrde & Associates Kimmeridge	01929 480064
Cannell & Associates, David M Wivenhoe	01206 823337
Clarke Designs LLP, Owen Dartmouth	01803 770495
Davies, Peter Wivenhoe	01206 823289
Down Marine Co Ltd Belfast	028 90480247
Green, James Plymouth	01752 660516
Greening Yacht Design Ltd, David Salcombe	01548 842000
Hansing & Associates North Wales/Midlands	01248 671291
JP Services – Marine Safety & Training Chichester	01243 537552
Marintec Lymington	01590 683414
Norwood Marine Margate	01843 835711
Quay Consultants Ltd Arundel	01243 673056
Scott Marine Surveyors & Consultants Conwy	01248 680759
Staton-Bevan, Tony Lymington	01590 645755
Swanwick Yacht Surveyors Southampton	01489 564822
Victoria Yacht Surveys Cornwall	0800 083 2113
Ward & McKenzie Woodbridge	01394 383222
Ward & McKenzie (North East) Pocklington	01759 304322
Yacht Designers & Surveyors Association Bordon	01730 710425

MARINE ENGINEERS

AAS Marine Aberystwyth	01970 631090
Allerton Engineering Lowestoft	01502 537870
APAS Engineering Ltd Southampton	023 8063 2558
Ardmair Boat Centre Ullapool	01854 612054
Arisaig Marine Inverness-shire	01687 450224
Arun Craft Littlehampton	01903 723667
Attrill & Sons, H Bembridge	01983 872319
Auto & Marine Services Botley	01489 785009
Auto Marine Southsea	023 9282 5601
BJ Marine Ltd Bangor	028 9127 1434
Bristol Boat Ltd Bristol	01225 872032
Buzzard Marine Engineering Yarmouth	01983 760707

C & B Marine Ltd
Chichester Marina   01243 511273

Caddy, Simon Falmouth Marina,
Falmouth   01326 372682

Caledonian Marine
Rhu Marina   01436 821184

Caratek
Hull   07957 922301

Cardigan Outboards
Cardigan   01239 613966

Channel Islands Marine Ltd
Guernsey   01481 716880

Channel Islands Marine Ltd
Jersey   01534 767595

Clarence Marine Engineering
Gosport   023 9251 1555

Cook's Diesel Service Ltd
Faversham   01795 538553

Cragie Engineering
Kirkwall   01856 874680

Wartsila
Havant   023 9240 0121

Crinan Boatyard Ltd
Crinan   01546 830232

Cutler Marine Engineering, John
Emsworth   01243 375014

Dale Sailing Co Ltd
Milford Haven   01646 603110

Davis Marine Services
Ramsgate   01843 586172

Denney & Son, EL
Redcar   01642 483507

DH Marine (Shetland) Ltd
Shetland   01595 690618

Emark Marine Ltd
Emsworth   01243 375383

Evans Marine Engineering, Tony
Pwllheli   01758 703070

Felton Marine Engineering
Brighton   01273 601779

Felton Marine Engineering
Eastbourne   01323 470211

Ferrypoint Boat Co
Youghal   +353 24 94232

Fettes & Rankine Engineering
Aberdeen   01224 573343

Fleming Engineering, J
Stornoway   01851 703488

Floetree Ltd (Loch Lomond Marina)
Balloch   01389 752069

Fowey Harbour Marine Engineers
Fowey   01726 832806

Fox Marine Services Ltd
Jersey   01534 721312

Freeport Marine Jersey 01534 888100

French Marine Motors Ltd
Colchester   01206 302133

GH Douglas Marine Services
Fleetwood Harbour Village Marina,
Fleetwood   01253 877200

Golden Arrow Marine
Southampton   023 8071 0371

Goodchild Marine Services
Great Yarmouth   01493 782301

Goodwick Marine
Fishguard   01348 873955

Gosport Marina
Gosport   023 9252 4811

Griffins Garage Dingle Marina,
Co Kerry   +353 66 91 51178

Hale Marine, Ron
Portsmouth   023 9273 2985

Hamnavoe Engineering
Stromness   01856 850576

Hampshire Marine Ltd
Stubbington   01329 665561

Harbour Engineering
Itchenor   01243 513454

Hardway Marine Store
Gosport   023 9258 0420

Hartlepool Marine Engineering
Hartlepool   01429 867883

Hayles, Harold
Yarmouth   01983 760373

Herm Seaway Marine Ltd
St Peter Port   01481 726829

HNP Engineers (Lerwick Ltd)
Lerwick   01595 692493

Home Marine Emsworth Yacht Harbour,
Emsworth   01243 374125

Hook Marine Ltd
Troon   01292 679500

Humphrey, Chris
Teignmouth   01626 772324

Instow Marine Services
Bideford   01271 861081

Jones (Boatbuilders), David
Chester   01244 390363

Keating Marine Engineering Ltd, Bill
Jersey   01534 733977

Kingston Marine Services
Cowes   01983 299385

Kippford Slipway Ltd
Dalbeattie   01556 620249

Lansdale Pannell Marine
Chichester   01243 512374

Lencraft Boats Ltd
Dungarvan   +353 58 68220

Llyn Marine Services
Pwllheli   01758 612606

Lynx Engineering
St Helens, Isle of Wight   01983 873711

M&G Marine Services
Mayflower International Marina, Plymouth
          01752 563345

MacDonald & Co Ltd, JN
Glasgow   0141 810 3400

Mackay Marine Services
Aberdeen   01224 575772

Mainbrayce Marine
Alderney   01481 722772

Malakoff and Moore
Lerwick   01595 695544

**Mallaig Boat Building and
Engineering** Mallaig 01687 462304

Marindus Engineering
Kilmore Quay   +353 53 29794

Marine Engineering Looe
Brixham   01803 844777

Marine Engineering Looe
Looe   01503 263009

Marine General Engineers Beaucette
Marina, Guernsey   01481 245808

Marine Maintenance
Portsmouth   023 9260 2344

Marine Propulsion
Hayling Island   07836 737488

Marine & General Engineers
St. Sampsons Harbour, Guernsey
          01481 245808

Marine-Trak Engineering Mylor Yacht
Harbour, Falmouth   01326 376588

Marlec Marine
Ramsgate   01843 592176

Martin Outboards
Galgate   01524 751750

MMS Ardrossan   01294 604831

Mobile Marine Engineering Liverpool
Marina, Liverpool   01565 733553

Motortech Marine Engineering
Portsmouth   023 9251 3200

Mount's Bay Engineering
Newlyn   01736 363095

MP Marine Maryport   01900 810299

New World Yacht Care
Helensburgh   01436 820586

North Western Automarine Engineers
Largs   01475 687139

Noss Marine Services
Dart Marina, Dartmouth   01803 833343

Owen Marine, Robert
Porthmadog   01766 513435

Pace, Andy Newhaven   01273 516010

**Penzance Dry Dock and Engineering
Co Ltd** Penzance   01736 363838

Pirie & Co, John S
Fraserburgh   01346 513314

Portavon Marine
Keynsham 0117 986 1626

Power Afloat, Elkins Boatyard
Christchurch 01202 489555

Powerplus Marine Cowes Yacht Haven,
Cowes 01983 200036

Pro-Marine Queen Anne's Battery
Marina, Plymouth 01752 267984

PT Marine Engineering
Hayling Island 023 9246 9332

R & M Marine
Portsmouth 023 9273 7555

R & S Engineering Dingle Marina,
Ireland +353 66 915 1189

Reddish Marine
Salcombe 01548 844094

RHP Marine
Cowes 01983 290421

River Tees Engineering & Welding Ltd
Middlesbrough 01642 226226

RK Marine Ltd Hamble 01489 583585

RK Marine Ltd
Swanwick 01489 583572

Rossiter Yachts Ltd
Christchurch 01202 483250

Ryan & Roberts Marine Services
Askeaton +353 61 392198

Salve Marine Ltd
Crosshaven +353 21 4831145

Seamark-Nunn & Co
Felixstowe 01394 275327

Seapower Ipswich 01473 780090

Seaward Engineering
Glasgow 0141 632 4910

Seaway Marine
Gosport 023 9260 2722

Shearwater Engineering Services Ltd
Dunoon 01369 706666

Silvers Marina Ltd
Helensburgh 01436 831222

Starey Marine
Salcombe 01548 843655

Strickland Marine Engineering, Brian
Chichester 01243 513454

Tarbert Marine Arbroath 01241 872879

Tollesbury Marine Engineering
Tollesbury Marina,
Tollesbury 01621 869919

Vasey Marine Engineering, Gordon
Fareham 07798 638625

Volspec Ltd
Tollesbury 01621 869756

Wallis, Peter Torquay Marina,
Torquay 01803 844777

WB Marine Chichester 01243 512857

West Coast Marine
Troon 01292 318121

West, Mick Brighton 01273 626656

Western Marine Power Ltd
Plymouth 01752 408804

**Weymouth Marina Mechanical
Services** Weymouth 01305 779379

Whittington, G Lady Bee Marine,
Shoreham 01273 593801

Whitewater Marine
Malahide +353 1 816 8473

Wigmore Wright Marine Services
Penarth Marina 029 2070 9983

Wright, M Manaccan 01326 231502

Wyko Industrial Services
Inverness 01463 224747

Ynys Marine
Cardigan 01239 613179

Youngboats
Faversham 01795 536176

1° West Marine Ltd
Portsmouth 023 9283 8335

MASTS, SPARS & RIGGING

1° Degree West Ltd
Portsmouth 02392 755155

A2 Rigging
Falmouth 01326 312209

Allspars Plymouth 01752 266766

Amble Boat Co Ltd
Morpeth 01665 710267

Arun Canvas & Rigging
Littlehampton 1903 732561

Buchanan, Keith
St Mary's 01720 422037

Bussell & Co, WL
Weymouth 01305 785633

Carbospars Ltd Hamble 023 8045 6736

Cable & Rope Works
Bexhill-on-Sea 0101424 220112

Coates Marine Ltd
Whitby 01947 604486

Composite Rigging
Southampton 023 8023 4488

Dauntless Boatyard Ltd
Canvey Island 01268 793782

Davies Marine Services
Ramsgate 01843 586172

Eurospars Ltd Plymouth 01752 550550

Exe Leisure Exeter 01392 879055

Fox's Marine Ipswich Ltd
Ipswich 01473 689111

Freeland Yacht Spars Ltd
Dorchester on Thames 01865 341277

Gordon, AD Portland 01305 821569

Harris Rigging Totnes 01803 840160

Heyn Engineering
Belfast 028 9035 0022

Holman Rigging
Chichester 01243 514000

Irish Spars and Rigging
Malahide +353 86 209 5996

Kildale Marine Hull 01482 227464

Lowestoft Yacht Services
Lowestoft 01502 585535

Laverty, Billy
Galway +353 86 3892614

Leitch, WB
Tarbert, Loch Fyne 01880 820287

Marine Resource Centre
Oban 01631 720291

Martin Leaning Masts & Rigging
Hayling 023 9237 1157

Mast & Rigging Services
Largs 01475 670110

Mast & Rigging Services
Kip 01475 522700

MP Marine Maryport 01900 810299

Ocean Rigging
Lymington 01590 676292

Owen Sails Oban 01631 720485

Premier Spars Poole 01202 677717

Pro Rig S Ireland +353 87 298 3333

Ratsey, Stephen
Aberystwyth 01646 601561

Rig Magic Ipswich 01473 655089

Rig Shop Southampton 023 8033 8341

Roberts Marine Ltd, S
Liverpool 0151 707 8300

Salcombe Boatstore
Salcombe 01548 843708

Seldén Mast Ltd
Southampton 01489 484000

Silvers Marina Ltd
Helensburgh 01436 831222

Silverwood Yacht Services Ltd
Portsmouth 023 9232 7067

Southern Spar Services
Northam 023 8033 1714

Southern Masts & Rigging
Brighton 01273 668900

Storrar Marine Store
Newcastle upon Tyne 0191 266 1037

Tedfords Rigging & Rafts
Belfast 028 9032 6763

TJ Rigging Conwy 07780 972411

TS Rigging Malden 01621 874861

Windjammer Marine
Milford Marina 01646 699070

Yacht Rigging Services
Plymouth 01752 226609

Yacht Shop, The
Fleetwood 01253 879238

Yacht Solutions Ltd
Portsmouth 02392 755155

XW Rigging Gosport 023 9251 3553

Z Spars UK Hadleigh 01473 822130

NAVIGATION EQUIPMENT – GENERAL

Belson Design Ltd, Nick
Southampton   077 6835 1330

Brown Son & Ferguson Ltd
Glasgow   0141 429 1234

Cooke & Son Ltd, B Hull 01482 223454

Diverse Yacht Services
Hamble   023 8045 3399

Dolphin Maritime Software Ltd
Lancaster   01524 841946

Dubois Phillips & McCallum Ltd
Liverpool   0151 236 2776

Eland Exeter   01392 255788

Garmin Southampton   02380 524000

Geonav UK Ltd Poole   0870 240 4575

Imray Laurie Norie and Wilson Ltd
St Ives, Cambs   01480 462114

Kelvin Hughes
Southampton   023 8063 4911

Lilley & Gillie Ltd, John
North Shields   0191 257 2217

Marine Chart Services
Wellingborough   01933 441629

PC Maritime Plymouth 01752 254205

Navico UK Romsey   01794 510010

XM Yachting Navimo
Hedge End   01489 778850

B G Manufacturing
Romsey   01794 521079

Price & Co, WF Bristol 0117 929 2229

Raymarine Ltd
Portsmouth   023 9269 3611

Robbins Marine Electronics
Liverpool   0151 709 5431

Royal Institute of Navigation
London   020 7591 3130

Sea Chest Nautical Bookshop
Plymouth   01752 222012

Seath Instruments (1992) Ltd
Lowestoft   01502 573811

Smith (Marine) Ltd, AM
London   020 8529 6988

South Bank Marine Charts Ltd
Grimsby   01472 361137

Southcoasting Navigators
Devon   01626 335626

Stanford Charts
Bristol   0117 929 9966
London   020 7836 1321
Manchester   0870 890 3730

Todd Chart Agency Ltd
County Down   028 9146 6640

UK Hydrographic Office
Taunton   01823 337900

Warsash Nautical Bookshop
Warsash   01489 572384

Yachting Instruments Ltd
Sturminster Newton   01258 817662

PAINT & OSMOSIS

Advanced Blast Cleaning Paint
Tavistock   01822 617192/07970 407911

Blakes Paints
Southampton   02380 232000

Herm Seaway Marine Ltd
St Peter Port   01481 726829

Gillingham Marina   01634 280022

International Coatings Ltd
Southampton   023 8022 6722

Marineware Ltd
Southampton   023 8033 0208

NLB Marine Ardrossan 01563 521509

Pro-Boat Ltd
Burnham on Crouch   01621 785455

Rustbuster Ltd
Peterborough   0870 9090093

Smith & Son Ltd, EC
Luton   01582 729721

SP Systems
Isle of Wight   01983 828000

Teal & Mackrill Ltd Hull 01482 320194

Troon Marine Services Ltd
Troon   01292 316180

PROPELLERS & STERNGEAR/REPAIRS

CJR Propulsion Ltd
Southampton   023 8063 9366

Darglow Engineering Ltd
Wareham   01929 556512

Gori Propellers Poole 01202 621631

Propeller Revolutions
Poole   01202 671226

Sillette – Sonic Ltd
Sutton   020 8337 7543

Vetus Den Ouden Ltd
Southampton   02380 454507

RADIO COURSES / SCHOOLS

Bisham Abbey Sailing & Navigation School Bisham   01628 474960

East Coast Offshore Yachting – Les Rant Perry   01480 861381

Hamble School of Yachting
Hamble   023 8045 6687

Pembrokeshire Cruising
Neyland   01646 602500

Plymouth Sailing School
Plymouth   01752 493377

Southern Sailing
Swanwick   01489 575511

Start Point Sailing
Kingsbridge   01548 810917

REEFING SYSTEMS

Atlantic Spars Ltd
Brixham   01803 843322

Calibra Marine International Ltd
Southampton   08702 400358

Eurospars Ltd Plymouth 01752 550550

Holman Rigging
Chichester   01243 514000

Navimo UK Ltd
Hedge End   01489 778850

Sea Teach Ltd Emsworth 01243 375774

Southern Spar Services
Northam   023 8033 1714

Wragg, Chris Lymington 01590 677052

Z Spars UK Hadleigh   01473 822130

REPAIR MATERIALS AND ACCESSORIES

Akeron Ltd
Southend on Sea   01702 297101

Howells & Son, KJ
Poole   01202 665724

JB Timber Ltd
North Ferriby   01482 631765

Robbins Timber Bristol 0117 9633136

Sika Ltd
Welwyn Garden City   01707 394444

SP Systems Newport,
Isle of Wight   01983 828000

Technix Rubber & Plastics Ltd
Southampton   01489 789944

Tiflex Liskeard   01579 320808

Timage & Co Ltd
Braintree   01376 343087

Trade Grade Products Ltd
Poole   01202 820177

Wessex Resins & Adhesives Ltd
Romsey   01794 521111

ROPE AND WIRE

Cable & Rope Works
Bexhill-on-Sea   01424 220112

Euro Rope Ltd
Scunthorpe   01724 280480

Marlow Ropes Hailsham 01323 444444

Mr Splice Leicester   0800 1697178

Spinlock Ltd Cowes   01983 295555

TJ Rigging Conwy   07780 972411

SAFETY EQUIPMENT

AB Marine Ltd
St Peter Port   01481 722378

Adec Marine Ltd
Croydon   020 8686 9717

Anchorwatch UK
Edinburgh   0131 447 5057

Avon Inflatables
Llanelli   01554 882000

Cosalt International Ltd
Aberdeen   01224 588327

Crewsaver Gosport   023 9252 8621

Glaslyn Marine Supplies Ltd
Porthmadog   01766 513545

Guardian Fire Ltd
Norwich   01603 787679

Hale Marine, Ron
Portsmouth   023 9273 2985

Herm Seaway Marine Ltd
St Peter Port   01481 722838

IBS Boats South Woodham Ferrers
    01245 323211/425551

KTS Seasafety Kilkeel   028 41762655

McMurdo Pains Wessex
Portsmouth   023 9262 3900

Met Office Bracknell   0845 300 0300

Nationwide Marine Hire
Warrington   01925 245788

Norwest Marine Ltd
Liverpool   0151 207 2860

Ocean Safety So'ton   023 8072 0800

Navimo UK Ltd
Hedge End   01489 778850

Polymarine Ltd Conwy   01492 583322

Premium Liferaft Services
Burnham-on-Crouch   0800 243673

Ribeye Dartmouth   01803 832060

Secumar Swansea   01792 280545

South Eastern Marine Services Ltd
Basildon   01268 534427

Suffolk Sailing
Ipswich   01473 833010

Whitstable Marine
Whitstable   01227 262525

Winters Marine Ltd
Salcombe   01548 843580

SAILMAKERS & REPAIRS

Allison-Gray Dundee   01382 505888

Alsop Sailmakers, John
Salcombe   01548 843702

AM Trimming
Windsor   01932 821090

Arun Canvas & Rigging
Littlehampton   01903 732561

Arun Sails Chichester   01243 573185

Bank Sails, Bruce
Southampton   01489 582444

Barford Sails Weymouth 01305 768282

Batt Sails Bosham   01243 575505

Bissett and Ross
Aberdeen   01224 580659

Breaksea Sails Barry   01446 730785

Bristol Sails Bristol   0117 922 5080

Buchanan, Keith
St Mary's   01720 422037

C&J Marine Textiles
Chichester   01243 782629

Calibra Sails Dartmouth 01803 833094

Canard Sails Swansea   01792 367838

Coastal Covers
Portsmouth   023 9252 0200

Covercare Fareham   01329 311878

Crawford, Margaret
Kirkwall   01856 875692

Crusader Sails Poole   01202 670580

Cullen Sailmakers
Galway   +353 91 771991

Dawson (Sails), J
Port Dinorwic   01248 670103

Dolphin Sails Harwich   01255 243366

Doyle Sails
Southampton   023 8033 2622

Downer International Sails & Chandlery
Dun Laoghaire   +353 1 280 0231

Duthie Marine Safety, Arthur
Glasgow   0141 429 4553

Dynamic Sails
Emsworth   01243 374495

Flew Sailmakers
Portchester   01329 822676

Fylde Coast Sailmaking Co
Fleetwood   01253 873476

Garland Sails Bristol   01275 393473

Goldfinch Sails
Whitstable   01227 272295

Gowen Ocean Sailmakers
West Mersea   01206 384412

Green Sailmakers, Paul
Plymouth   01752 660317

Henderson Sails & Covers
Southsea   023 9229 4700

Hood Sailmakers
Lymington   01590 675011

Hooper, A Plymouth   01752 830411

Hyde Sails
Southampton   0845 543 8945

Jackson Yacht Services
Jersey   01534 743819

Jeckells and Son Ltd (Wroxham)
Wroxham   01603 782223

Jessail Ardrossan   01294 467311

JKA Sailmakers
Pwllheli   01758 613266

Kemp Sails Ltd
Wareham   01929 554308/554378

Kildale Marine Hull   01482 227464

Lawrence Sailmakers, J
Brightlingsea   01206 302863

Leitch, WB
Tarbert, Loch Fyne   01880 820287

Leith UK
Berwick on Tweed   01289 307264

Lodey Sails Newlyn   01736 719359

Lossie Sails
Lossiemouth   07989 956698

Lucas Sails Portchester 023 9237 3699

Malakoff and Moore
Lerwick   01595 695544

McCready and Co Ltd, J
Belfast   028 90232842

McKillop Sails, John
Kingsbridge   01548 852343

McKillop Sails (Sail Locker)
Ipswich   01255 678353

McNamara Sails, Michael
Great Yarmouth   01692 584186

McWilliam Sailmaker (Crosshaven)
Crosshaven   +353 21 4831505

Mitchell Sails Fowey   01726 833731

Montrose Rope and Sails
Montrose   01674 672657

Mountfield Sails
Hayling Island   023 9246 3720

Mouse Sails Holyhead   01407 763636

Nicholson Hughes Sails
Rosneath   01436 831356

North Sea Sails
Tollesbury   01621 869367

North West Sails
Keighley   01535 652949

Northrop Sails
Ramsgate   01843 851665

Owen Sails Benderloch 01631 720485

Parker & Kay Sailmakers –
East Ipswich   01473 659878

Parker & Kay Sailmakers –
South Hamble   023 8045 8213

Penrose Sailmakers
Falmouth   01326 312705

Pinnell & Bax
Northampton   01604 592808

Pollard Marine
Port St Mary   01624 835831

Quantum Sails
Ipswich Haven Marina   01473 659878

Quantum-Parker & Kay Sailmakers
Hamble   023 8045 8213

Quay Sails (Poole) Ltd
Poole   01202 681128

Ratsey & Lapthorn
Isle of Wight   01983 294051

Ratsey Sailmakers, Stephen
Milford Haven   01646 601561

Relling One Design
Portland   01305 826555

Richardson Sails
Southampton   023 8045 5106

Rig Shop, The
Southampton   023 8033 8341

Rockall Sails
Chichester   01243 573185

Sail Locker
Woolverstone Marina   01473 780206

Sail Style Hayling Is   023 9246 3720

Sails & Canvas Exeter   01392 877527

Saltern Sail Co
West Cowes   01983 280014

Saltern Sail Company
Yarmouth   01983 760120

Sanders Sails
Lymington   01590 673981

Saturn Sails Largs 01475 689933

Scott & Co, Graham
St Peter Port 01481 259380

Shore Sailmakers
Swanwick 01489 589450

SKB Sails Falmouth 01326 372107

Sketrick Sailmakers Ltd
Killinchy 028 9754 1400

Storrar Marine Store
Newcastle upon Tyne 0191 266 1037

Suffolk Sails
Woodbridge 01394 386323

Sunset Sails Sligo +353 71 62792

Torquay Marina Sails and Canvas
Exeter 01392 877527

Trident UK Gateshead 0191 490 1736

UK McWilliam Cowes 01983 281100

Underwood Sails Queen Anne's
Battery, Plymouth 01752 229661

W Sails Leigh-on-Sea 01702 714550

Warren Hall
Beaucette, Guernsey 07781 444280

Watson Sails
Dublin 13 +353 1 846 2206

WB Leitch and Son
Tarbert 01880 820287

Westaway Sails
Plymouth Yacht Haven 01752 892560

Wilkinson Sails
Burnham-on-Crouch 01621 786770

Wilkinson Sails
Teynham 01795 521503

Yacht Shop, The
Fleetwood 01253 879238

SOLAR POWER

Ampair Ringwood 01425 480780

Barden UK Ltd Fareham 01489 570770

Marlec Engineering Co Ltd
Corby 01536 201588

SPRAYHOODS & DODGERS

A & B Textiles
Gillingham 01634 579686

Allison–Gray Dundee 01382 505888

Arton, Charles
Milford-on-Sea 01590 644682

Arun Canvas and Rigging Ltd
Littlehampton 01903 732561

Buchanan, Keith
St Mary's 01720 422037

C & J Marine Textiles
Chichester 01243 785485

Covercare Fareham 01329 311878

Covercraft Southampton 023 8033 8286

Jeckells and Son Ltd
Wroxham 01603 782223

Jessail Ardrossan 01294 467311

Lomond Boat Covers
Alexandria 01389 602734

Lucas Sails
Portchester 023 9237 3699

Poole Canvas Co Ltd
Poole 01202 677477

Saundersfoot Auto Marine
Saundersfoot 01834 812115

Teltale Sails Prestwick 01355 500001

Trident UK Gateshead 0191 490 1736

SURVEYORS AND NAVAL ARCHITECTS

Amble Boat Company Ltd
Amble 01665 710267

Ark Surveys East Anglia/South Coast
01621 857065/01794 521957

Atkin & Associates
Lymington 01590 688633

Barbican Yacht Agency Ltd
Plymouth 01752 228855

Battick, Lee St Helier 01534 611143

Booth Marine Surveys, Graham
Birchington-on-Sea 01843 843793

Byrde & Associates
Kimmeridge 01929 480064

Bureau Maritime Ltd
Maldon 01621 859181

Cannell & Associates, David M
Wivenhoe 01206 823337

**Cardiff Commercial Boat Operators
Ltd** Cardiff 029 2037 7872

CE Proof Hamble 023 8045 3245

Clarke Designs LLP, Owen
Dartmouth 01803 770495

Cox, David Penryn 01326 340808

Davies, Peter N
Wivenhoe 01206 823289

Down Marine Co Ltd
Belfast 028 90480247

Evans, Martin
Kirby le Soken 07887 724055

Goodall, JL Whitby 01947 604791

Green, James Plymouth 01752 660516

Greening Naval Architect Ltd, David
Salcombe 01548 842000

Hansing & Associates
North Wales/Midlands 01248 671291

**JP Services – Marine Safety &
Training** Chichester 01243 537552

MacGregor, WA
Felixstowe 01394 676034

Mahoney & Co, KPO
Co Cork +353 21 477 6150

Norwood Marine
Margate 01843 835711

Quay Consultants Ltd
West Wittering 01243 673056

**Scott Marine Surveyors &
Consultants** Conwy 01492 573001

S Roberts Marine Ltd
Liverpool 0151 707 8300

Staton-Bevan, Tony
Lymington 01590 645755/07850 315744

Swanwick Yacht Surveyors
Southampton 01489 564822

Thomas, Stephen
Southampton 023 8048 6273

Ward & McKenzie
Woodbridge 01394 383222

**YDSA Yacht Designers & Surveyors
Association** Bordon 0845 0900162

TAPE TECHNOLOGY

Adhesive Technologies
Braintree 01376 346511

CC Marine Services (Rubbaweld) Ltd
London 020 7402 4009

Trade Grade Products Ltd
Poole 01202 820177

UK Epoxy Resins
Burscough 01704 892364

3M United Kingdom plc
Bracknell 01344 858315

TRANSPORT/YACHT DELIVERIES

Anglo European Boat Transport
Devon 01803 868691

Boat Shifters
07733 344018/01326 210548

Convoi Exceptionnel Ltd
Hamble 023 8045 3045

Debbage Yachting
Ipswich 01473 601169

East Coast Offshore Yachting
01480 861381

Forrest Marine Ltd
Exeter 08452 308335

Hainsworth's UK and Continental
Bingley 01274 565925

Houghton Boat Transport
Tewkesbury 07831 486710

Moonfleet Sailing
Poole 01202 682269

Performance Yachting
Plymouth 01752 565023

Peters & May Ltd
Southampton 023 8048 0480

Reeder School of Seamanship, Mike
Lymington 01590 674560

Seafix Boat Transfer
North Wales 01766 514507

Sealand Boat Deliveries Ltd
Liverpool 01254 705225

Shearwater Sailing
Southampton 01962 775213

Southcoasting Navigators
Devon 01626 335626

West Country Boat Transport
01566 785651

Wolff, David 07659 550131

TUITION/SAILING SCHOOLS

Association of Scottish Yacht Charterers Argyll 07787 363562
01880 820012

Bisham Abbey Sailing & Navigation School Bisham 01628 474960

Blue Baker Yachts Ipswich 01473 780008

Britannia Sailing (East Coast) Ipswich 01473 787019

British Offshore Sailing School Hamble 023 8045 7733

Coastal Sea School Weymouth 0870 321 3271

Conwy School of Yachting Conwy 01492 572999

Corsair Sailing Banstead 01737 211466

Dart Sailing School Dartmouth 01803 833973

Dartmouth Sailing Dartmouth 01803 833399

Drake Sailing School Plymouth 01635 253009

East Anglian Sea School Ipswich 01473 659992

East Coast Offshore Yachting – Les Rant Perry 01480 861381

Five Star Sailing Southampton 01489 885599

Gibraltar Sailing Centre Gibraltar +350 78554

Glenans Irish Sailing School Baltimore +353 28 20154

Go Sail Ltd East Cowes 01983 280220

Hamble School of Yachting Hamble 023 8045 6687

Haslar Sea School Gosport 023 9252 0099

Hobo Yachting Southampton 023 8033 4574

Hoylake Sailing School Wirral 0151 632 4664

Ibiza Sailing School 07092 235 853

International Yachtmaster Academy Southampton 0800 515439

Island Sea School Port Dinorwic 01248 352330

JP Services – Marine Safety & Training Chichester 01243 537552

Lymington Cruising School Lymington 01590 677478

Marine Leisure Association (MLA) Southampton 023 8029 3822

Menorca Cruising School 01995 679240

Moncur Sailing School, Bob Newcastle upon Tyne 0191 265 4472

Moonfleet Sailing Poole 01202 682269

National Marine Correspondence School Macclesfield 01625 262365

Northshore King's Lynn 01485 210236

On Deck Sailing Southampton 023 8033 3887

Pembrokeshire Cruising Neyland 01646 602500

Performance Yachting Plymouth 01752 565023

Plain Sailing Dartmouth 01803 853843

Plymouth Sailing School Plymouth 01752 493377

Port Edgar Marina & Sailing School Port Edgar 0131 331 3330

Portsmouth Outdoor Centre Portsmouth 023 9266 3873

Portugal Sail & Power 01473 833001

Reeder School of Seamanship, Mike Lymington 01590 674560

Safe Water Training Sea School Ltd Wirral 0151 630 0466

Sail East Harwich 01473 689344

Sally Water Training East Cowes 01983 299033

Sea-N-Shore Salcombe 01548 842276

Seafever 01342 316293

Solaris Mediterranean Sea School 01925 642909

Solent School of Yachting Southampton 023 8045 7733

Southcoasting Navigators Devon 01626 335626

Southern Sailing Southampton 01489 575511

Start Point Sailing Dartmouth 01548 810917

Sunsail Port Solent/Largs 0870 770 6314

Team Sailing Gosport 023 9252 4370

Tiller School of Navigation Banstead 01737 211466

Workman Marine School Portishead 01275 845844

Wride School of Sailing, Bob North Ferriby 01482 635623

WATERSIDE ACCOMMODATION & RESTAURANTS

Abbey, The Penzance 01736 366906

Arun View Inn, The Littlehampton 01903 722335

Baywatch on the Beach Bembridge 01983 873259

Beaucette Marina Restaurant Guernsey 01481 247066

Bella Napoli Brighton Marina 01273 818577

Bembridge Coast Hotel Bembridge 01983 873931

Budock Vean Hotel Porth Navas Creek 01326 252100

Café Mozart Cowes 01983 293681

Caffé Uno Port Solent 023 9237 5227

Chandlers Bar & Bistro Queen Anne's Battery Marina, Plymouth 01752 257772

Chiquito Port Solent 02392 205070

Cruzzo Malahide Marina, Co Dublin +353 1 845 0599

Cullins Yard Bistro Dover 01304 211666

Custom House, The Poole 01202 676767

Dart Marina River Lounge Dartmouth 01803 832580

Deer Leap, The Exmouth 01395 265030

Doghouse Swanwick Marina, Hamble 01489 571602

Dolphin Restaurant Gorey 01534 853370

Doune Knoydart 01687 462667

El Puertos Penarth Marina 029 2070 5551

Falmouth Marina Marine Bar and Restaurant Falmouth 01326 313481

Ferry Boat Inn West Wick Marina, Nr Chelmsford 01621 740208

Ferry Inn, The (restaurant) Pembroke Dock 01646 682947

First and Last, The Braye, Alderney 01481 823162

Fisherman's Wharf Sandwich 01304 613636

Folly Inn Cowes 01983 297171

Gaffs Restaurant Fenit Harbour Marina, County Kerry +353 66 71 36666

Godleys Hotel Fenit, County Kerry +353 66 71 36108

Harbour Lights Restaurant Walton on the Naze 01255 851887

Haven Bar and Bistro, The Lymington Yacht Haven 01590 679971

Haven Hotel Poole 01202 707333

HMS Ganges Restaurant Mylor Yacht Harbour 01326 374320

Jolly Sailor, The Bursledon 023 8040 5557

Kames Hotel Argyll 01700 811489

Ketch Rigger, The Hamble Point Marina Hamble 023 8045 5601

Kota Restaurant Porthleven 01326 562407

La Cala Lady Bee Marina, Shoreham 01273 597422

Le Nautique St Peter Port 01481 721714

Lighter Inn, The Topsham 01392 875439

Mariners Bistro Sparkes Marina, Hayling Island 023 9246 9459

Mary Mouse II Haslar Marina, Gosport 023 9252 5200

Martha's Vineyard
Milford Haven   01646 697083

Master Builder's House Hotel
Buckler's Hard   01590 616253

Millstream Hotel
Bosham   01243 573234

Montagu Arms Hotel
Beaulieu   01590 612324

Oyster Quay Mercury Yacht Harbour,
Hamble   023 8045 7220

Paris Hotel Coverack   01326 280258

Pebble Beach, The
Gosport   023 9251 0789

Petit Champ Sark   01481 832046

Philip Leisure Group
Dartmouth   01803 833351

Priory Bay Hotel Seaview,
Isle of Wight   01983 613146

Quayside Hotel
Brixham   01803 855751

Queen's Hotel Kirkwall   01856 872200

Sails Dartmouth   01803 839281

Shell Bay Seafood Restaurant
Poole Harbour   01929 450363

Simply Italian Sovereign Harbour,
Eastbourne   01323 470911

Spinnaker, The
Chichester Marina   01243 511032

Spit Sand Fort
The Solent   01329 242077

Steamboat Inn Lossiemouth Marina,
Lossiemouth   01343 812066

Taps Shamrock Quay,
Southampton   023 8022 8621

Tayvallich Inn, The
Argyll   01546 870282

Villa Adriana Newhaven Marina
Newhaven   01903 722335

Warehouse Brasserie, The
Poole   01202 677238

36 on the Quay
Emsworth   01243 375592

WEATHER INFO

Met Office Exeter   0870 900 0100

WOOD FITTINGS

Howells & Son, KJ
Poole   01202 665724

Onward Trading Co Ltd
Southampton   01489 885250

Robbins Timber
Bristol   0117 963 3136

Sheraton Marine Cabinet
Witney   01993 868275

YACHT BROKERS

ABC Powermarine
Beaumaris   01248 811413

**ABYA Association of Brokers & Yacht
Agents** Bordon   0845 0900162

Adur Boat Sales
Southwick   01273 596680

Ancasta International Boat Sales
Southampton   023 8045 0000

Anglia Yacht Brokerage
Bury St Edmunds   01359 271747

Ardmair Boat Centre
Ullapool   01854 612054

Barbican Yacht Agency, The
Plymouth   01752 228855

Bates Wharf Marine Sales Ltd
     01932 571141

BJ Marine
Bangor   028 9127 1434

Bluewater Horizons
Weymouth   01305 782080

Boatworks + Ltd
St Peter Port   01481 726071

Caley Marina Inverness   01463 236539

Calibra Marine International Ltd
Southampton   08702 400358

Camper & Nicholsons International
London   020 7009 1950

Clarke & Carter Interyacht Ltd
Ipswich/Burnham on Crouch
     01473 659681/01621 785600

Coastal Leisure Ltd
Southampton   023 8033 2222

Dale Sailing Brokerage
Neyland   01646 603105

Deacons
Southampton   023 8040 2253

Exe Leisure
Topsham   001392 879055

Ferrypoint Boat Co
Youghal   +353 24 94232

Gweek Quay Boatyard
Helston   01326 221657

International Barge & Yacht Brokers
Southampton   023 8045 5205

Iron Wharf Boatyard
Faversham   01795 537122

Jackson Yacht Services
Jersey   01534 743819

Kings Yacht Agency
Beaulieu   01590 616316

Kippford Slipway Ltd
Dalbeattie   01556 620249

Lencraft Boats Ltd
Dungarvan   +353 58 68220

Liberty Yachts Ltd
Plymouth   01752 227911

Lucas Yachting, Mike
Torquay   01803 212840

Network Yacht Brokers
Dartmouth   01803 834864

Network Yacht Brokers
Plymouth   01752 605377

New Horizon Yacht Agency
Guernsey   01481 726335

Oyster Brokerage Ltd
Ipswich   01473 602263

Pearn and Co, Norman
(Looe Boatyard) Looe   01503 262244

Performance Boat Company
Maidenhead   07768 464717

Peters Chandlery
Chichester   01243 511033

Portavon Marina
Keynsham   0117 986 1626

Prosser Marine Sales Ltd
Glasgow   0141 552 2005

Retreat Boatyard
Topsham   01392 874720

Scanyachts
Southampton   023 8045 5608

SD Marine Ltd
Southampton   023 8045 7278

Sea & Shore Ship Chandler
Dundee   01382 202666

South Pier Shipyard
St Helier   01534 711000

South West Yacht Brokers Group
Plymouth   01752 401421

Sunbird Marine Services
Fareham   01329 842613

Trafalgar Yacht Services
Fareham   01329 823577

Transworld Yachts
Hamble   023 8045 7704

WA Simpson Marine Ltd
Dundee   01382 566670

Walton Marine Sales
Brighton   01273 670707

Walton Marine Sales
Portishead   01275 840132

Walton Marine Sales
Wroxham   01603 781178

Watson Marine, Charles
Hamble   023 8045 6505

Western Marine
Dublin   +353 1280 0321

Westways of Plymouth Ltd
Plymouth   01752 670770

Woodrolfe Brokerage
Maldon   01621 868494

Youngboats Faversham   01795 536176

YACHT CHARTERS & HOLIDAYS

Ardmair Boat Centre
Ullapool   01854 612054

**Association of Scottish Yacht
Charterers** Argyll   01880 820012

Blue Baker Yachts
Ipswich   01473 780111/780008

Camper & Nicholsons International
London   020 7009 1950

Coastal Leisure Ltd
Southampton   023 8033 2222

Crusader Yachting
Turkey   01732 867321

Dartmouth Sailing
Dartmouth   01803 833399

Dartmouth Yacht Charters
Kingswear   01803 752935

Doune Marine Mallaig 01687 462667

Four Seasons Yacht Charter
Gosport   023 9251 1789**Golden Black Sailing**
Cornwall   01209 715757

Hamble Point Yacht Charters
Hamble   023 8045 7110

Haslar Marina & Victory Yacht Charters Gosport   023 9252 0099

Indulgence Charters
Wendover   01296 696006

Liberty Yachts West Country, Greece, Mallorca & Italy   01752 227911

Nautilus Yachting Mediterranean & Caribbean   01732 867445

Ondeck
Gosport   02392 583000

Patriot Charters & Sail School
Milford Haven   01437 741202

West Country Yachts
Plymouth/Falmouth
            01752 606999/01326 212320

Puffin Yachts
Port Solent   01483 420728

Rainbow Sailing School
Swansea   01792 467813

Sailing Holidays Ltd
Mediterranean   020 8459 8787

Sailing Holidays in Ireland
Kinsale   +353 21 477 2927

Setsail Holidays Greece, Turkey, Croatia, Majorca   01787 310445

Shannon Sailing Ltd
Tipperary   +353 67 24499

Sleat Marine Services
Isle of Skye   01471 844216

Smart Yachts
Mediterranean   01425 614804

South West Marine Training
Dartmouth   01803 853843

Sunsail Worldwide   0870 770 0102

Templecraft Yacht Charters
Lewes   01273 812333

TJ Sailing Gosport   07803 499691

Top Yacht Sailing Ltd
Havant   02392 347655

Victory Yacht Charters
Gosport   023 9252 0099

West Wales Yacht Charter
Pwllheli   07748 634869

Westways of Plymouth Ltd
Plymouth   01752 670770

39 North (Mediterranean)
Kingskerwell   07071 393939

YACHT CLUBS

Aberaeron YC
Aberdovey   01545 570077

Aberdeen and Stonehaven SC
Nr Inverurie   01569 764006

Aberdour BC   01383 860029

Abersoch Power BC
Abersoch   01758 712027

Aberystwyth BC
Aberystwyth   01970 624575

Aldeburgh YC   01728 452562

Alderney SC   01481 822959

Alexandra YC
Southend-on-Sea   01702 340363

Arklow SC   +353 402 33100

Arun YC Littlehampton 01903 716016

Axe YC Axemouth   01297 20043

Ayr Yacht and CC   01292 476034

Ballyholme YC Bangor 028 91271467

Baltimore SC   +353 28 20426

Banff SC   01464 820308

Bantry Bay SC   +353 27 50081

Barry YC   01446 735511

Beaulieu River SC
Brockenhurst   01590 616273

Bembridge SC
Isle of Wight   01983 872237

Benfleet YC
Canvey Island   01268 792278

Blackpool and Fleetwood YC   01253 884205

Blackwater SC Maldon 01621 853923

Blundellsands SC   0151 929 2101

Bosham SC Chichester 01243 572341

Brading Haven YC
Isle of Wight   01983 872289

Bradwell CC   01621 892970

Bradwell Quay YC
Wickford   01268 776539

Brancaster Staithe SC 01485 210249

Brandy Hole YC
Hullbridge   01702 230320

Brightlingsea SC
Colchester   01206 303275

Brighton Marina YC
Peacehaven   01273 818711

Bristol Avon SC   01225 873472

Bristol Channel YC
Swansea   01792 366000

Bristol Corinthian YC
Axbridge   01934 732033

Brixham YC   01803 853332

Burnham Overy Staithe SC   01328 730961

Burnham-on-Crouch SC
                         01621 782812

Burnham-on-Sea SC
Bridgwater   01278 792911

Burry Port YC   01554 833635

Cabot CC   01275 855207

Caernarfon SC (Menai Strait)
Caernarfon   01286 672861

Campbeltown SC   01586 552488

Island YC
Canvey Island   01702 510360

Cardiff YC   029 2046 3697

Cardiff Bay YC   029 20226575

Carlingford Lough YC
Rostrevor   028 4173 8604

Carrickfergus SC
Whitehead   028 93 351402

Castle Cove SC
Weymouth   01305 783708

Castlegate Marine Club
Stockton on Tees   01642 583299

Chanonry SC Fortrose 01463 221415

Chichester Cruiser and Racing Club
                         01483 770391

Chichester YC   01243 512918

Christchurch SC   01202 483150

Clyde CC Glasgow   0141 221 2774

Co Antrim YC
Carrickfergus   028 9337 2322

Cobnor Activities Centre Trust
                         01243 572791

Coleraine YC   028 703 44503

Colne YC Brightlingsea 01206 302594

Conwy YC Deganwy   01492 583690

Coquet YC   01665 710367

Corrib Rowing & YC
Galway City   +353 91 564560

Cowes Combined Clubs
                         01983 295744

Cowes Corinthian YC
Isle of Wight   01983 296333

Cowes Yachting   01983 280770

Cramond BC   0131 336 1356

Creeksea SC
Burnham-on-Crouch   01245 320578

Crookhaven SC   087 2379997 mobile

Crouch YC
Burnham-on-Crouch   01621 782252

Dale YC   01646 636362

Dartmouth YC   01803 832305

Deben YC Woodbridge 01394 384440

Dell Quay SC Chichester 01243 785080

Dingle SC	+353 66 51984	**Hardway SC** Gosport	023 9258 1875	**Lilliput SC** Poole	01202 740319
Douglas Bay YC	01624 673965	**Hartlepool YC**	01429 233423	**Littlehampton Yacht Club**	
Dovey YC Aberdovey	01213 600008	**Harwich Town SC**	01255 503200	Littlehampton	01903 713990
Dun Laoghaire MYC	+353 1 288 938	**Hastings and St Leonards YC**		**Loch Ryan SC** Stranraer	01776 706322
Dunbar SC		Hastings	01424 420656	**Lochaber YC** Fort William	01397 772361
Cockburnspath	01368 86287	**Haven Ports YC**		**Locks SC** Portsmouth	023 9282 9833
East Antrim BC	028 28 277204	Woodbridge	01473 659658	**Looe SC**	01503 262559
East Belfast YC	028 9065 6283	**Hayling Ferry SC; Locks SC**		**Lossiemouth CC**	
East Cowes SC	01983 531687	Hayling Island	023 80829833	Fochabers	01348 812121
East Dorset SC Poole	01202 706111	**Hayling Island SC**	023 92463768	**Lough Swilly YC** Fahn	+353 74 22377
East Lothian YC	01620 892698	**Helensburgh SC** Rhu	01436 672778	**Lowestoft CC**	01502 574376
Eastney Cruising Association		**Helensburgh**	01436 821234	**Lyme Regis Power BC**	01297 443788
Portsmouth	023 92734103	**Helford River SC**		**Lyme Regis SC**	01297 442373
Eling SC	023 80863987	Helston	01326 231006	**Lymington Town SC**	0159 674514
Emsworth SC	01243 372850	**Herne Bay SC**	01227 375650	**Lympstone SC** Exeter	01395 278792
Emsworth Slipper SC	01243 378881	**Highcliffe SC**		**Madoc YC** Porthmadog	01766 512976
Essex YC Southend	01702 478404	Christchurch	01425 274874	**Malahide YC**	+353 1 845 3372
Exe SC (River Exe)		**Holyhead SC**	01407 762526	**Maldon Little Ship Club**	
Exmouth	01395 264607	**Holywood YC**	028 90423355		01621 854139
Eyott SC Mayland	01245 320703	**Hoo Ness YC** Sidcup	01634 250052	**Manx Sailing & CC**	
Fairlie YC	01294 213940	**Hornet SC** Gosport	023 9258 0403	Ramsey	01624 813494
Falmouth Town SC	01326 373915	**Howth YC**	+353 1 832 2141	**Marchwood YC**	023 80666141
Falmouth Watersports Association		**Hoylake SC** Wirral	0151 632 2616	**Margate YC**	01843 292602
Falmouth	01326 211223	**Hullbridge YC**	01702 231797	**Marina BC** Pwllheli	01758 612271
Fareham Sailing & Motor BC		**Humber Yawl Club**	01482 667224	**Maryport YC**	01228 560865
Fareham	01329 280738	**Hundred of Hoo SC**	01634 250102	**Mayflower SC** Plymouth	01752 662526
Felixstowe Ferry SC	01394 283785	**Hurlingham YC** London	020 8788 5547	**Mayo SC (Rosmoney)**	
Findhorn YC Findhorn	01309 690247	**Hurst Castle SC**	01590 645589	Rosmoney	+353 98 27772
Fishguard Bay YC		**Hythe SC** Southampton	02380 846563	**Medway YC** Rochester	01634 718399
Lower Fishguard	01348 872866	**Hythe & Saltwood SC**	01303 265178	**Menai Bridge BC**	
Flushing SC Falmouth	01326 374043	**Ilfracombe YC**	01271 863969	Beaumaris	01248 810583
Folkestone Yacht and Motor BC		**Iniscealtra SC**		**Mengham Rythe SC**	
Folkestone	01303 251574	Limerick	+353 61 338347	Hayling Island	023 92463337
Forth Corinthian YC		**Invergordon BC**	01349 852265	**Merioneth YC**	
Haddington	0131 552 5939	**Irish CC**	+353 214870031	Barmouth	01341 280000
Forth YCs Association		**Island CC** Salcombe	01548 531176	**Monkstone Cruising and SC**	
Edinburgh	0131 552 3006	**Island SC** Isle of Wight	01983 296621	Swansea	01792 812229
Fowey Gallants SC	01726 832335	**Island YC** Canvey Island	01268 510360	**Montrose SC** Montrose	01674 672554
Foynes YC Foynes	+353 69 91201	**Isle of Bute SC**		**Mumbles YC** Swansea	01792 369321
Galway Bay SC	+353 91 794527	Rothesay	01700 502819	**Mylor YC** Falmouth	01326 374391
Glasson SC Lancaster	01524 751089	**Isle of Man YC**		**Nairn SC**	01667 453897
Glenans Irish Sailing School		Port St Mary	01624 832088	**National YC**	
	+353 1 6611481	**Itchenor SC** Chichester	01243 512400	Dun Laoghaire	+353 1 280 5725
Glenans Irish SC (Westport)		**Keyhaven YC**	01590 642165	**Netley SC** Netley	023 80454272
	+353 98 26046	**Killyleagh YC**	028 4482 8250	**New Quay YC**	
Gosport CC Gosport	02392 586838	**Kircubbin SC**	028 4273 8422	Aberdovey	01545 560516
Gravesend SC	07538 326623	**Kirkcudbright SC**	01557 331727	**Newhaven & Seaford SC**	
Greenwich YC London	020 8858 7339	**Langstone SC** Havant	023 9248 4577	Seaford	01323 890077
Grimsby and Cleethorpes YC		**Largs SC** Largs	01475 670000	**Newport and Uskmouth SC**	
Grimsby	01472 356678	**Larne Rowing & SC**	028 2827 4573	Cardiff	01633 271417
Guernsey YC		**Lawrenny YC**	01646 651212	**Newtownards SC**	028 9181 3426
St Peter Port	01481 722838	**Leigh-on-Sea SC**	01702 476788	**Neyland YC**	01646 600267
Hamble River SC		**Lerwick BC**	01595 696954	**North Devon YC**	
Southampton	023 80452070			Bideford	01271 861390
Hampton Pier YC					
Herne Bay	01227 364749				

YACHT CHARTERS & HOLIDAYS · YACHT CLUBS

North Fambridge Yacht Centre
01621 740370

North Haven YC Poole 01202 708830

North of England Yachting Association Kirkwall 01856 872331

North Sunderland Marine Club
Sunderland 01665 721231

North Wales CC
Conwy 01492 593481

North West Venturers YC (Beaumaris) Beaumaris 0161 2921943

Oban SC Ledaig by Oban
01631 563999

Orford SC Woodbridge 01394 450997

Orkney SC Kirkwall 01856 872331

Orwell YC Ipswich 01473 602288

Oulton Broad Yacht Station
01502 574946

Ouse Amateur SC
Kings Lynn 01553 772239

Paignton SC Paignton 01803 525817

Parkstone YC Poole 01202 743610

Peel Sailing and CC
Peel 01624 842390

Pembroke Haven YC 01646 684403

Pembrokeshire YC
Milford Haven 01646 692799

Penarth YC 029 20708196

Pentland Firth YC
Thurso 01847 891803

Penzance YC 01736 364989

Peterhead SC Ellon 01779 75527

Pin Mill SC Woodbridge 01394 780271

Plym YC Plymouth 01752 404991

Poolbeg YC +353 1 660 4681

Poole YC 01202 672687

Porlock Weir SC
Watchet 01643 862702

Port Edgar YC Penicuik 0131 657 2854

Port Navas YC
Falmouth 01326 340065

Port of Falmouth Sailing Association
Falmouth 01326 372927

Portchester SC
Portchester 023 9237 6375

Porthcawl Harbour BC
Swansea 01656 655935

Porthmadog SC
Porthmadog 01766 513546

Portrush YC Portrush 028 7082 3932

Portsmouth SC 02392 820596

Prestwick SC Prestwick 01292 671117

Pwllheli SC Pwllheli 01758 613343

Queenborough YC
Queenborough 01795 663955

Quoile YC
Downpatrick 028 44 612266

R Towy BC Tenby 01267 241755

RAFYC 023 80452208

Redclyffe YC Poole 01929 557227

Restronguet SC
Falmouth 01326 374536

Ribble CC
Lytham St Anne's 01253 739983

River Wyre YC 01253 811948

RNSA (Plymouth) 01752 55123/83

Rochester CC 01634 841350

Rock Sailing and Water Ski Club
Wadebridge 01208 862431

Royal Dart YC
Dartmouth 01803 752496

Royal Motor YC Poole 01202 707227

Royal Anglesey YC (Beaumaris)
Anglesey 01248 810295

Royal Burnham YC
Burnham-on-Crouch 01621 782044

Royal Channel Islands YC (Jersey)
St Aubin 01534 745783

Royal Cinque Ports YC
Dover 01304 206262

Royal Corinthian YC (Burnham-on-Crouch)
Burnham-on-Crouch 01621 782105

Royal Corinthian YC (Cowes)
Cowes 01983 293581

Royal Cork YC
Crosshaven +353 214 831023

Royal Cornwall YC (RCYC)
Falmouth 01326 312126

Royal Dorset YC
Weymouth 01305 786258

Royal Forth YC
Edinburgh 0131 552 3006

Royal Fowey YC Fowey 01726 833573

Royal Gourock YC
Gourock 01475 632983

Royal Highland YC
Connel 01852 300460

Royal Irish YC
Dun Laoghaire +353 1 280 9452

Royal London YC
Isle of Wight 019 83299727

Royal Lymington YC 01590 672677

Royal Mersey YC
Birkenhead 0151 645 3204

Royal Motor YC Poole 01202 707227

Royal Naval Club and Royal Albert YC Portsmouth 023 9282 5924

Royal Naval Sailing Association
Gosport 020 9252 1100

Royal Norfolk & Suffolk YC
Lowestoft 01502 566726

Royal North of Ireland YC
028 90 428041

Royal Northern and Clyde YC
Rhu 01436 820322

Royal Northumberland YC
Blyth 01670 353636

Royal Plymouth Corinthian YC
Plymouth 01752 664327

Royal Scottish Motor YC
0141 881 1024

Royal Solent YC
Yarmouth 01983 760256

Royal Southampton YC
Southampton 023 8022 3352

Royal Southern YC
Southampton 023 8045 0300

Royal St George YC
Dun Laoghaire +353 1 280 1811

Royal Tay YC Dundee 01382 477133

Royal Temple YC
Ramsgate 01843 591766

Royal Torbay YC
Torquay 01803 292006

Royal Ulster YC
Bangor 028 91 270568

Royal Victoria YC
Fishbourne 01983 882325

Royal Welsh YC (Caernarfon)
Caernarfon 01286 672599

Royal Welsh YC
Aernarfon 01286 672599

Royal Western YC
Plymouth 01752 226299

Royal Yacht Squadron
Isle of Wight 01983 292191

Royal Yorkshire YC
Bridlington 01262 672041

Rye Harbour SC 01797 223136

Salcombe YC 01548 842593

Saltash SC 01752 845988

Scalloway BC Lerwick 01595 880409

Scarborough YC 01723 373821

Schull SC +353 28 37352

Scillonian Sailing and BC
St Mary's 01720 277229

Seasalter SC
Whitstable 07773 189943

Seaview YC
Isle of Wight 01983 613268

Shoreham SC Henfield 01273 453078

Skerries SC
Carlingdford Lough +353 1 849 1233

Slaughden SC Duxford   01728 689036

Sligo YC Sligo   +353 71 77168

Solva Boat Owners Association
Fishguard   01437 721538

Solway YC
Kirkdudbright   01556 620312

South Caernavonshire YC
Abersoch   01758 712338

South Cork SC   +353 28 36383

South Devon Sailing School
Newton Abbot   01626 52352

South Gare Marine Club - Sail
Section Middlesbrough   01642 505630

South Shields SC   0191 456 5821

South Woodham Ferrers YC
Chelmsford   01245 325391

Southampton SC   023 8044 6575

Southwold SC   01986 784225

Sovereign Harbour YC
Eastbourne   01323 470888

St Helier YC   01534 721307/32229

St Mawes SC   01326 270686

Starcross Fishing & CC (River Exe)
Starcross   01626 891996

Starcross YC Exeter   01626 890470

Stoke SC Ipswich   01473 624989

Stornoway SC   01851 705412

Stour SC   01206 393924

Strangford Lough YC
Newtownards   028 97 541202

Strangford SC
Downpatrick   028 4488 1404

Strood YC Aylesford   01634 718261

Sunderland YC   0191 567 5133

Sunsail Portsmouth   023 92222224

Sussex YC
Shoreham-by-Sea   01273 464868

Swanage SC   01929 422987

Swansea Yacht & Sub-Aqua Club
Swansea   01792 469096

Tamar River SC
Plymouth   01752 362741

Tarbert Lochfyne YC   01880 820376

Tay Corinthian BC
Dundee   01382 553534

Tay YCs Association   01738 621860

Tees & Hartlepool YC   01429 233423

Tees SC Aycliffe Village   01429 265400

Teifi BC - Cardigan Bay
Fishguard   01239 613846

Teign Corinthian YC
Teignmouth   01626 777699

Tenby SC   01834 842762

Tenby YC   01834 842762

Thames Estuary YC   01702 345967

Thorney Island SC   01243 371731

Thorpe Bay YC   01702 587563

Thurrock YC Grays   01375 373720

Tollesbury CC   01621 869561

Topsham SC   01392 877524

Torpoint Mosquito SC -
Plymouth   01752 812508

Tralee SC   +353 66 7136119

Troon CC   01292 311190

Troon YC   01292 315315

Tudor SC Portsmouth   023 92662002

Tynemouth SC
Newcastle upon Tyne   0191 2572167

Up River YC
Hullbridge   01702 231654

Upnor SC   01634 718043

Vanguard SC
Workington   01228 674238

Wakering YC Rochford   01702 530926

Waldringfield SC
Woodbridge   01394 283347

Walls Regatta Club
Lerwick   01595 809273

Walton & Frinton YC
Walton-on-the-Naze   01255 675526

Warrenpoint BC   028 4175 2137

Warsash SC
Southampton   01489 583575

Watchet Boat Owner Association
Watchet   01984 633736

Waterford Harbour SC
Dunmore East   +353 51 383389

Watermouth YC
Watchet   01271 865048

Wear Boating Association
0191 567 5313

Wells SC
Wells-next-the-sea   01328 711190

West Kirby SC   0151 625 5579

West Mersea YC
Colchester   01206 382947

Western Isles YC   01688 302371

Western YC Kilrush   +353 87 2262885

Weston Bay YC
Portishead   07867 966429

Weston CC
Southampton   02380 466790

Weston SC
Southampton   02380 452527

Wexford HBC   +353 53 22039

Weymouth SC
Weymouth   01305 785481

Whitby YC   07786 289393

Whitstable YC   01227 272942

Wicklow SC   +353 404 67526

Witham SC Boston   01205 363598

Wivenhoe SC
Colchester   01206 822132

Woodbridge CC   01394 386737

Wormit BC   01382 553878

Yarmouth SC   01983 760270

Yealm YC
Newton Ferrers   01752 872291

Youghal Sailing Club   +353 24 92447

YACHT DESIGNERS

Cannell & Associates, David M
Wivenhoe   01206 823337

Clarke Designs LLP, Owen
Dartmouth   01803 770495

Giles Naval Architects, Laurent
Lymington   01590 641777

Harvey Design, Ray
Barton on Sea   01425 613492

Jones Yacht Design, Stephen
Warsash   01489 576439

Wharram Designs, James
Truro   01872 864792

Wolstenholme Yacht Design
Coltishall   01603 737024

YACHT MANAGEMENT

Barbican Yacht Agency Ltd
Plymouth   01752 228855

Coastal Leisure Ltd
Southampton   023 8033 2222

O'Sullivan Boat Management
Dun Laoghaire   +353 86 829 6625

Swanwick Yacht Surveyors
Swanwick   01489 564822

YACHT VALETING

Autogleam
Lymington   0800 074 4672

Blackwell, Craig
Co Meath   +353 87 677 9605

Bright 'N' Clean
South Coast   07789 494430

Clean It All
Nr Brixham   01803 844564

Kip Marina Inverkip   01475 521485

Mainstay Yacht Maintenance
Dartmouth   01803 839076

Mobile Yacht Maintenance
07900 148806

Shipshape Hayling Is   023 9232 4500

Smith Boat Care, Paul
Isle of Wight   01983 754726

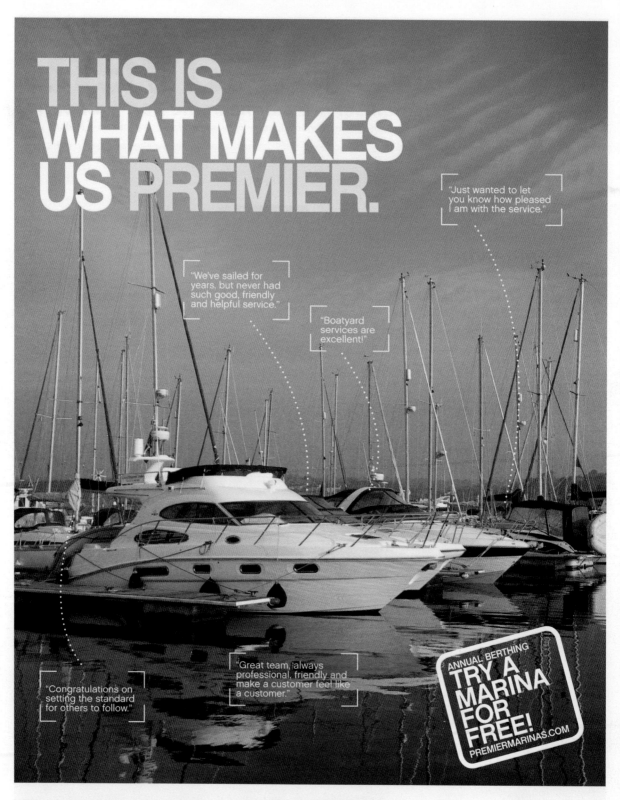

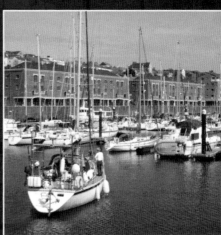

AB Marine 119
Advance Marine 104
Airsaig Marine 83
Ancaster International 22, 39
Anodes 128
Aqua Togs 29
Ardfern Yacht Club 83
Ardoran 82
ASAP 61
Atlantic Spars 16
B Cooke & Son 69
Beaucette Marina 117
Ben Sutcliffe 101
Blackwater Marina 58
Blagdons Boatyard 10
Boat Electrics 88
Boat Shed (The) 96
Boatworks + ...119, 120
Burham Yacht Club 55
BWML 69, 94
Carrickfergus Waterfront 114
Chatham Marine 6
Chelsea Harbour 53
Clyde Marina 89
Cowes Yacht Harbour 28
Darthaven Marina 14
Dean & Reddyhoff 147
Dicky B Marine 13
Dometic 17, 122
DRS Rigging 57
Duncan Yacht Charter 83
Dunlaoghaire Marina 106
Dunlaoghaire Marina Services . . .108
Elgin & Lossiemouth 76
Endeavour Quay 35
Falmouth Visitors Yacht Harbour . . .7
Fambridge Yacht Harbour 56
Firmhelm 98
Freemantle Yacht Rigging 101
G P Barnes 42
Gallions Point 50
Garmin 142
George Hammond 45
Gillingham Marina 48
Gosport Boat Yard 35
H20 Marine 10
Hafan Pwllheli 128
Hamble Sailing Services 32

Harbour Marine 65
Harry King & Sons 63
Holdsworth Hotels 124
Holman Rigging 38, 43
Howth Marina 107
insurance-4-boats.co.uk 145
Iron Stores 120
Island Sailing Club 28
James Watt Dock Marina 87
Jersey Harbours 121
Jessail .90
Kildale Marine 69
Kingfisher Marine 19
Kip Marina 84
Kyle Chandlers 88
Lee Rogers Rigging 15
Lindon Lewis 53
Liverpool Marina 96
Lowesoft Haven 63
Lymington Yacht Harbour 27
Manx Marine 131
Marine & General 119
Marval Marine 26
Maryport Development 91
Milford Haven 159
N U Signs 12
Navigators Marine Service Ltd . . .38
Neptune Marina Ltd 128
Neyland Marine Services 101
Neyland Yacht Harbour 101
Noonan Boats 107
Norwest Marine 96
Novasoil 23
Ocean Engineering 9
Old Forge (The) 82
Orkney Marinas 80
Padstow Harbour 9
Pantaenius 4
Pascall Atkey 28
Pirates Cave Ltd 51
Plymouth Yacht Harbour 13
Poole Harbour Sea Survival 24
Port Flair Ltd 56
Pratt Navel Architecture 62
Premier Marinas 21, 158
Preston Marina 95
Principal Power 24
PYD 132

Quay Marinas 5, 66
Quayside Fuels 18
Quayside Marina 118
R J Wells 37
R Pearce and Co 9
Ramsgate 40
Richardsons Yacht Services 29
Rossiter Yachts 24
Royal Harwich 61
Russler Yachts 8
S Roberts Marine 92
Sailport Plc 11
SCD Ltd 139
Seabridge Marine 123
Seafit Marine Services Ltd 130
Second Wind Sailing 90
Severn Sails 103
Ship Inn (The) 14
Shipshape Services 36
Shotley Marina 60
SMR 43
South Coast Yacht Care 43
Southcoast 38
Southdock Marina 52
Stephen Ratsey 100
Stephen Ratsey 119
Swansea Watersports 102
T S Marine 32
Tim Beck Marine 12
Titchmarsh Marina 59
Tollesbury Marina 46, 58
TYHA 5
Upper Deck 7, 12
Warsash Nautical 32
Waypoint 1 Marine 12
Whitehaven Marina 94
Whitehills Harbour 77
Wilkinson Sails 48
Yacht Works 18